Science in the countryside

Lifelong learning for ecological citizenship

Margaret Pilkington

promoting adult learning

Published by the National Institute of Adult Continuing Education (England and Wales)

21 De Montfort Street
Leicester LE1 7GE
Company registration no. 2603322
Charity registration no. 1002775

NIACE has a broad remit to promote lifelong learning opportunities for adults. NIACE works to develop increased participation in education and training, particularly for those who do not have easy access because of barriers of class, gender, age, race, language and culture, learning difficulties and disabilities, or insufficient financial resources.

NIACE's website on the internet is **www.niace.org.uk**

Cataloguing in Publication Data
A CIP record of this title is available from the British Library

ISBN 1 86201 213 X

Typeset by Book Production Services, London
Printed by Antony Rowe Ltd, Chippenham

S̶c̶i̶e̶n̶c̶e̶ in the countryside

*To my mother and father, who shared with me
their love of botany and the natural world*

Contents

Preface

For all of us…lifelong opportunities to learn should build our experience and confidence,
encourage us to learn by doing and to give our energies and expertise back to the
community in a variety of roles

(Carlton and Soulsby, 1999, p. 2).

Context and objectives

This book is born out of the joys and frustrations of teaching a science subject
in an arts-orientated environment. Joys, because of the satisfaction of seeing a
growing scientific maturity in my students, which enables them to engage
intelligently with the many science-based ethical issues, particularly
environmental issues, of the day. Frustrations because, in the academic world,
the gulf between arts and sciences persists in attitudes to teaching, in
vocabulary, and in differing perceptions about the nature of our subject
matter. My experience of science and science teaching has been acquired over
a period of 30 years in a wide range of academic establishments: a marine
science laboratory and a university department of zoology in New Zealand;
and subsequently in England at the Open University, and in the Centre for
Continuing Education at the University of Sussex. The way forward
articulated in the rest of the book has grown out of this experience supported
by my recent research using student voices to evaluate learning. In the Centre
for Continuing Education, arts and science courses are taught within the same
administrative infrastructure, which has led me to a heightened awareness of
the inherent differences and tensions. Within the rest of the University of
Sussex the divide persists despite the insistence of second Vice-Chancellor,
Asa Briggs, that the gulf should be bridged.

Recent advances in science have confronted us with ethical questions that
go far beyond their scientific and technological origins. Answers to these
questions cannot be left merely to 'experts'. There must be an aware body of
scientifically literate citizens who are capable of entering into debate and of
critically understanding public policy. A major aim of science education for
mature students is to contribute to their development into such citizens. This
evidently requires that the arts/science divide be bridged for them, and that is
no easy task. This book explores science teaching in the context of a particular

subject, natural history, which could be seen as being closer to the arts than many science subjects. If it contributes to an awareness of the difficulties of bridging the arts/science divide and, in some part, to resolving them, its aims will have been achieved.

Ecological citizenship

Ecology is a word of biological origin, defined by biologists as the study of 'the interrelationships between organisms and their environment and each other' (Lawrence, 1995, p. 167), but the term has been taken into general vocabulary and has been used to refer to anything vaguely to do with the natural world. This book focuses on the scientific meaning of ecology and is concerned with the study of interrelationships between all living organisms, including humans, and their physical environment. Similarly, ideas about ecological citizenship have been extended by ecofeminists and radical environmental activists to include the notion that elements of the natural world, such as bears, trees, rivers and oceans, have rights, and to call into question '…the notion of a human at the centre of moral community' (Moore 2003, p. 101). I would want to turn this around and focus on the responsibilities of human citizens for understanding and maintaining the complex web of interrelationships that sustains life on this planet. This scientific aspect of citizenship, which is missing from the social and political context of most current debates (e.g. Apel and Franz-Balsen, 1998; Schemann, 2001; Moore, 2003), is the subject of this book. It includes the scientific research objectives of biological conservation and the educational objectives of creating a scientifically literate population able to participate in a truly democratic debate about environmental issues. Here we are coming from a different direction from the ecofeminists and environmental activists, but aiming for the same end point. As we shall see in Chapters 4 and 5, such a scientific view will also embrace an aesthetic appreciation of the natural world and ideas about valuing local wildlife habitats.

How to read this book

This book has been written for several different audiences. First, I am writing for science educators across the higher education sector, including those in mainstream departments, where there is considerable concern about the future of science and where more and more they will be dealing with continuing (or mature) students. As a field biologist, my examples are drawn from a particular branch of science, but the principles underlying the examples should have general applicability.

Second, I am writing for my colleagues in adult education, whether scientists or not, because I think it is very important that we deal with adult education as a whole and not allow it to become more and more Arts-focused. Also, it is crucial that we engage together in the current debates about the environment. Preservation of biodiversity depends on our overcoming the gap between the technical-scientific world of environment scientists and natural resource managers, and the creators and transmitters of cultural symbols and values such as artists, writers and social scientists (Engel, 1993, p. 198). My type of science is not difficult to understand and I am used to explaining scientific concepts to non-scientist students, so I hope non-scientist colleagues will find the text sufficiently interesting to follow the lines of reasoning. The territory of woodland plants and wildflower meadows may be unfamiliar, but it is the milieu in which my role as an educator is acted out, and education out of context is not worth talking about. I hope I have come to meet you half-way because I, for my part, have tried to engage with the unfamiliar discourse of social scientists and educationalists. You will find the part that deals with plants and science is wrapped in its educational context in the introduction and conclusion to each chapter. 'It is not the ecologists, economists, or earth scientists who will save spaceship earth, but the poets, priests, artists and philosophers' (Hamilton, 1993, p. 1), but for this to happen the science needs to be made accessible.

And third, and very importantly, I am writing for those interested in nature conservation, from site managers and experienced field biology students to the new enthusiast coming on to a natural history open course or walking round a nature reserve for the first time. You, I hope, will be interested in most of this book: the student voices, the fieldwork, and the habitats studied. And maybe the educational aspects which introduce and conclude most chapters since, even if you are not in a formal teaching position, you will be concerned about how we pass on knowledge to others.

In a book such as this, which aims to appeal to non-botanists as well as the plant enthusiast, there is always a debate about the use of scientific names. These are said to be off-putting to the non-specialist and yet are essential to the specialist since their universality prevents confusion over which plant we are talking about. Regional differences between the common names given to different plants means that the same name sometimes refers to different plants in different parts of the country (for example bluebell means *Campanula rotundifolia* in Scotland and *Hyacinthoides non-scripta* in England) and, since many common plants have a plethora of names (Mabey, 1996) any one name may be unfamiliar to many people. I have tried to square this circle by using common names throughout the text, but have included a list of botanical names at the end of the book (Appendix 1), so that there is no doubt about which species I am referring to. A further difficulty is making the name stand out in the text. Scientific names stand out because as foreign words they are given in italics.

Chapter outlines

Chapter 1 sets out the need for UK citizens to understand how science works so that current debates about the environment can be properly democratic. I suggest that this ecological citizenship could be achieved by using an approach to science literacy similar to that used by the Brazilian educationist Paulo Freire, and that today's adult education natural history classes are ripe for such a transformation. The fieldwork approach advocated also leads to the acquisition of the skills required for active participation in biological conservation work, both paid and voluntary. Although the issues addressed are applicable to the teaching of science to adults generally: for example at Further Education and Community Colleges, and within the WEA (Workers Education Association) and U3A (University of the Third Age); my particular focus is continuing education (hereafter CE) science courses within the university sector. The chapter finishes with a brief history of CE university teaching leading into the present serious situation in which the number of CE science courses and CE science tutors continues to decline. In spite of lip-service to lifelong learning for citizenship, government policies for education continue to be driven by economic concerns, in which education for career and the work place is financed, while lifelong learning for citizenship is neglected. The future of CE science teaching depends on reasserting the dual role of science for career and science for citizenship.

 Chapter 2 provides examples of a problem-posing approach to science education using vegetation studies. It uses examples from woodland and heathland habitats to illustrate how a very widely used system of classification can be extended to provide genuine open-ended exercises for adult natural history and field biology students. By following a standard method, areas of vegetation (plant communities) can be designated as nationally recognisable types. Data on the frequency of plant species occurring within a series of samples are compared with standard data to determine the 'best fit' community type. This gives scope for genuinely open-ended exercises because each particular example examined will be unique. During the data-collection process, identification skills will be reinforced across a range of plants from mosses to trees, and in arriving at the 'best fit' answer, students will use data analysis skills and learn the art of balancing evidence to arrive at a substantiated conclusion. They are thus learning the skills that are needed to participate in biodiversity conservation either as a career or as an ecological citizen.

 This problem-posing approach to teaching emphasises active learning and fieldwork rather than knowledge acquisition and, it will be argued, needs to be adopted across the range from mainstream university departments to school level if we are to achieve the goal of learning throughout life. Fieldwork is disappearing as part of the curriculum of both university and school, and this trend too needs to be reversed if we are to have sufficient biological recorders for the future.

Chapter 3 puts the adult learner centre-stage and looks at how scientific knowledge and the way science operates can be taught by starting with the concerns of ordinary adults. This is crucial to 21st century citizenship, because many of the environmental problems confronting the world today require a scientifically literate population to engage in the debate. We start with a shared enjoyment of bluebell woods and show how a topic such as global warming, which is remote and disconnected from most people's view of the world, can be presented in a way that will engage with this appreciation. An understanding of how scientific investigations are conducted, and the problem of uncertainty in biological data, is developed through participation in two long-term projects. The ideas discovered through a study of the local scene are then extended to global concerns. Student voices are used to illustrate the practice, which is applicable to science teaching in general.

Chapter 4 begins the process of looking at how adult education can contribute to the achievement of biodiversity conservation targets. We start by defining what is meant by 'biodiversity' and then we hear from the students who took part in the class exercises described in the last two chapters. Why did they decide to join their class, and how has participation changed their perspectives on nature conservation and the environment? In what ways were they now equipped, as ecological citizens, to contribute to biodiversity conservation in their local areas? The chapter celebrates adult learner achievements and highlights the importance of education for citizenship, especially for the older learner. The importance of financial support from the government for this type of adult education is stressed.

However, if the biodiversity targets set by the 1992 UK Government are to be achieved adult educators also need to move beyond the confines of the classroom environment to the wider community. In **Chapter 5** the education is taken into a community setting in the context of an ecological experiment in a Local Nature Reserve. Here the education is at many levels: the local authority, which manages the site; the general public using the site recreationally; and the CE students collecting biological data from the experiment each summer. We consider the importance of education that puts people in touch with nature.

Participation in the experiment enabled the students to extend their learning beyond the more formal learning of their part-time courses. Their voices explore the nature of this learning and how it was mediated. Currently there is a shortage of people with the necessary skills for biological monitoring and consequently this aspect of nature conservation is frequently neglected. The skills learnt by these students are exactly the skills needed for this task, so their learning provides a blueprint, which can be used to inform the training of other biological monitors. As local communities seek to meet their biodiversity targets, we will need more people with these skills, so such training is an important aspect of ecological education for career and citizenship. People like these students, who have recently retired and have an interest in natural history, represent an immediate resource which could be harnessed for biological monitoring tasks.

In **Chapter 6,** adult student voices, identified by a distinctive sans-serif face, are used to illustrate the practice of science teaching, using a hands-on approach with the countryside as the laboratory. We start by exploring the issues raised by the public perception of science and, in particular, the need for wider understanding of scientific method and of the limitations of science if we are all to participate in the search for answers to pressing environmental questions. In this context, it is important that people practise science rather than just hear or read about it. But the numbers of students studying science at school and university continue to decline, and science is widely perceived as being difficult and unrelated to everyday life. A new approach is needed which is not based on knowledge acquisition through lectures or science programmes.

Student voices are used to show that CE natural history classes can provide a non-intimidating route into science and that learning through fieldwork leads to an understanding of how science works. This leads to empowerment for ordinary adults by enabling them to participate in public debates about science from a position of knowledge rather than emotion. Such an approach to science teaching is applicable at all levels and across all sectors of education.

In **Chapter 7,** we turn again to the ecological experiment discussed in Chapter 5, but here we consider whether the students are participating in research or just acquiring identification skills. The goals of genuine participative research are set out and participation in the experiment is compared with fieldwork in other disciplines, such as archaeology, in which enthusiastic amateurs work alongside professionals.

We then turn our attention to the research itself. What sort of research is needed for nature conservation objectives to be achieved and how does this sort of research fit within current trends in ecological research? This will take us into a consideration of what we mean by an experiment and the current need to move away from simplified laboratory-type experiments with a high degree of statistical certainty to less certain, but more realistic, situations, which deal with the management of habitats. The implications for the policy and practice of conservation bodies, local government and ecological education are discussed.

In **Chapter 8** we continue the research theme by looking at another type of field research which can be used to build up our understanding of species-rich habitats. Here observational techniques are used rather than experimental manipulations and best examples are studied in relation to their management history. Again, there is an essential synthesis between teaching and research which is likely to be lost as continuing education tutors become located within mainstream departments. We take wildflower meadows as our habitat. They represent the species-rich end of a widespread but declining habitat, and as such are an important priority for biological conservation research (Soule and Orians, 2001). The observational techniques used, based on the National Vegetation Classification, will be familiar to conservation professionals and to the students whose voices we have heard throughout this book. I hope that this account will lead to a greater appreciation of the importance of such research and will stimulate participation from biological recorders and site managers as well as academic ecologists.

We start by looking at the best examples of wildflower meadows which we can find in Sussex to build up a picture of an ideal Sussex meadow. This will inform our management objectives in the meadow management experiment, but, because these are small pockets within an intensively managed landscape, we need to move further afield to find examples which can be studied in relation to more sustainable, and biodiverse, land management. We have chosen the Republic of Ireland because it has predominantly the same grassland plant species as England, but includes areas of incredibly species-rich grassland maintained by a continuing tradition of non-intensive grazing. The difficulty of maintaining the biodiversity of such grassland in a conservation context is illustrated with contrasting data from a nature reserve in Norfolk.

Chapter 9, the concluding chapter, provides a summary of the book with implications for policy and practice, and suggests a way forward.

Acknowledgements

I would like to thank my students for their crucial participation in this venture; my colleague John Lowerson, who first suggested that this book should be written; the many people (colleagues, students and family) who gave helpful comments on draft chapters; the Royal Society for a COPUS grant for setting up the Meadow Management Experiment; and Mid Sussex District Council for their collaboration in the Experiment.

CHAPTER 1

Science in crisis?

I think it is deplorable that, at a time when science and science-related topics are becoming increasingly important to society as a whole, Continuing Education provision has been almost completely eroded

(Gron Tudor Jones, Science Tutors' Questionnaire, 2003).

The need for scientifically literate citizens

As the quotation at the head of this chapter suggests, continuing education (CE) science teaching is at the crossroads. Over the last ten years much of this provision has disappeared and yet there is an urgent need for the general public to understand how science works, as society struggles to make decisions on scientific matters (Carlton, 2001). We cannot leave such decisions to the scientific experts because there are moral and ethical dimensions to these matters which science, by its very nature, cannot address. In today's world, where technological and scientific discoveries have given us immense power, we need citizens who are scientifically literate as well as able to read and write. Mainstream university science teaching requires a foundation of knowledge that students must acquire before embarking on their university learning, but this is not the only way to learn about science. This book presents a way forward based on an approach to science literacy similar to that used by the Brazilian educationist Paulo Freire. By rooting the learning in the countryside rather than in a laboratory or lecture room, we can build on people's innate curiosity and appreciation of the natural world, in an active and hands-on way. As they learn about science through doing science, these people will be acquiring the skills needed to participate in scientific aspects of the biodiversity conservation agenda agreed in 1992 at the United Nations Conference on Environment and Development in Rio de Janeiro. Such participation is urgently needed as there is a critical shortage of biological recorders with appropriate skills to undertake species and site monitoring. This is part of *Agenda 21*; the 800-page document agreed at Rio, which attempted to set an international agenda for the 21st century. Even within *Agenda 21*, current debates on citizenship have focused on social, political and environmental rights (e.g. Apel and Franz-Balsen, 1998; Schemann, 2001), and have largely ignored such scientific aspects.

A Freirean approach to science literacy

In the 1970s, when Freire introduced his literacy for empowerment programme among Brazilian peasants, he argued that people who did not have access to literacy skills were being denied their rights as citizens as they were unable to participate effectively in a world that increasingly relied on the written word for decision-making processes (Freire, 1970; 1996). In a similar way, people in Britain today are unable to participate effectively in the development of their future, and that of Western society in general, because they have not been given appropriate tools to understand scientific method. Such science literacy is crucial for democratic participation, as science pushes the boundaries on such complex subjects as genetic modification of crops and the role of human intervention in global warming. Individuals are being expected to make decisions based on scientific research without understanding the processes and methods by which science operates. What then can Freire's pedagogy of the excluded tell us about teaching science literacy in Britain today?

Freire found that the subject of literacy texts was often detached from the wider picture of his students' view of life, and so his first concern was to connect the subject matter to their experience (Freire 1996, p. 52). In a similar way, scientific knowledge and the way science operates can seem remote from everyday life for many adults in Britain today. A popular strategy for rooting science in everyday experiences is to take the science out of laboratories into the more familiar arena of the work or leisure place with courses such as 'The science of brewing' or 'The chemistry of glass' (Nicholson, 1998). This enables the teacher to start from where the students are and build on local issues of immediate concern to them before extending the discussion to a wider and less familiar context. Many students join in CE natural history classes because they are interested in the countryside and in finding out more about the plants and animals they encounter when out walking. The science behind an issue such as global warming will seem remote. On the other hand, the idea that global warming may lead to the loss of bluebells from a local wood is of immediate concern. In Chapter 3 we look at how a programme of scientific enquiry to detect early signs of bluebell decline can lead towards scientific literacy while at the same time encouraging engagement with the wider issues of global warming. And in Chapter 6, students talk about their progression from a general interest in countryside matters to science literacy.

For Freire (1996, p. 62) the beginning of a correct approach lay in finding out, through visiting and observation, where the people he was teaching came from. This is akin to the human constructivist's view that 'the goal of education is the construction of shared meanings' within which students and teachers can exchange ideas within a common framework of understanding (Kirchin, 2000, p 61). In both, the teacher is required to understand not only the subject matter, but also student perspectives on the world. In terms of science literacy, our experience as academics and scientists may be very different from the CE students we are seeking to educate and, like Freire, we need to invest time and effort into understanding student perspectives so that we use a common vocabulary and shared meanings. Freire (1974) found that he had to reject a purely mechanistic literacy programme and instead teach adults how to read 'in relation to their awakening consciousness' (p. 43). What might this mean in terms of science teaching? 'Science consciousness' requires an understanding of the process of science, and of the role of government and scientists in democratic engagement with citizens. In particular it requires a contextual understanding of the interface between the objective world of scientific experimentation and the subjective, but no less important, world of ethical values. And nowhere is this more important than in the debate about the contribution of human activities to climate change. An understanding of scientific method and its limitations is most readily acquired through doing science, and here fieldwork is ideal since genuinely open-ended exercises can be devised. Biological data are inherently untidy, so projects where students collect real data from the countryside teach students about the uncertainty which, contrary to popular belief, exists in many scientific investigations and makes precise predictions difficult. As discussed in Chapter 3, the existence of a scientifically literate population would militate against political manipulation of, for example, the debate on climate change and perhaps make it unacceptable to continue to postpone unpopular decisions on the pretext of waiting for absolute certainty.

Freire suggests that the wrong way of teaching is to try to fill passive students with knowledge as if you were depositing money in a bank account, with the students only receiving, filing and storing the deposits (Freire 1996, p. 53). There is a great temptation for science teachers to operate like this. Science subjects have an enormous knowledge base, and in CE we are usually teaching science to adults who lack a traditional background in science education such as A-level qualifications. This is one of the reasons why mature students are not always welcomed in mainstream university departments like biological sciences, even when they have formal qualifications for entry into Higher Education (HE) such as that gained by passing specially-designed access courses (Bourgeois et al, 1999, pp. 104–5). The attitude of an admissions tutor from Biological Sciences at Warwick University is typical:

We have had a great deal of problems with these access courses. To say that you can do a one-year course and it gives you the biology and chemistry background to get into what students have done for two years at 'A' level and if you have been out of it for a long period of time is absolutely ridiculous. It is scandalous

(Bourgeois *et al,* 1999, pp. 104–5).

This becomes more and more of a problem as scientific knowledge increases year by year. Compare the amount of knowledge required for A-level Botany and Zoology (two separate subjects) 40 years ago with the amount of factual information required for current A-level Biology (single subject). The size of the text books has increased enormously. And how much of this information, so laboriously filed and stored by today's A-level students, will still be useful in 20 years time? Surely we should be concentrating on teaching full-time undergraduates and schoolchildren, as well as mature adults, how to make sense of information rather than to try to amass ever-greater amounts. And here, the continuing education context becomes an asset. Operating within an arts culture, where a 24–credit course at our institution has a time budget of 36 contact hours out of the notional 240 hours of study, it is not possible for us to even attempt to fill in the knowledge base which our students lack. Instead we have been forced into the position of thinking creatively about what we are doing.

Freire also draws attention to the 'Teacher–Student Contradiction' inherent in the lecture approach, where the teacher knows everything and the students know nothing and listen meekly. He argues that this contradiction must be resolved by reconciliation in which 'both are simultaneously teachers and students' and that this happens when a problem-posing approach is taken. The task of the teacher is then to re-present the universe to the people not as a lecture but as a problem (Freire, 1996, p. 90). A problem-solving approach to the teaching of biology gained prominence in the late 1950s and early 1960s in the Nuffield Ordinary Level Biology Project (Gould, 1983) and was later extended to the Nuffield Advanced Biology Course for A-level students in 1986 (Lock, 1994). The idea was 'to encourage a more scientific, experimental study of biology through the method of guided discovery. (Gould, 1983). While the method has its enthusiastic supporters (Lock, 1994), a number of difficulties have been identified with this approach. The practical work needs to be closely structured in order to lead students to an understanding of key concepts, and this tends to produce closed-ended exercises which lead to a single outcome, rather than encouraging open-ended, problem-solving investigation (Gould, 1983). Recent European-wide debate about how to arrest falling numbers of children studying science (European Commission, 2001) comes to the same conclusion: 'Experimentation yes if it is genuine enquiry, but it doesn't work if you already know the answer' (p. 9). Fieldwork classes in biology and natural history provide ideal situations for open-ended science exercises, and there is a particular need for continuing education to espouse this route, since fieldwork is disappearing from mainstream university programmes. In a recent study of graduate biologists training to be teachers, less than one-third had significant experience of fieldwork, and a further one-third had no experience of fieldwork at all (Tilling, 2001). Chapter 2 provides examples of a problem-posing, fieldwork approach using vegetation studies. Students work in groups to collect data from an area of woodland or heathland and, by comparing the class data with standard data, they draw out ecological principles relating to the habitat in general and to the particular example which they have studied. Since each example is unique, the teacher is discovering along with the students. Freire called this 'discovering together' process 'co-intentional education' (1996, p. 51).

By moving along this route of shared investigation rather than tutor-imparted knowledge we can enable genuine participation by our students in one of today's most pressing endeavours: to prevent the destruction of our planet Earth. The need to conserve as much biodiversity as possible has been given new impetus by the recent suggestion that the stability of the physical state of our planet may be due to the interactions of many species in complex ecosystems. Loss of species and simplification of ecosystems may have unpredictable consequences, perhaps leading to unstoppable changes in the state of the Earth (Hambler, 2004). In Chapter 4, students from natural history and field biology classes talk about how participation in the class exercises described in earlier chapters enabled them to play an active part in biodiversity conservation and in Chapter 5 how this learning was extended by participation in a community conservation project, the Meadow Management Experiment.

In the Meadow Management Experiment, students carried out vegetation monitoring to enable the effect of different management regimes to be scientifically assessed. Such monitoring is a crucial part of all site management for nature conservation, but at the moment very little of this is being done because there is a gap between the size of the agenda and the size of the professional human resource available to site managers. Anderson (1999), a consultant ecologist responsible for creating new habitats and management schemes, discusses the difficulties associated with adequate monitoring. Monitoring is written into management plans, but how well it is carried out depends on the interest of the client and the money available. The same is true for management plans for local nature reserves. English Nature and local wildlife trusts do not have the resources to carry out the monitoring, so although monitoring is written into management plans there are likely to be continual problems with implementation for councils relying on professional help. This was certainly the case in Mid Sussex in the early 1990s when two local nature reserves were designated. Monitoring was written into the management plans, but when it came to implementation, professional help from English Nature, and the Wildlife Trust who had advised on the management plan, was not available, and freelance professional help was too expensive. In recent years university continuing education students have contributed to their local conservation agenda by monitoring the response of the vegetation to the management each year. As local communities seek to meet their biodiversity targets within *Agenda 21* the need for this sort of monitoring expertise will increase, providing many opportunities for co-intentional education.

As well as co-intentional education at the community level, there is also the possibility of 'discovering together' at the national level. In Britain there has been a long tradition of amateur recording (Davis, 2001) and this continues today, with many professional bodies making use of the knowledge and enthusiasm of members of the general public who have contributed to national surveys such as the Dormouse Survey of 1993, Vole-Watch in 1998 and the cowslip survey organised by Plantlife in 2000. The dormouse survey turned out to be the largest survey of the dormouse ever undertaken in Europe, with more than 5,850 people taking part in The Great Nut Hunt which was launched during National Dormouse Week at the end of October 1993. Hazelnuts form an important part of the diet of dormice, so the distribution of empty nuts opened with the distinctive neat round hole, characteristic of the action of dormice teeth, betrays the presence of these shy nocturnal animals. Volunteers searched the woodland floor and identified and then counted all the nuts opened by dormice. These nuts demonstrated the presence of dormice at 295 sites in England and Wales compared with the previous total (Biological Records Centre) of only 52 records since 1980 (English Nature, 1994a). This represented thousands of searching hours by the 'Nutters' and enabled the experts to concentrate their efforts on confirming identification of the holes in sample nuts sent in. By combining resources in this way, the agenda for dormouse conservation has been advanced in a way which would not have been possible if all the work had been done by the experts. A follow-up survey is currently under way, providing further evidence of the success of this type of collaboration.

Such national surveys can stimulate interest and involve the general public in science in an active way, but we need to build on this in order to achieve our objective of a scientifically literate citizenry. In the past, much of this task was undertaken by CE university teaching, and we turn now to a brief history of this sector before discussing the way forward.

Liberal adult education in Britain, and the question of accreditation

In the 1980s, the era before all courses had to carry credit, traditional liberal adult education (LAE) was the mainstay of university continuing education in Britain. Courses were designed to interest and engage students, and to be the presence of the university in the region by taking place at centres outside the university. Education for the workplace was a very small part of the overall provision. Such an ethos had its origins in a UK Government report from 1919 which stated that the aims of adult education were to foster personal development and citizenship (Ministry of Education, 1919). These courses were an ideal way of getting the general public to engage with science, and twenty years ago CE departments in universities such as Birmingham had a large programme of science courses, which attracted an annual student body equivalent to 500 full-time undergraduates (Gron Tudor Jones, 2003 questionnaire).

When I came into LAE, in the second half of the 1980s, students in natural history classes mostly engaged in a fairly passive way and expected to be entertained with illustrated lectures (slide shows!) for indoor sessions and guided walks in the field. Although we encouraged active discussion, and the book list was often read avidly, we were only doing slightly better than television programmes about wildlife, where participation is entirely passive. However, the basis for more active participation was there in our student body. In many cases there was a culture of note-taking which could be built on to sharpen skills of recording and the keeping of a field notebook. Some long-standing students produced wonderful records of the sites visited each year, and these provided inspiration to newcomers to the class; but it was entirely up to the students how they responded to the course. Getting students to collect data in the field had to be introduced very carefully, and I can remember slightly bemused students, who had attended other LAE classes in the past, telling me that they had never done anything like this before! Other students voted with their feet, telling me that they were not interested in such a detailed approach to the subject. Most students on these courses were not aware that they were taking a university course, so perhaps we were not fulfilling our university-in-the-region role very well.

All this was to change with the advent of HEFCE circular 18/93 in 1993, closely followed by HEFCE circular 3/94 in January 1994. Suddenly we were faced with the prospect that in future the government would only fund courses which carried credit. Worse, there was the implication that students would have to progress and use the credit to achieve named awards.

In 1995–96 and beyond, continuing education provision which results in a recognised HE award, and also that continuing education which is accredited and can contribute to an HE award (or is credit-bearing within a credit accumulation framework), will be eligible for funding .

(HEFCE circular 3, 1994).

In order to gain the credit, students would have to do work for assessment. Tutors would have to be paid for the additional workload that this would entail, leading in turn to increased fees. What effect would the prospect of some form of test, perhaps coupled with increased fees to pay for the assessment, have on enrolments?

Pre-accreditation survey of LAE

In 1993, the Centre for Continuing Education at the University of Sussex looked at the existing situation in 26 universities and asked how they proposed to respond to accreditation (Holloway 1994). This research was set in the context of a limited 'in house' study of tutor and student reactions to the proposed changes.

Most departments were planning to increase their accredited work and most already provided some sort of accredited provision. Respondents from some departments were worried about the effect of accreditation on the enjoyment of learning:

LAE is about self-development and making education an enjoyable process, a two-way thing between students and tutors. Accreditation is only worthwhile if you want to cash it in for something. ... Students come for the joy of learning and don't seem to want to do the accreditation, it is the learning they enjoy.

(Quoted in Holloway, 1994, p. 52)

Others could see advantages to the new system, although they acknowledged that it would be catering for students who wanted the credit rather than those studying purely for interest:

Accreditation will...attract a different clientele, that is, younger people who want access to degree courses. [...] The courses in science, maths and social sciences we shall be offering in the future will be extremely popular with younger students.

(Quoted in Holloway 1994, p. 50)

There were considerable concerns about the effect on existing students:

Whereas practitioners might perceive accreditation as making CE focus on learning rather than teaching and/or motivating the students, students tend to regard this as making greater demands on their time and having a detrimental effect on their classroom experience.

(Quoted in Ambrose and Holloway, 1994, p. 86)

There was considerable anxiety about the effect of the introduction of accreditation on student numbers, but most institutions were confident that they could find a way through the difficulties. At Sussex, we conducted a survey of our tutors and students (Mayhew, 1994) to find out their response to the forthcoming changes. Tutor concerns were summed up by the following tutor who wrote:

If student assessment were involved, most of my present students probably would not come, and, more generally, a whole segment of students would no longer attend.... My expectation is that I might get students who wanted some kind of formal certification, perhaps just to prove they can do it, perhaps with a view to moving on to university... to put it in market terms, whole blocs of potential consumers will take their custom elsewhere.

(Mayhew, 1994, p. 62)

Student responses showed that tutors had reason to be concerned: accreditation was perceived to be off-putting by a clear majority of existing students. A retired teacher expressed the feeling of many respondents:

There is no overwhelming need to prove oneself after 40 years of professional work ... further qualifications are irrelevant. I'm contented with what I have at this stage of life!

(Mayhew, 1994, p. 76)

Other students were worried about finding the time for extra work between sessions, or felt that being assessed would destroy the pleasure they got from attending the course. However, there were some students who indicated that, although they were opposed to accreditation, they would not allow it to prevent them attending a course. A small minority of students thought it would enhance the value of the course.

The results of these surveys informed our way forward as an institution. Along with many other institutions, we thought that given time we could change our clientele to embrace a younger age of student who would value the credit and would engage with the new courses we were developing as part of named awards such as certificates and part-time degrees. In the meantime, we would continue to cater for our traditional LAE learners throughout the region by providing accredited Open Courses. Students on these courses would be required to produce work for assessment, but this did not need to be an essay and would be built into the course as an integral part of the learning. In this way we hoped to retain most of our traditional LAE students. We would lose some tutors, but again it was hoped that new tutors would be found who would welcome the more dynamic approach.

Post-accreditation survey of science LAE

In June 2000, we conducted another survey of university CE departments (Fisher, unpublished survey 2000), this time focusing specifically on science teaching – because it seemed to us that science courses had been particularly vulnerable to accreditation and might reveal any negative effect of accreditation before arts courses. It was easy to see reasons why this might be: if people generally perceived science as being difficult and threatening, the thought that they were going to be tested in some way would not encourage them to enrol. Our own Open Course science provision had decreased and the neighbouring University of Kent no longer had any CE science provision. A questionnaire was sent to the 26 CE departments who had responded to the earlier survey (Holloway, 1994), asking about the science courses they had run in the previous year. We received 13 replies from other institutions, but four of these were from institutions that no longer had anything corresponding to the old LAE programme. The replies revealed an interesting picture of this transitional period, with many respondents trying to see accreditation as a positive development. Long-standing tutors had been lost, but new tutors had been recruited who were enthusiastic about the opportunities offered by accreditation, such as better-structured learning and the ability to accumulate credits towards an award. Similarly, the student body was slowly being replaced by younger students who had no experience of pre-accreditation courses. Replies were equally divided between those reporting better provision and those saying it was worse, but reasons other than accreditation were often given for the change. Departments which reported bigger and better programmes of science courses, such as Leeds, had managed to combine open courses to make certificates. Most science courses were short (10 credits or fewer) and there were very few courses beyond Level 1. Leeds had tried Level 2 courses in their most popular subject, geology, but had had very few students moving from Level 1 onto these courses.

In Autumn 2000, NIACE (National Institute of Adult and Continuing Education) conducted a survey of science in relation to adult learners, published as a discussion paper (Carlton, 2001) to coincide with the British Association's Festival of Science at Glasgow University in September 2001. The aim of the paper was to encourage policy-makers and practitioners concerned with broad adult education, including further education, higher education and work-related learning, to commit themselves to widening participation. Examples of good practice were used, but it was not intended to be an audit of science provision. The paper concluded that there were many examples of good and innovative practice, but that this was on a relatively small and disconnected scale. It recommended that case studies and methods of good practice for adult teaching and learning in science should be published. This book is offered as a contribution to this process.

CE science: the present situation

At Sussex we still have a good programme of science open courses predominantly in field-based subjects such as natural history, geology, and garden design, but with astronomy gaining in popularity in recent years. Many of the students on these courses are not actively seeking credit, but have bought into the argument that the assessment is an integral part of the learning process. A small minority are keen to acquire the credit and have used it as advanced standing within a part-time interdisciplinary degree in landscape studies. This contains a strong science component at Level 1, Level 2 and Level 3. We also have 120-credit Certificates in Field Biology and Field Geology which recruit well and provide option courses within the degree.

In order to find out about the situation in other universities I sent out a questionnaire in December 2003 to university CE science tutors through an email discussion group. The email group, which was established in 2000 following a meeting at Cambridge University, was assumed to include a majority of tutors who were still active in this field. Of the nine tutors who responded, six were full-time faculty members who had been in their present jobs for 13 to 28 years; the other three were more recent part-time faculty. Seven were from English universities, one was from a Welsh university, and one was from a Scottish university, so although the sample was small it represented a spread of location.

The picture that emerged was not a happy one. Four of the respondents reported that their science programmes had been reduced almost to zero. At the University of Birmingham a particle physicist had seen his programme of extra-mural science, which 20 years ago generated 500 FTEs, reduced to nothing but a few IT courses. This he attributed to accreditation:

The onset of the 'credit culture' has steadily eroded our science provision.

The kinds of people that came were interested in science, but did not want to be assessed. I felt terrible trying to persuade students – several in their 70s and 80s – to come in to do tests and write assignments!

Similarly, a physicist at the University of Southampton had lost his programme for the general public by 2002–03. But it was not just physicists. The earth scientist at the University of Leeds, who three years previously was running 30 geology courses, expected to lose his last three courses in the next year.

In contrast, two respondents reported expanding programmes mainly in life and environmental sciences. A key factor in the survival of CE science programmes, emerging from this very limited study, seems to be the development of appropriate pathways from open courses into named awards such as the Landscape Studies degree at Sussex. The earth scientist at Leeds attributed the demise of his programme to the lack of a natural science tutor who would have enabled the development of an interdisciplinary degree similar to the Sussex Landscape Studies one. Some institutions had moved a long way down this road. For example, the CE department at the University of Sheffield had been restructured into part-time degrees five years ago, with the Workers Education Association (WEA) taking over the LAE provision. The respondent thought that this had worked well. Although there were now fewer courses, the student experience was richer and students were encouraged to move from the WEA classes onto the degrees. Jan Martin, from University of Wales, Aberystwyth, reported that her institution had just decided that all open courses should be part of certificates, and a respondent from the University of Surrey reported that, while their open course programme was contracting, their Landscape Studies degree was expanding slightly. But is this what we want to happen? A thriving open course programme which feeds into named awards is fine, since it caters for both those wanting to use their credit and for those who do not want to progress in this way. However, if all open course provision becomes part of named certificates there is no room for a horizontal type of progression where people use their learning to develop their confidence and the skills needed to participate fully in a chosen area of science, such as field-based biological monitoring (Pilkington and Stuart, 2001, p. 13). Jan Martin put it this way:

> *The Government prioritises paper qualifications, but many of our students appear to feel education is not about certificates. The more mainstream HE provision, however, recruits a different type of student. As the department becomes better known for the new type of provision, it is likely that numbers of such students will grow. In the old extra-mural open studies system, students would attend the same class many times (although it might have been run under a different name each year). This cannot be sustained – students studying for named certificates or diplomas have a finite 'lifetime' within the department.*

Another respondent thought that CE in general, not just science, was 'struggling to hang on to its values in the face of credit-driven policy'. In the past we had been able to do 'really innovative things such as blending sciences and humanities', but this was becoming increasingly difficult to do as more and more of our efforts had to be spent on fully accredited provision that dovetailed into degree structures. This, I think, is particularly true if the provision has to feed into mainstream degree programmes, and one of the strengths of the University of Sussex part-time Landscape Studies degree is that it is run within a CE department while at the same time being fully recognised by the rest of the university as a University of Sussex BA. This is, of course, no longer possible where CE departments have been closed and part-time provision spread throughout the university as has happened at several institutions. Under these conditions it is difficult for one CE person to maintain the different ethos needed for genuine part-time adult provision within a large body of scientists pursuing a different agenda. One respondent, David Hill at Bristol University, was 'mainstreamed' in August 1998 when the separate department of CE was closed. He suggested that his ability to deliver CE science teaching had been hampered by the resulting inefficiency and 'lack of a positive environment for continuing education and dedicated services available through the old CE department.' Absorption into mainstream departments also has serious implications for the type of research which can be undertaken. We will return to this in Chapter 8.

The full extent of the crisis becomes apparent when such trends within CE science are set in the context of what is happening within university CE departments more generally. It has been estimated that the number of adult and continuing education departments based in higher education (HE) institutions across the UK has reduced by fifty per cent over the past decade (O'Kane 2002, p. 7) and this trend has continued into 2005, with several more departments closed or threatened with closure. Nor is the picture any better outside the HE sector. A recent NIACE participation survey showed that the number of adults participating in learning had fallen from a high in 2001 back to 1996 levels (Tuckett and Aldridge, 2003).

Science education for citizenship: the way forward

We have, then, a very serious situation. There is a decline in adults studying and a decline in the array of science courses available to them, and yet at the same time we have an urgent need for the general public to understand how science works. In the field of ecology there is an additional need because we have a human resource problem as well as a general lack of understanding about the issues. We need to equip ordinary adults to be ecological citizens and to participate in their local biodiversity conservation agenda. Without such participation the objectives set at the Earth Summit in Rio de Janeiro in 1992 cannot be achieved.

So how can we go about doing this? For CE generally, O'Kane (2002, p. 7) suggests that 'it is critically important to stimulate demand by building upon activities which already interest and involve people.' Clearly this must be our starting point and there is huge interest in natural history on which we can build. It has been estimated (Marren, 2002, p. 16) that for every species of bird breeding in this country there are 4000 RSPB members (Royal Society for the Protection of Birds). So here we have the possibility of building links between activities which already interest people, such as natural history, and learning about science. The 2003 Science Tutors', Email Questionnaire showed some expanding provision in the broadly defined area of natural history/ environmental sciences. Such courses can be extended beyond the illustrated lecture and guided walk programme of pre-accreditation, to a more active learning-by-doing approach which will enable students to engage with scientific method while at the same time acquiring the identification and fieldwork skills needed for voluntary or career participation in biodiversity conservation work. In this book, we start by describing the type of hands-on science we are referring to (Chapters 2 and 3) and then the 'voices' of students who have participated in this way are used to show that such courses can provide popular and non-intimidating routes into science learning, and empowerment for ecological citizenship (Chapters 4, 5, 6 and 7).

Education for citizenship, in the context of this book, also embraces the science literacy which is needed for democratic participation in current debates on the environment and here it is important that we include a wider cross-section of the adult population. This book is addressed to all those interested in this debate, both scientists and non-scientists, because the way forward requires a joint effort. There must be careful articulation from scientists particularly about the limits of scientific knowledge and the problems of uncertainty in scientific data, but we also need the participation of a scientifically literate population because 'governments have no answers which are independent of the attitudes and behaviours of individual citizens' (Field, 2000, p. 33). This has major implications for the teaching of science in many contexts, from school to university and community, in a truly continuing and lifelong learning agenda. Neither scientific literacy nor the more practical concerns of ecological citizenship are going to be achieved simply by building routes into traditional university science learning. As we shall see, students need time and space to develop these skills and this is rarely provided in credit-driven programmes. Until there is a new approach to science teaching, the present direction of continuing education in which remnants of the old liberal adult education programme are being linked into mainstream degree programmes will not achieve science literacy objectives.

CHAPTER 2

A problem-posing approach to teaching: vegetation analysis using the NVC

The standing objection to botany has always been, that it is a pursuit that amuses the fancy and exercises the memory, without improving the mind, or advancing any real knowledge; and, where the science is carried no farther than a mere systematic classification, the charge is but too true. But the botanist that is desirous of wiping off this aspersion should be by no means content with a list of names; he should study plants philosophically, should investigate the laws of vegetation .... Not that system is by any means to be thrown aside; without system the field of Nature would be a pathless wilderness; but system should be subservient to, not the main object of, pursuit .

(Gilbert White, 1789, p. 226).

The first chapter set out a philosophy of science teaching, which relates to fostering independent learning while preparing people to take part in biological conservation work either as volunteers or as a career. We have rejected the idea that we can fill our students with a large amount of factual knowledge and have opted instead for using open-ended, fieldwork exercises to help them develop as independent learners and to make sense of the information they collect: to discover for themselves and in so doing 'to develop the impatience and vivacity which characterises search and invention' (Freire 1974, p. 43). Previous research with schoolchildren suggests that this will only work if the exercises are genuinely open-ended and if we as teachers do not know the answers (European Commission, 2001, p. 9). At the same time, in order to prepare people for biological conservation work, perhaps as site managers or ecological consultants, or as volunteers involved in biological survey, we need to develop biological identification and fieldwork skills. Identification skills in particular take a long time to develop and we will want to get our students to do more than compile lists of species seen. And in addition to all this, we will have to ensure that our students are familiar with the most widely used system of classification of vegetation (the National Vegetation Classification or NVC), which is the starting point these days for everything from site description to management plans and prescriptions.

Exercises that involve the collection of data in the countryside are ideal because each data set will be unique and will involve both teacher and students in new challenges, both during the data collection and at the data analysis stage.

Setting some of these exercises within the context of the NVC will help us fulfil the last requirement, but in addition, using the NVC will give lots of practice with identification of plants from tiny mosses to trees because the method is based on rigorous identification of species. It provides a framework that can be used on virtually any site since it embraces all habitats (Rodwell, 1991a), and the system has been put together in such a way that data analysis leads to the discovery of the interrelationships between plants and their environment.

Before coming on to the use of the NVC in class exercises, we look first at the ideas behind classification and the particular characteristics of the NVC system.

Making sense of plant communities

As the quote from Gilbert White at the head of this chapter suggests, botanists over the centuries have been obsessed with naming plants and writing long lists of the species that they have seen, a bit like stamp collecting. We are all guilty of this at times – who does not thrill at the discovery of an orchid not encountered before? And these lists have their place: when combined in a systematic geographical way they can be built up into a picture of the distribution of our flora as exemplified in the *New Atlas of the British and Irish Flora* (Preston *et al*, 2002). However, in natural history classes and in training nature conservation professionals, we must move beyond this stage to 'investigate the laws of vegetation'. And of particular help in this task is the new National Vegetation Classification system (NVC). For many years, ecologists in continental Europe, such as Braun-Blanquet (1932), have looked at the sociology of plants and have classified vegetation into a hierarchical system of plant communities. Until recently a different approach was taken in Britain, which stressed the variety of ways in which plants associate. British ecologists were more interested in how vegetation works than in a classification of plant associations. However, it became increasingly clear that some systematic account of the communities in which plants occur was needed if we were to plan effectively for the conservation of our flora. In the early 1990s, fifteen years of work by a team of ecologists under the leadership of John Rodwell came to fruition and provided us with our own national system of classification (Rodwell, 1991a). Since then the NVC has been widely used for describing and mapping vegetation during surveys of nature conservation sites and in putting together management plans, but, although it was always envisaged as being much more than this, its predictive potential has been largely ignored. Too often, site managers are trained to use the system simply to assign types to areas of vegetation rather than learning how to analyse the data they have collected. Such data analysis provides accessible scientific training without the need for complicated maths and the answer is not known in advance. There is space for genuine discovery by all the participants: both teacher and learners.

Why classify?

As Gilbert White recognised, a system of classification is essential if we are to make sense of the natural world. We need to identify, or put names to plants so that we can communicate about them. In a sense the name is a shorthand, that enables someone who hasn't seen the specimen we are talking about to have a mental picture of it. This picture may be based on knowledge from other examples of the same plant species or from a picture in a book or written description. Ultimately, a species is defined by a type specimen in a museum. In a similar way we can classify vegetation into plant communities using the NVC, and anyone familiar with the system will then have a mental picture of the vegetation we are talking about. However, plant communities are much more variable than plant species, and one community tends to grade into another. The type descriptions are based on a large number of samples taken throughout the country and so represent a generally prevailing picture of the community. Particular examples of a plant community will differ from the type description in many ways, but by giving the plant community a name we are cutting down on the amount of extra description needed. For example, we might describe an area of woodland as 'oak – bramble – bracken woodland, with a high frequency of beech and very little bramble'. This type of woodland normally contains only a low frequency of beech and a lot of bramble, so the essential characteristics of this particular example of a familiar woodland type would be immediately clear to a fellow researcher without the need to wade through a long description about oak and bracken and the other plants occurring in the wood. This shorthand description is obviously very useful when it comes to describing sites and writing management plans, but the British system has an added advantage in that the classification also reflects the underlying ecology of the plant communities (Rodwell, 1991a, p. 67). This means that differences between a particular example of a plant community and the type description can be linked to particular features of the environment, such as soil characteristics or past management of the site. It is this aspect that takes us beyond site description and allows us to make sense of the plant communities.

In this chapter, examples from heath and woodland plant communities are used to illustrate how the system can be extended beyond site description to provide genuinely open-ended exercises for natural history and ecology students. Although the particular examples used come from Sussex, the habitats themselves are widespread, and the principles used can be easily extended to other NVC types and other parts of the country. Later in Chapter 8, the same principles are used to extend the system to research using grassland communities.

The NVC method

The NVC is based on the idea that the vegetation of Britain can be separated out into plant communities, that is: 'recognisable types of vegetation with a species composition and range of characteristics of particular conditions' (Rodwell, 1991a, p. 266). The method for determining the community type requires the selection of areas of vegetation that look uniform in composition and structure, and within this the placing of square samples, known as quadrats, to provide representative examples of the vegetation. To begin with the sampling avoids boundaries and transitional zones, but later the way in which the community grades into adjacent communities is looked at. This pragmatic and commonsense approach provides a good starting point for students lacking a scientific background, and is also quicker than more objective methods of sampling, so fitting more comfortably within the limited time available for most class exercises. The plants within each quadrat are listed and given a quantitative score as a measure of abundance. Particular attention is paid to accurate identification because the system was founded on a belief that 'it really does matter which plants grow where' (Rodwell, 1991a, p. 267). Following the fieldwork, the frequency with which each species occurs in the quadrats is calculated and this value, together with the range of abundance scores for each species, provides the features used to determine the community type. Five quadrats provide a reasonable sample size and this number also makes it easy to determine frequency values, which range from I to V, because the number of quadrats in which the species occurs will give the frequency value directly.

The process of identification of community type using this 'floristic' description is analogous with the way you might go about identifying a wildflower. If you come across a new wildflower that you want to put a name to, you might compare your specimen with a picture in a field guide or a written description. If you are more experienced you might use a key to arrive at an answer first and then check the answer by looking at the illustration or the written description. In a similar way, the determination of a plant community type in the NVC starts by using a key to arrive at a community type and this is then checked by comparison with the floristic table for the community type; here the floristic table is serving the same function as the wildflower picture. Finally, the conclusion about community type needs to be checked against the written description provided for each community; the equivalent of the written description of a species in the field guide or flora.

The NVC keys are a bit daunting for the inexperienced. Just as a botanical key requires knowledge of the terms used to describe the particular plant group being dealt with, so the NVC keys require an understanding of terms such as *constant, occasional* and *rare,* which refer to frequency, and are distinct from terms such as *dominant,* which refer to abundance. Abbreviated keys that focus on the plant communities occurring in a particular geographical location can help students learn to find their way through these terms without being overwhelmed by too many choices.

Example 1: Lowland heath from two contrasting natural areas

Introduction

A lowland dry heath community provides a good starting point for understanding how the NVC works. There are not too many species for students to identify and species lists for the vegetation samples are of a manageable size. The habitat is open and dominated by one or two constant species, so it is easy for students to see uniformity of structure and composition within the vegetation and to select appropriate samples. Most of the plants within the quadrats will be relatively easy for students to identify, but there will be two or three grasses to challenge their developing skills and there is the excitement of the possible discovery of a tiny moss or lichen hiding between the heather plants. Many heathland lichens are exquisitely beautiful and never fail to elicit delight. In Sussex we are particularly fortunate in having a very varied geology, and in this example a comparison of similar heath on different geology is used to demonstrate the strengths of the NVC as a data analysis tool. At the end of the section, these types are discussed in relation to the country as a whole.

English Nature's current strategy for nature conservation (outlined in *Beyond 2000)* is based on the division of England into 120 'Natural Areas', reflecting the distribution of wildlife and natural features (English Nature, 1997a). Seven of these extend inside the administrative boundary of Sussex, illustrating the rich diversity of habitats and plant communities found within the county. Heathland occurs in two of these Sussex Natural Areas: High Weald in the east of the county and Wealden Greensand in the west. The two areas of heathland both contain the H2 dry heath community of ling heather – dwarf furze heath (Rodwell, 1991b), but the communities differ in subtle ways, reflecting the different geology of the two areas.

The data analysis table for the High Weald site (Ellisons Pond, Ashdown Forest, map reference TQ 462287)

The data analysis for this heath community is relatively uncomplicated because there are only three sub-communities and the floristic table fits on a single sheet of A4 paper. In order to compare quadrat data from a particular example, the data have to be ordered in the same way as the standard floristic table with which the data are being compared. Floristic tables look complicated, but they are all constructed in the same way. In this example students learn about constructing a comparison table without getting lost in a vast array of species. Table 2.1 shows a comparison table for a particular example of a dry heath community from the High Weald. Constant species, those species that are likely to occur in every quadrat, are listed first. These are followed by preferential species, which are particularly useful in deciding which sub-community one is dealing with. And finally there is a long list of associate species, which fill in the detail of the community but are not particularly diagnostic. Ordering our data in this way allows us to compare the quantitative measures of frequency directly with standard values, and we have added a 'comments' column at the extreme right so that we can highlight species with values that differ markedly from the standard data while at the same time facilitating a quick assessment of the measure of agreement.

In this example we have compared our data with the H2c sub-community data (Rodwell, 1991b, pp. 388–9), rather than with all three communities. This is because the simplified key (based on Rodwell, 1991b, pp. 359–60) gave a fairly conclusive answer. First, H2 heath was separated out from the more continental heath of East Anglia (H1) on the basis of the presence of bell heather and either dwarf furze or western gorse, and from the more western heath of the New Forest (H3) on the basis that bristle bent grass was absent. Then, the purple moorgrass (H2c) sub-community was indicated because this grass was very common and had totally displaced wavy hairgrass, and cross-leaved heath was more frequent than bell heather.

The standard data set for the H2c sub-community looks a bit sparse because most of the preferential species for the H2a and H2b sub-community do not occur in this sub-community. Our data from the High Weald show a reasonably good fit with the sub-community data from the standard floristic table, except that we have no wavy hairgrass; and bell heather is much less frequent, while cross-leaved heath is more frequent. If we turn to the written description in Rodwell 1991b, we find an account on p. 386, which matches our situation. We read that this sub-community is characteristic of areas where the soil becomes waterlogged at certain times of the year, and that this waterlogging leads to the replacement of wavy hairgrass by purple moorgrass, and bell heather by cross-leaved heath.

Table 2.1. NVC Floristic table comparing data from 4 m by 4 m quadrats on heath in the High Weald with standard data for H2 ling – dwarf furze heath.

For simplicity, only the frequency values have been included, as these are more important than abundance values in determining community type. Common names are used (except for lichens), but botanical names are listed in the appendix to avoid confusion.

Constant species	Standard data for H2c	Heath on High Weald	
		Data	Comments
ling heather	V	V	agrees
dwarf furze	V	IV	slightly lower
bell heather	IV	III	**much lower**
wavy hairgrass	II		**none**
Preferentials for H2a			
fork moss			
cupressus moss			
red fescue			
Cladonia fimbriata (a lichen)			
Cladonia coccifera (a lichen)		II	not in H2c
Cladonia chlorophaea (a lichen)			
hair moss			
Preferentials for H2b			
bracken	II	II	agrees
bilberry			
oak seedling			
birch seedling		I	not in H2c
pine seedling			
rowan seedling			
bramble			
Preferentials for H2c			
purple moorgrass	V	V	agrees
cross-leaved heath	III	V	**much higher**
petty whin	I	present in area	
Associates present in quadrats			
common gorse	I	I	agrees
Cladonia impexa (a lichen)		II	not in H2c

The High Weald site is an area on Ashdown Forest where the open heath is being invaded by birch, and considerable efforts have been made to control the spread of birch trees. It is good news for the site managers that birch seedlings only occurred in one quadrat. They will also be pleased to see the presence of some lichen species characteristic of the more species-rich H2a sub-community, suggesting that with appropriate management to curb the purple moorgrass this community might become more species-rich. This part of the Ashdown Forest is now being grazed by sheep and cattle, and it will be interesting to see how the H2 heath community changes under this new management.

The data analysis table for the Wealden Greensand site (Sullington Warren, map reference TQ 099142)

In this case, although the key suggested that the heathland community was H2, it was not clear whether the sub-community was H2a or H2b. There were lots of seedlings of oak, birch and pine, which suggested the H2b sub-community, but there was no bilberry, which should have been constant, and there were also patches of some of the mosses and lichens characteristic of the H2a sub-community. So the comparison table (see Table 2.2) contains data from the standard table (Rodwell 1991b, pp. 338–9) for both these sub-communities.

There is a dramatic contrast with the data set from the High Weald. We have no purple moorgrass or cross-leaved heath this time; and both wavy hairgrass and bell heather occur in every quadrat. This can be related directly to the different geology of the two areas. Ashdown Forest in the High Weald lies on the Hastings Beds, characterised by silty sand, which was laid down in estuarine conditions (English Nature, 1997a, pp. 9–10). The high level of river-borne silt makes this type of sand soft and silky, almost clay-like, to the touch when rolled between fingers. The silt traps water and leads to waterlogging of the ground in winter. In contrast, Sullington Warren lies on the Wealden Greensand, which is a sea-deposited, acidic sand. The Greensand was laid down under the sea and became covered with chalk, which then eroded away (English Nature, 1997b, p. 7). Frost-shattered flints lie in the surface deposits and the sand feels hard and gritty when rubbed between the fingers. There is no silt to retain the water and the sand is very free-draining, leading to the development of a much more typical heathland soil, known as a podzol, than on Ashdown Forest. Under these free-draining conditions bell heather and dwarf furze are often co-dominant with the ling heather, and cross-leaved heath may be totally absent (Rodwell, 1991b, pp. 383–85).

From the comments column it can be seen that the constant species show a good fit with the H2 community, but some preferential species (such as

Table 2.2. NVC Floristic Table comparing data from 4 m by 4 m quadrats on heath on the Wealden Greensand with standard data for H2 ling – dwarf furze heath.

For simplicity, only the frequency values have been included, as these are more important than abundance values in determining community type. Common names are used (except for lichens), but botanical names are listed in the appendix to avoid confusion.

Constant species	Standard data for		Heath on Wealden Greensand	
	H2a	H2b	Data	Comments
ling heather	V	V	V	agrees
dwarf furze	V	V	IV	slightly lower
bell heather	IV	V	V	agrees with b
wavy hairgrass	IV	V	V	agrees with b
Preferentials for H2a				
fork moss	II	II	III	slightly higher
cupressus moss	II	II	IV	**much higher**
red fescue	II	I		**none**
Cladonia fimbriata (a lichen)	II		II	agrees with a
Cladonia coccifera (a lichen)	II			none
Cladonia chlorophaea (a lichen)	I			none
hair moss	I		II	slightly higher
Preferentials for H2b				
bracken	II	IV		none
bilberry		**V**		agrees with a
oak seedling	I	III	IV	nearest to b
birch seedling	I	III	III	agrees with b
pine seedling		I	III	nearest to b, but higher
rowan seedling		I		agrees with a
bramble		I	I	agrees with b
Preferentials for H2c				
purple moorgrass	II	III		**none**
cross-leaved heath	II			agrees with b
petty whin		I		agrees with a
Associates present in quadrats				
common gorse	I	I	III	higher
Cladonia impexa (a lichen)	I	I	II	reasonable agreement

bilberry, and the mosses and lichens) suggest a better fit with H2a and other preferential species (such as the tree seedlings and bramble) with H2b. This is where the analysis gets interesting, and vegetation characteristics have to be set within the wider context of the management of the site to make sense. The spread of this type of vegetation in south-east England was encouraged by human activity in the Bronze Age and possibly earlier, and management treatments continue to be of prime importance in maintaining the plant community (Rodwell, 1991b, p. 386). In the absence of grazing it progresses to woodland: the early stages of this can be seen in the H2b sub-community characterised by tree seedlings and bilberry. In contrast, the typical sub-community, H2a, develops where there are gaps in the ling heather, created by the leggy nature of ageing heather bushes (Rodwell, 1991b, p. 384) or by management designed to increase biodiversity. The site, consisting of just over 25 hectares, is an island of heathland within a belt of stockbroker housing, and is owned by the National Trust. As part of the intensive management, bracken is removed and the heather is cut, thus producing a similar effect to grazing, which would be difficult to implement on this site. This is pushing the community towards the more species-rich H2a sub-community, but the management is retaining a screen of oak, birch and pine trees round the area, which gives rise to large numbers of tree seedlings in the quadrats and pushes the community towards the H2b sub-community. Thus, analysis of the data makes ecological sense and, in coming to a conclusion, students develop the skills required to present an argument and to weigh up conflicting pieces of evidence.

Extending the exercise to other regions

The ling – dwarf furze heath from Sussex which we have been discussing in this example is easily related to other lowland dry heaths. Such heaths occur across a wide geographical circle from East Anglia through the Weald and Hampshire Basin to Somerset, Dorset, Devon, Cornwall and South Wales; up the western side of Britain to North Wales and the Isle of Man; across the southern Pennines; and down into northern Norfolk (Rodwell 1991b, p. 351). For learners living further north, the best starting point will be the ling – bilberry heath (Rodwell 1991b, pp. 492–503) which predominates on grouse-moors and in sub-montane regions and extends to the far north of Scotland. The ling sub-community of this heath is much more species-rich than the two lowland heaths of our example, but the same principles apply, and most of the key players, the constant and preferential species, occurred in our quadrats. The additional species-richness is largely made up from a very long list of associate mosses and lichens occurring in only 20 per cent of samples. Having followed the procedure for our less species-rich example, you will be able to move with ease to this and other examples of upland heaths.

Example 2: The woodland section of the NVC

Having got to grips with heath, students are then ready to go on and tackle the more complicated situation found in woodlands. Woodlands present difficult scales for us to deal with, both spatially and in time. It is much less easy to see uniform areas on the large scale of woodland trees than it is in open habitats: to start with, one is usually standing underneath them, and there may be a dense under-storey of shrubs. Large quadrats are needed to sample the tree and shrub component of the woodland. These are difficult to set out and it is difficult to judge how much of the quadrat is covered by each species. The vegetation growing on the woodland floor, wildflowers and mosses, is on a totally different scale, and so a second, smaller, quadrat is required within each large quadrat to build up a complete picture of the woodland. This leads to massive floristic tables with the canopy species listed first, followed by shrub species and finally the woodland-floor species. Trees grow and age on a much longer time-scale than humans and this makes interpretation of woodland change challenging.

However, having taken on board these complications, students enjoy working with the woodland section of the NVC. Most people with an interest in natural history will be able to identify common tree and shrub species, as well as many of the woodland wildflowers. So one is starting from where they are, and the rarer plants, such as wild service trees, which one is introducing, will be of special interest because of their rarity. Mosses will be new to most of these students, but many woodland mosses are distinctive, and their study is gaining in popularity with the publication of habitat field guides such as Carol Crawford's guide *Bryophytes of Native Woods* (2002), which uses common names. And there is special appeal in finding out about their own local little bit of woodland. Indeed many students have gone on from class sessions to discover about this for themselves, and student projects have contributed to research (Pilkington, 2003a).

Woodland section of NVC in relation to soil

A calendar featuring the British countryside will usually contain a picture of a bluebell wood, and this represents for many people their idea of an ideal wood. So local bluebell woods will provide a good starting point for learning about the ecology of woodlands. Such woods are abundant in the Weald of Sussex, where they occur on a range of brown-earth soils from acidic sandy soils through to more base-rich calcareous clays. Two different NVC communities are represented by these woods, oak – bracken – bramble woodland (W10) on the first, and ash – field maple – dogs mercury woodland (W8) on the second (Rodwell, 1991c). By looking at an example of each, students discover for themselves general ecological principles and are able to relate differences in the vegetation to soil characteristics, such as pH, and past management of the woodland. The relationship between these examples and woods in other parts of the country is discussed in a section at the end of this chapter.

Measuring soil pH in the field is difficult and I have used a range of techniques over the years, from colorimetric methods to various meters and probes. Students like to use meters: it feels like real science and they expect them to be foolproof. This is far from the case (see chapter 8 for a fuller discussion) and it may be difficult to convince them that the reading on the dial may be giving them a misleading answer. However, I have found that the following standard method, using a portable, battery-operated pH meter, gives consistent results with reasonably experienced students:

> Fill a calibrated bottle to the 50 ml mark with distilled water and add soil up to the 70 ml mark. Shake for 5 minutes and then allow to settle for 20 minutes before decanting. Dip the electrode of the meter into 2 cm of supernatant, stir gently for 20 seconds and take the reading as soon as the display has stabilised.

Two contrasting types of woodland and two methods for dealing with them

The full NVC method for woodland requires tree and shrub data to be collected from 50 m by 50 m quadrats, and then the plants growing on the woodland floor, the 'field layer', to be recorded from a 4 m by 4 m quadrat within each of the large quadrats. The two records are combined to make a single data set. Putting out 50 m tapes through trees and shrubs to demark the quadrats is a difficult operation, and doomed to failure with inexperienced students if there is any quantity of under-storey. So, an area of woodland with a very sparse under-storey was chosen to demonstrate this method and then students used an alternative method developed by Kirby *et al* (1991, p. 75) in a contrasting wood with a very dense shrub layer. In the second method, a 4 m by 4 m quadrat is set out first and the plants on the woodland floor (the 'field layer') within this are recorded. Then students take 12 paces out from the sides of the quadrat to visually demark an area of about 25–30 m square, and within this they record the tree and shrub species. This visual quadrat is not as large as the 50 m by 50 m quadrats, but Kirby *et al* (1991, p. 75) suggest that this slightly reduced area will not be significantly different for classification purposes. This 'minimum quadrat' method also has the advantage that it can be used by someone working on their own. In each case, a bulb-planter is used to extract two soil samples from each field layer quadrat at a depth of 10 cm, for measurement of pH.

The two woods chosen also belong to different NVC woodland types. The first, Nap Wood (TQ 5833), lies on a spur of Tunbridge Wells Sandstone near Marks Cross in East Sussex. Marren (1992, p. 94) describes it as 'a well-preserved wood typical of the High Weald'. The area chosen was near the entrance, at the top of a north-facing slope where a very shallow acidic soil overlies the parent sandstone bedrock. The second wood, Blackbrook Wood (TQ 3417), is in the Low Weald and lies on Wealden Clay to the south-east of Ditchling Common in East Sussex. The area chosen was in the eastern part of this 43 hectare block of rather fragmented woodland, where a band of Paludina limestone gives rise locally to an area of neutral soil.

The data analysis table for Nap Wood

The key for the woodland section of the NVC (Rodwell,1991c, pp. 35–45) starts by separating off a number of woodlands that clearly do not apply to this case; woodlands on wet soils, dominated by willow, downy birch or alder, and woodlands dominated by beech, yew, scots pine or juniper. We then get on to oak woodlands and, again, some woods that do not fit are separated off first: those with a carpet of great fork moss or wood sorrel or wavy hairgrass. This brings us to our two bluebell woods both of which have pedunculate oak as a canopy constant. Nap Wood comes out as W10, oak – bracken – bramble wood (Rodwell, 1991c, p. 43) because pedunculate oak and silver birch are constant. On the woodland floor, bracken, which likes an acid soil, dominates and dogs mercury, which is only found on more alkaline soils, is absent. At the sub-community level, the anemone sub-community, where wood anemone replaces bluebell as the dominant species on the woodland floor, is separated off first. Our example lacks wood anemone, so we move on to a series of sub-communities, which we also reject, dominated in turn by ivy, creeping soft-grass, and sycamore with wood sorrel. This leaves us with the typical sub-community W10a, and so we can set up our comparison table using the standard data for this sub-community (see Table 2.3). In the comments column of this table, we have only commented when a frequency value for a species in our quadrats differs from the standard data by more than one. Otherwise we have accepted that there is reasonable agreement.

This sample from Nap Wood represents an extreme example of W10 woodland almost on the boundary with W16 oak – birch – wavy hairgrass woodland (Rodwell, 1991c, pp. 263–77), which occurs typically on more acidic

Table 2.3. NVC Floristic Table comparing Nap Wood data with standard
W10 data for oak – bracken – bramble wood.

For simplicity, only the frequency values have been included, as these
are more important than abundance values in determining
community type. Common names are used (except for some mosses),
but botanical names are listed in the appendix to avoid confusion.

	Standard data for W10a	Nap Wood, High Weald Data	Comments
Canopy constants			
pedunculate oak	III	V	**more frequent**
silver birch	III	V	**more frequent**
beech	I	III	**more frequent**
rowan	I	II	
holly	I		
alder	I		
wild cherry	I		
downy birch	I	IV	**much more frequent**
yew	I		
hornbeam	I		
aspen	I		
Canopy preferentials			
sessile oak	III	II	
sweet chestnut	I		
Scots pine	II	II	
sycamore	II		
ash	I		
oak hybrids	I		
Under-storey			
hazel	III		**none**
common hawthorn	II	I	
holly	II		
hornbeam sapling	I		
guelder rose	I		
beech sapling	II	II	
rhododendron	I	II	
rowan	I	II	
silver birch sapling	I	II	
crab apple	I		
pedunculate oak sapling	I	II	

	standard data for W10a	Nap Wood, High Weald	
		Data	Comments
Field layer			
Preferentials for W10a			
bramble	V	I	**much less frequent**
bracken	IV	V	
honeysuckle	III	I	**slightly less frequent**
Other sub-communities			
Catherine's moss	I	I	
feather moss	II	II	
forest star	II	I	
tamarisk moss	I	II	
ordinary moss	I	III	**higher**
neat moss	I	I	
Associates			
bluebell	III	II	
Dicranella heteromalla (moss)	I	I	
cypress moss	I	V	**much more frequent**
pedunculate oak seedling	I	I	
rowan seedling	I	I	
pincerwort (a liverwort)	I	II	
beech seedling	I	II	
holly seedling	I	I	
fork moss	I	IV	**much more frequent**
average pH 4.0–5.5		3.9	**more acidic**

soils than W10, but, as its name suggests, is carpeted with wavy hairgrass rather than bluebells. The sandy soil ,with an average pH of 3.9, is very acid for W10, which typically occurs on soils from pH 4.0 to 5.5 (Rodwell 1991c, p. 182), and lying as a thin layer over sandstone will be very free-draining and lacking in nutrients. Most of the differences highlighted in the comments column of the comparison table can be related to these soil characteristics. Thus, among the canopy constants, birch, which is typical of sandy soils, and beech, which is frequently dominant on well-drained sands (Clapham, Tutin and Warburg, 1962), are both more frequent. In the under-storey, hazel, which likes damp, neutral or moderately acid soils (Clapham, Tutin and Warburg, 1962) is absent. In the field layer, bramble, which likes a nutrient-rich soil, has a low frequency, while bracken, which favours acid soils, is rampant with high abundance values (not shown in the table). And finally, two heathland mosses (Watson, 1981), cypress moss and fork moss, present as low-frequency associates in the standard data, are present in almost every quadrat. Bluebell was slightly less frequent than the standard data in the area sampled at the top of the slope, but became much more frequent lower down the slope as the depth of soil overlying the sandstone bedrock increased.

Other differences in our data can be linked to past management of the wood. For example, pedunculate oak was planted into many Sussex woods in the mid 1800s, and this legacy is evident in the high frequency of this species in data collected from many Sussex woods (Pilkington, 2003, p. 33). In our particular example, pedunculate oak occurred in every quadrat.

The data analysis table for Blackbrook Wood

We follow through the key (Rodwell,1991c, pp. 35–45) to the point where we left off for Nap Wood, with pedunculate oak as a canopy constant, but this time we have ash and field maple as canopy constants instead of silver birch, reflecting the requirement of these species for a more alkaline soil. This brings us out to W8, ash – field maple – dogs mercury woodland (Rodwell 1991c, p. 43) for Blackbrook Wood. For the sub-communities, we can reject the communities that are dominated by tufted hairgrass or ivy, and this leaves us with the sub-community in which wood anemone and lesser celandine are constant, and the typical sub-community in which these two species are rare. Our quadrat data set suggests the typical sub-community, because lesser celandine is absent and wood anemone has a low frequency, but we will include both sub-communities in our table of comparison because lesser celandine occurs within the part of Blackbrook Wood sampled and the flora of the woodland floor was growing in patches, which made sampling difficult.

Within W8 woodland there is a clear difference between woodlands occurring in the south-east of England and those occurring in the north and west. The floristic table separates out sets of types from these two regions on the basis of characteristic species in the canopy and in the under-storey, and we have followed this in our table of comparison (Table 2.4). Looking at this table we can see that the two principal canopy constants, ash and field maple, and the south-east of Britain preferential species, pedunculate oak, are all very frequent, thus confirming our assignment of Blackbrook Wood to ash – field maple – dogs mercury woodland (W8). Similarly, the field layer constants bramble and dogs mercury agree with the typical sub-community, but we will need to explain why feather moss has such a low frequency. The under-storey constants are very different with a low frequency of hazel and high frequencies of several other shrubs. We will deal with the discrepancies in the shrub layer first: here past management practices rather than soil characteristics provide the explanation.

As Rodwell (1991c, pp. 116–17) explains, south-eastern communities of W8 woodland were almost universally treated as coppice and this has led to increased amounts of hazel, except where the coppice crop comprised trees like hornbeam or lime, which cast a deep shade. The adjacent area of Blackbrook Wood consists of overgrown hornbeam coppice, which now shares the canopy with the ash and oak, and casts a very deep shade. Consequently, the shrub layer is absent apart from very small amounts of hawthorn. In contrast, our area has no hornbeam and the comparatively light shade cast by the ash and oak canopy has allowed a very dense shrub layer to develop. Most of the rest of Blackbrook Wood contains overgrown hornbeam coppice, apart from one other area, also adjacent to our area which also lacks hornbeam and contains planted horse chestnut coppice. Presumably, the hornbeam was taken out to allow the chestnut coppice to grow. It is possible that our area was also cleared of hornbeam in preparation for coppice planting which never took place. However, whatever the process, the effect of canopy hornbeam on the shrub layer is clearly demonstrated in the two areas.

And what about the low frequency of feather moss? This is more likely to be linked to climate than to past management. Wealden woods tend to have a more Atlantic climate than generally prevails in the south-east, and this is often reflected in the moss flora (Rose, 1995, p. 18). In these wetter woods on the weald, feather moss is less frequent than in the more usual W8 woodland of southern Britain.

We turn now to look at the field layer preferential species which will help us to decide whether we have the 'a' or 'b' sub-community. We have included both in our table, and the comments column strongly suggests that we have the 'a' or typical sub-community. We have also listed the preferential species from other sub-communities which occurred in our quadrats. Again these agree

Table 2.4. NVC Floristic Table comparing Blackbrook Wood data with standard W8 data for ash – field maple – dogs mercury wood.

For simplicity, only the frequency values have been included, as these are more important than abundance values in determining community type. Common names are used (except for some mosses), but botanical names are listed in the appendix to avoid confusion.

| | Standard Data for | | Blackbrook Wood, Low Weald | |
	W8a	W8b	Data	Comments
Canopy constants				
ash	IV	IV	V	
field maple	II	I	III	agrees with a
crab apple	I		I	agrees with a
S.E. preferentials				
pedunculate oak	IV	III	IV	agrees with a
hornbeam	II	II		agrees with a
silver birch	II	I		none
elm species	I			agrees with b
sweet chestnut	I	I		none
wild service	I			present in area - agrees with a
Under-storey constants				
hazel	V	IV	II	**much less frequent**
common hawthorn	III	IV	III	agrees with a
field maple	II	I	III	agrees with a
ash sapling	II	II		none
elder	I	II	V	**much more frequent**
dogwood	II	I	I	agrees with b
blackthorn	I	I	V	**much more frequent**
spindleberry	I		V	**much more frequent**
S.E. Preferentials				
woodland hawthorn	I	I	V	**much more frequent**
hornbeam	I	I		none
Field Layer Constants				
dogs mercury	IV	III	IV	agrees with a
feather moss	IV	IV	I	**much less frequent**
bramble	IV	III	IV	agrees with a

| | Standard Data for | | Blackbrook Wood, Low Weald | |
	W8a	W8b	Data	Comments
Preferentials for W8a				
rough meadow grass	III	II	IV	agrees with a
ground ivy	III	II	IV	agrees with a
primrose	III	II	I	agrees with b
dog violet	II	II	IV	slightly more frequent
			IV	than a
bugle	II	II		slightly more frequent
Preferentials for W8b				
wood anemone	I	V	I	agrees with a
celandine	I	IV		present in area –
			I	agrees with a
yellow archangel	I	II		agrees with a
wood dock	I	II	II	agrees with b
Other preferentials				
ivy	II	II	I	agrees
goosegrass	I	II	IV	**much more frequent**
herb Robert	I	I	I	agrees
stripe moss	I	I	II	agrees
Thamnobryum alopecurum (moss)	I	I	II	agrees
hard shield fern	I		I	agrees with a
Main associates				
bluebell	III	IV	III	agrees with a
ordinary moss	III	II	III	agrees with a
wavy flat moss	III	III	I	less frequent
enchanter's nightshade	III	I	II	between a and b
wood avens	III	I	II	between a and b
Average pH	4.5–7.0	4.5–7.0	5.4	

with the 'a' sub-community, except for goosegrass, which was much more frequent in our quadrats. This species is more frequent in northern and western sub-communities not shown in our table (Rodwell, 1991c, p. 151), and again points to the more Atlantic nature of Wealden woods.

Extending the exercise to other regions

The two dry woodland types, ash – field maple – dogs mercury woodland (W8) and oak – bracken – bramble woodland (W10), which we have used in this example extend throughout most of Britain (Figure 9 in Rodwell, 1991b, p. 23), although they are particularly characteristic of the warm, dry south-eastern lowland zone. The two equivalent woodland types characteristic of the cool, wet north-western sub-montane zone, ash – rowan – dogs mercury woodland (W9) and oak – birch – wood sorrel woodland (W11), do not occur over the rest of Britain, so you are fortunate if you live in this north-western zone. You will probably be able to find examples of W8 and W10 woodland to compare with our two Sussex woods and then you will be able to go on and apply the same principles to the north-western equivalents which we in the south do not have easy access to.

The beauty of the NVC for teaching

The NVC approach outlined here has many advantages as a framework for teaching people about natural science and the skills needed to work as a professional wildlife surveyor or conservation manager. Identification skills, particularly of less well-known plant groups, such as grasses and mosses, may be taught as part of an undergraduate course, but there is rarely sufficient time to practise these skills and acquire proficiency. Identification exercises as an end in themselves are unlikely to excite the interest of the adult learner, and learning these skills by oneself while on the job is at best a slow and frustrating process. Learning about the NVC by collecting quadrat data from a range of habitats is an ideal way to get lots of practice in identification. Students can work in groups and help each other remember salient features. Different students will have different strengths, will learn to identify species in a different order and so will be able to teach each other. And there is always the tutor as well. Sometimes no-one will be able to identify a particular specimen: then a team effort will be needed, using a key to arrive at an answer. Plants will be learned in context and as part of a community in a particular habitat, thus reinforcing general ecological principles at the same time without any additional effort. Since the NVC uses the whole range of plants from mosses to trees, the student acquires broad–ranging rather than narrow specialist skills, and an appreciation of the importance of paying attention to correct identification, a feature lamentably absent from many so-called professional wildlife surveys.

In addition to identification skills, students learn in a pragmatic way about how to sample vegetation and make sense of their fieldwork. There is no daunting statistical maths to get in the way of their understanding, but at the same time the approach is objective, using quantitative values for frequency and abundance of the plants in the community being studied. Thus general data analysis skills are learned, which can be applied to other situations.

And, finally, the art of balancing conflicting evidence to arrive at a conclusion is practised. The answers are rarely cut and dried, so it will be a case of presenting a good line of reasoning and contributing to a discussion, skills which will be essential for wildlife conservation. As Peter Marren suggests, wildlife conservation is not just about surveys and monitoring, but about politics and arguing one's case. 'In practice looking after wildlife is not based on scientific rationalisation alone, but on negotiation and politics.' (Marren, 2002, p. 27). In the Blackbrook Wood example, the exercise could be extended to include an adjacent area of overgrown hornbeam coppice as a contrast to the area without hornbeam that was studied. Data from this area, collected by a student as part of a field biology research project, showed that wood anemones and bluebells were more frequent and abundant under the overgrown hornbeam coppice than in the average picture represented by the standard data for this type of woodland (Pilkington 2003a, p. 32). Having collected their data, students could be introduced to the current debate about whether coppicing should be re-introduced to hornbeam woods in Sussex, which were last coppiced 50 or 60 years ago during the Second World War. Ted Green (2000) has suggested that it is dangerous to coppice a stool outside its original coppicing cycle, and hornbeam in particular is sometimes a reluctant producer of coppice re-growth, so there is no guarantee that the hornbeam would coppice successfully after this length of time. In addition, deer are increasing in number in lowland Britain and pose a major problem to coppice re-growth on sites where coppice management has been recently re-introduced (Putman and Moore, 1998). Against this, the beneficial effects on the ground flora of coppicing have been well-documented (Fuller and Warren, 1995, p. 30) and sites can be found where hornbeam has been successfully coppiced in recent years. The additional data from Blackbrook Wood would suggest that because we already have more frequent wood anemones and bluebells under the overgrown hornbeam coppice than is to be expected in this sort of woodland, re-coppicing this amenity woodland may not be a good idea.

Implications

This chapter has articulated, and illustrated with examples, a particular approach to using the NVC which has two aims. First, it provides open-ended science learning and, second, a framework in which we can begin to make sense of the vegetation that lies like a mantle over our countryside.

The science learning here focuses on 'active learning' (Kolb, 1984) rather than the usual model for science teaching, which tends to focus on knowledge acquisition through lectures. The importance of learning through doing, particularly for science, has been emphasised (Grace, 2002), but to implement this will require a major shift in thinking about science teaching. We cling tenaciously to the idea that we must fill peoples' heads with information, in spite of the fact that, in today's world, much of this information will be out of date by the time it is used. The idea that we are teaching people to learn is beginning to be accepted within the arts and the humanities, but has made little impression on science teaching apart from traditional laboratory teaching, and this type of laboratory work tends to concentrate on closed investigations with a 'right' answer rather than enabling the exploratory learning which will lead to independent learners (Knapper and Cropley, 2000). If we are to pay more than lip-service to the notion of learning throughout life, a shift has to be made within universities and colleges to '... a common goal that focuses on the process of learning instead of just the content.' (Knapper and Cropley, 2000, p. 200). And, as John Field points out (2000) we will not achieve our goal if we limit our attention to post-school curricula. Children need to learn how to learn at school. It is too late by the time they are adults. Again, the importance of science investigation at school level has been emphasised in the past, but, as discussed in Chapter 1, this has fallen down partly because the exercises have not been genuinely open-ended. There are examples of schools taking part in environmental projects linked to research establishments (van Marion, 1995) and here the key to success was the extent to which the data collected by the schoolchildren were used by the research establishment. Prompt feedback from the researcher was strongly motivating and ensured high quality student work and learning (p. 26). Using the local countryside, even if it is only a nearby park, can provide another alternative.

In post-liberal CE science teaching, we have had to come to terms with this shift from tutor-imparted knowledge to independent learning. Our students do not come to us with an A-level foundation of assimilated knowledge on which we can build, and yet we are required to document the learning that they have achieved at the end of a course. Within university continuing education, we are also limited by an Arts model of contact hours which, in our department, means that a 24-credit course has a time budget of only 36–40 hours of contact time out of the 240 hours total study time. Arts colleagues find this time allocation generous, but mainstream science colleagues think it is unworkable. The lack of background knowledge and the limited time available mean that it is essential for us to put the emphasis on independent learning. By using the countryside as the laboratory, open-ended science exercises can be devised which leave plenty of room for this learning, and students can be led from tutor-led investigations like those described in this chapter, to conducting their own investigations in their own local habitats. From here it is a natural progression to research projects and work at HE (Higher Education) Level 3. This is what mature students do well and is part of the joy of teaching adults. There are always surprises. Individual students follow up site visits with their own investigations and unearth old maps or documentary evidence, fragments of oral history or old management plans, which shed light on present enigmas. It is important to ensure that tasks are sufficiently open-ended to allow genuinely original contributions. With programmes that cross disciplines, such as landscape studies, students can be encouraged to provide the link between tutors from different disciplines and, for example, put the field biology into its historical context.

Currently, as we saw in Chapter 1, there are very few CE science courses beyond foundation and Level 1. The type of problem-posing approach to teaching science described in this chapter has made it possible to design HE science courses at Level 2 and Level 3 which fit comfortably within the limited contact hours of a department operating within an arts regime. The amount of independent study and research can be gradually expanded as students gain in confidence, resulting in final year degree students able to undertake a major piece of research and write it up as a 10,000-word dissertation. However, the benefits go much wider than such pragmatic considerations. This type of independent student research contributes to our knowledge of local habitats and can result in scientific publications. For example, the data collected by field biology students for their final Level 2 research projects contributed to a paper on Sussex woodlands published in a Joint Nature Conservancy Council report (Pilkington, 2003). There is also a great and increasing need for the fieldwork and biological identification skills achieved by these students. This need is not being addressed by mainstream ecology teaching. Many graduates from full-time degree courses lack basic identification skills and this may prevent them getting the type of job they aspire to. For example, one of my field biology students, Jo, had a first class degree in environmental science, but felt that her full-time degree course had not equipped her for the sort of career she was interested in. This is how she explained her reasons for joining the field biology class.

It was mostly because I wanted to get a job in this field and I needed some practical experience, which I didn't get at university. It was the only course that I found that had a lot of practical element to it, everything else, Masters degrees and all sorts of other courses I tried, were very theoretical which I already had.

(Jo, 2001)

Even where mainstream courses cover biological identification, students rarely get enough practice to become proficient in the identification of more difficult groups, such as mosses. Plant community data sets within the NVC include mosses and lichens, so building up data sets from quadrats in different habitats gives practice without it being a sterile exercise. There is the excitement of not knowing what will be found next. The ecology is learned in the context of particular sites and habitats, and so there is an immediacy about the learning not found in theoretical discussions divorced from actual situations.

At the other end of the spectrum, there has been a recent proliferation of short courses put on by the wildlife trusts for site managers and conservation volunteers which deal in a rather superficial way with the NVC and site management. For example, single-session courses on the NVC using a subjective approach and only a few species. Students come away from such courses thinking that they know all about the NVC and then become disillusioned when faced with the realities of quadrat work and rigorous identification. Similarly, vegetation monitoring can not be taught in a couple of 2–hour evening sessions, even if the participants already possess appropriate identification skills. To pretend that it can not only undercuts more rigorous provision, but leads to subsequent disappointment and possible disengagement by participants.

As well as providing open-ended exercises, this approach to the NVC is building up our knowledge of the detail of wildlife habitats, and it is this detail that is going to be of crucial importance as we make decisions about the future of our countryside. Competing claims for the same piece of land from agriculture, housing, airports and roads, as well as nature conservation, mean that these decisions become progressively more difficult. In the past, economic arguments have won (Green, 1981, p. 205), but there is hope that, as our wildlife resources continue to shrink, we will come to value them more and eventually move beyond the economic argument to wider considerations of the quality of life. It is hoped that 'the National Vegetation Classification will make us look again, with wonder and concern, at the mantle of vegetation which sustains and inspires us.' (Rodwell, 1991a, p. 268) Conserving what remains of our wildlife heritage will require an understanding of the composition and ecology of species-rich examples of plant communities. In Chapter 8 we explore how research using the NVC can contribute to this understanding.

As well as the threat from competing claims for the same piece of land, we have the threat of climate change on already fragmented wildlife habitats. We turn to this issue in the next chapter.

CHAPTER 3

Bringing global issues down to the local level for adult learners

The key difference between the investigations of scientists and those of poets and painters is an insistence on measurements to check the validity of scientific arguments.

(Philander, 1998, p. 14).

Adult learners

According to Freire, the task of educators is to present their subject in such a way as to engage with the learner's agenda. So, as adult educators, we need to start by considering what this might mean in the case of adult learners, and here we are particularly concerned with learning about science. 'Adult learners' have been defined as people aged 25 or over who have had a 'significant break from their initial education' (Carlton, 2001, p. 20). As such, they will bring additional skills to their study as well as a possibly impeding baggage of perceptions of themselves as learners. They will be better at the wider picture, able to use the knowledge and experience that they have acquired in the intervening years to develop a more holistic view of the subject, but they may also come with negative attitudes towards their ability to cope with academic study, particularly in areas where they experienced difficulty at school. For many this includes abstract subjects such as maths and science (Carlton, 2001, p. 13). For these students, context will be all important and the factual knowledge lying behind and forming the foundation of the subject will come later when the reason for knowing is clear. This is the reverse of the way science is usually taught – a systematic body of knowledge is gradually built up from first principles. Much science teaching falls into Freire's category of 'narrative education' (1996, p. 52) where the teacher is trying to 'fill' the students with the contents of his narrative. The contents are often detached from reality and disconnected from the wider picture of the students' experience and view of life. This will become an issue for mainstream university departments as the proportion of adult students increases. It is not just adult learners who have this difficulty with science: Millar (1991) suggests that this may be one of the main reasons why so many adolescent school children find science hard to learn.

In this chapter, global warming is used as an example of a topic which is remote and disconnected from the students' view of the world, and two long-term projects are used to illustrate the Freirean principle of starting from where the students are coming from, and building on local issues of immediate concern to them, before extending the discussion to a wider and less familiar context. The first project looks at the effect of warmer winters on bluebells in a local wood, and the second deals with the related topic of changes in the date on which familiar plants leaf and flower in spring. In both, we are interested in students learning about scientific method and not just scientific facts. Student voices, recorded in 2001 during the Ecological Citizenship Project described in Chapter 4, are used to illustrate the practice, and the relevance of this approach to science teaching in general is discussed.

Getting a handle on global warming: a long-term monitoring study of bluebells in a local wood

Introduction

Natural history classes are almost alone among science courses in being popular with the adult learner (Field, 1995). Many students join such classes because they are interested in the countryside and in finding out more about the plants and animals they encounter when out walking. This is how two students described their reasons for joining a natural history open course:

> *I was seduced by the course description which said 'Come out into the beautiful Sussex Countryside...'*

(Pam, 2001)

> *My main motivation and interest was in learning more about natural history of the local environment.*

(Shirley B, 2001)

To these students, the science behind an issue such as global warming will seem remote:

> *I had no scientific knowledge at all and I found that a great problem, because I found it very difficult to relate to a scientific approach.*

(Shirley B, 2001)

On the other hand, the idea that global warming may lead to the loss of bluebells from local woods is of immediate concern. This scenario was presented in a recent report by Plantlife (1991) *Death Knell for Bluebells*. Warmer winters, it was suggested, may lead to our woods being filled with grass rather than bluebells. Every year at bluebell time local woods suddenly fill with people out walking, so this loss would be a cause of sadness to a large section of the population of Britain.

So, what are the observations behind this prediction? Bluebell woods depend on a delicate balance between the timing or 'phenology' of leafing and flowering, and on the settled conditions prevailing in ancient woodlands which have been in existence for at least 400 years. Bluebell plants are adapted to start growth early in the year while temperatures are cold. This enables them to build up food reserves through photosynthesis, and then to flower and set seed, before the leaves emerge on the woodland trees overhead to cast a deep shade that makes both photosynthesis and pollination by insects difficult. Next year's growth is made ready in the underground bulb and then the current leaves decay, leaving the dry seed pods as the only evidence in summer of the spring haze of blue. The seeds are shed into the soil left bare by the departing leaves. It will be about seven years before the new plants coming from this year's seed will themselves start flowering, ensuring continuity of the population of bluebells as the older plants die. In contrast, grass requires warm temperatures to grow and grass growth in the past occurred well after the bluebells'.

The worry is that warmer winters will enable the grass to start growing earlier in the year (you may have noticed that you are mowing your lawn earlier these days) and that vigorous growth will over-top the bluebells before they have finished flowering. The Plantlife booklet (1991) is suggesting that, as a result of this, in fifty years our springtime woods will be filled with grass, not bluebells. This is dramatic stuff, but ecologists such as Grime (1993) also suggest that changes in the timing of growth and the relative abundance of these two types of plant are likely to provide us with early indications of the effect of climate change on our plant communities. So here is a project which is likely both to interest the adult learner and provide us with useful information about the effect of climate change on what is an important habitat on a world scale – bluebell woods are restricted to the British Isles and the west of mainland Europe. In the next section we look how these ideas can be used to set global warming and scientific method in an accessible context using an ongoing long-term study in Hoe Wood, a local wood in West Sussex. We start by considering scientific method.

Monitoring the flora of Hoe Wood

Posing the question

As the quotation at the head of this chapter asserts, the conduct of science requires that we test our arguments in an objective way, usually by making measurements. We often start with an anecdotal observation, but this has to be developed into a statement which can be tested in this way. In the Hoe Wood study, rather than using an observation that we have made, we are using a prediction from a book: that one effect of global warming will be warmer winters in Britain, and that this will lead to a decrease in bluebells and an increase in grass in our woods. It is the second half of this statement that we plan to test. Bringing this down to the local level, our statement or hypothesis is that:

> *over the next fifty years there will be a decrease in the abundance of bluebells in local woods and an increase in the abundance of grass.*

We can test this hypothesis by estimating the abundance of bluebells, grass and other plants growing on the ground in sample areas of a local wood and looking at how this varies over the years.

Setting out the quadrats

In order to detect early signs of a change in the relative amounts of bluebells and grass in local woods we needed to select a wood that was likely to stay relatively undisturbed for the foreseeable future and then record the abundances of different plants growing on the woodland floor in sample areas or quadrats. We used a piece of woodland called Hoe Wood at the county wildlife trust headquarters and countryside centre (National Grid Reference TQ 218134–218135), which has been set aside for research and is not open to the general public. It consists of large trees of pedunculate oak, ash and field maple with smaller specimens of field maple and hazel forming the understorey below. It is covered in a carpet of bluebells in the spring. In NVC terms it is ash – field maple – dogs mercury W8 woodland (Rodwell, 1991c) similar to Blackbrook Wood which we discussed in the last chapter, but it belongs to a different sub-community, W8b, with wood anemone, lesser celandine and bluebell constant in the field layer.

Quadrats were placed at regular intervals along a footpath to avoid damaging bluebell plants, which are very sensitive to trampling. For this reason we also chose a relatively small quadrat size, 1 m by 1 m, so that the whole quadrat could be easily viewed, and quadrats were set just 30 cm in from the edge of the path. The position of each quadrat was marked with a wooden post, but could also be relocated by measuring along the footpath. The first six quadrats were set out in 1993 at 5 m intervals, and after two years a further 15 quadrats were set out further along the path at 10 m intervals. The position of quadrats was adjusted to avoid discontinuities such as large trees. A simple distribution of samples, ensuring that they can be easily located by recorders even after a considerable lapse of time, has been found to be essential for long-term studies (Peterken, 2000).

When to record

The plan was to come back at the same time every year to record the abundance of all the plants occurring in the quadrats. The timing of observations was obviously going to be critical: woodland plants such as bluebell and wood anemone emerge from the ground, flower quickly and then decay, so the number of plants above ground changes considerably in a short space of time. We tried to base our observations on the time at which the plants reached a certain stage in development rather than on a calendar date. For the first six quadrats this was to be when wood anemone leaves had just appeared above-ground, which was some time in mid March for most years. In practice, this proved very difficult to do: wood anemone leaves emerge as thin spidery stalks and then open out and flower very quickly, and different plants do this at different times, so that some plants are flowering before other plants have even appeared above ground. So we decided to record from the second series of quadrats a month later, when all the wood anemone leaves would be fully expanded and timing would be less critical.

What to record

Records were to be based on percentage cover of each plant species in the quadrat. This is arrived at by mentally taking away all but one species and estimating how much of the square is covered by this species. In order to make the recording quick and accurate across a range of participants, the percentage cover values were grouped into ten categories using the Domin scale (Rodwell, 1991c, p. 6), with a value of 10 representing high cover and a value of 1 just one or two plants. Members of many different natural history classes have done the recording over the years, as this is an ideal exercise for inexperienced students. The plants are easy to identify, there are not too many of them, and it is relatively easy to see how much of the square is covered by each species (much easier than in more crowded habitats, such as grassland). Students usually worked in groups of three or four and consistency was checked by getting two groups to record from the same quadrat in turn. The results showed very consistent recording.

Declining bluebells?

Eleven years of data collected from the first six quadrats showed little sign of any significant decrease in bluebell cover or any increase in grass cover. We can look at the quadrat data in two ways: first, how the abundance changes within each quadrat over the eleven years; and, second, what happens to the abundance averaged over the six samples. In the first case, the abundance of bluebells changed by one or two Domin values, moving both up and down over the years: in only two of the six quadrats does this look anything like a falling trend. The abundance of grass varied much more, but increases did not happen in years when the bluebell abundance fell. Similarly, if we look at the averages for each year, the average Domin value for bluebells moves between 6.8 and 5.7, with a slight downward trend from 6.8 to 5.8. The grass varies from 3.2 to 6.5, with a rising trend to 6.5 in 1998, when it just over-topped the bluebells, followed by a falling trend to 3.3 in 2003.

In the much bigger sample of fifteen quadrats in the second series there is even less suggestion that bluebells might be declining. Average values varied from 7.1 to 8.1 starting at 7.6 and finishing at 7.7. Again, the grass was more variable, ranging from 2.6 to 4.5 and actually decreasing from 3.7 to 2.6 over the nine years of recording. Similar findings were recorded for wood anemone, another spring vernal, and for another warmth-demanding species, cow parsley.

So what have we established? Not evidence of change, but rather the constancy of the plant community growing on the woodland floor in this piece of undisturbed ancient woodland. This is very pleasing, as it indicates that we have a robust method of monitoring and if the study is continued we will be able to pick up any significant decline in the bluebells. There is just a hint that a very gradual decline might be taking place in the first series, which adds excitement to the continuing study and prevents any possible feeling of complacency about global warming. Students are aware that we are looking for a long-term effect and that, like planting trees, they are starting something which will be continued by the next generation:

> I don't know how long the Hoe Wood investigations are going to go on for but I doubt very much if I will be here when they finish but the little bit that I've done towards it will in fact be able to be used by somebody else in future because they will recognise that the method is a proper scientific method.
>
> (Pam, 2001)

The Plantlife time-scale for grass replacing bluebells was fifty years.

Moving from the local to the global

Taking part in the monitoring of bluebell abundance in a local wood taught students about using measurements to find out about a matter of particular interest to them: are bluebells on the decline? From here one could move on to discuss the scientific evidence for global warming which might cause bluebell populations to decline, such as the rapidly increasing levels of carbon dioxide in the earth's atmosphere, and how increased levels of this and other greenhouse gases prevent heat escaping into the stratosphere. These facts would have had little meaning divorced from the local hands-on situation, and needed to be assimilated by the students into their existing view of the world to create a new picture, but in addition an understanding of how science operates is central to current arguments about global warming. Many of the students who had started from a position of no science background did indeed feel that they had a better understanding of the way science operates:

> *My science education ended at 16 and I have had no real input since then at all ... I think I have a wider knowledge about how science works – the method, the way in which you study, the ways in which you record what it is that you are looking at, so that when you want to use that material you've got something concrete. You've got something that is recorded in a manner that other people will understand ...*
>
> (Pam, 2001)

> *I had done a couple of 'O' levels at school, physics and biology, and somehow associated that very much with pottering around in a laboratory, and it was interesting to see that you could in fact broaden the system, you took the same sort of method, the same ways of thinking, and you could apply it perfectly well to something totally different.*
>
> (Josephine, 2001)

> *I had no education or knowledge of science at school and I suppose in a way I was totally naïve about the subject and thought that science was something that was only carried on by academics.*
>
> (Mike, 2001)

Although initially it did not seem like science to some of the students, because it took place in a wood rather than in a laboratory, the experience was actually a more accurate reflection of the way science works than laboratory exercises because it was a genuinely open-ended investigation. As Knapper and Cropley (2000, p. 75) discuss, the sort of laboratory work used for student exercises tends to concentrate on the right answer rather than on the process of investigation. This gives the impression that science normally produces clear-cut answers to problems, whereas only certain types of investigation produce results which enable precise predictions to be made. Such investigations concern simple phenomena that can be studied in controlled, replicated laboratory experiments, not the complex interactions which determine climate. So although accurate predictions about global climate change are in principle possible on the basis of the laws of physics, such forecasts may be impossible in practice because the scientists are dealing with 'idealizations of reality' (Philander, 1998, p. 7). Since, like these students, most people's picture of science is laboratory science it is difficult for them to understand why precise prediction is not possible. This allows political manipulation of the debate because the unpopular decisions which would cut the emission of greenhouse gases can be postponed indefinitely while we wait for the point of absolute certainty. It also means that scientists can always be found to present an opposing view, and by focusing attention on this small group it is possible to create the impression that there is little agreement in the scientific community whereas in fact most scientists are convinced by the evidence that the current rapid increase in the atmospheric concentration of greenhouse gases will lead to global climate change (Philander, 1998, p. 9). Philander goes on to suggest, that in order 'to appreciate what is happening the public needs to become familiar with the methods and results of scientists, especially the reasons for the inevitable uncertainties that preclude precise predictions with which everyone agrees.' The study of biological systems, which are inherently variable, can help to develop this appreciation of uncertainty within science, which is a factor crucial to the global climate change debate. This was something which Bill, a retired engineer, came to understand:

> *There's a probability on the evidence that you've got at that time, but it isn't one hundred per cent. Very little of it you can say with a hundred percent certainty that this is right, or this is going to happen. This uncertainty is far greater in biology than in engineering. ... A lot of the uncertainty is because there are so many interactive areas. You're closing it down. Knowledge is slowly getting better but you're trying to predict and forecast aren't you?*
>
> (Bill, 2001)

Changing lifestyles

There is even more uncertainty when we come to study the effect of climate change on vegetation in the countryside. To begin with there is the difficulty of attributing vegetation change to climate change rather than to other causes (Marrs, 1990). In our study we may detect signs of change in the woodland vegetation, but we will not be able to attribute this unambiguously to climate change rather than to other environmental factors. However, we need to risk making predictions and to follow on with the corresponding adjustments to our behaviour (Barkham, 1994). This will only be effective if we can take the general public with us. An ideal way of doing this would be to involve adults in the monitoring of representative plant communities in their local area. They, like the students in this study, would then become effective ambassadors for changed lifestyles:

> *I talk about what I'm doing to other people and I try to explain that it's a very minor part of the research into possible global warming, and even if I've only interested one person, that's one person more.*
>
> (Pam, 2001)

As well as the science, the students enjoyed being in a beautiful wood, and their aesthetic pleasure reinforced the desire to contribute to the conservation of such places for future generations to enjoy:

> *... we should ensure that we're passing on good environment to our future generations.*
>
> (Mike, 2001)

This was seen as being part of citizenship:

> *... the undertaking of various projects and surveys – it all comes down really to, I don't know what the consensus was of the meaning of the word citizen, a responsible person, and one who is willing to try to improve his own area for the environment ...*
>
> (Mike, 2001)

> *I think you are giving your time to monitor an area and keep the data which perhaps will be useful to citizens in, say, a hundred years' time. Even if it is only a small ten-year monitoring, they will be able to come back and say 'that's how this wood was for ten years one hundred years ago'.*
>
> (Fabae, 2001)

As well as the actual monitoring and survey work which had been done as part of class work, the classes had provided the skills and knowledge that the students needed for this type of conservation work:

> *... the classes provide one with the knowledge to be able to go off and do responsible things in the countryside.*
>
> (Josephine, 2001)

Preparing mainstream HE students for responsible citizenship has been seen as just as important as preparing them for future careers (Knapper and Cropley, 2000, p. 108). With current demographic trends tilting towards the over-60 age-group (Knapper and Cropley, 2000, p. 7), this has to be even more important in the context of adult learners, many of whom will be retired or nearing retirement. Here we are talking about ecological aspects of citizenship, such as taking part in biological monitoring and survey work, but also, as Julia says in the following quote, about energy efficiency and recycling:

> *I was going to say about recycling and doing your very best to use less energy, drive less and generally be environmentally friendly.*

(Julia, 2001)

This age group is likely to exert a considerable influence on the younger generation as well:

> *And very importantly I think, I have been able to pass on my enthusiasm and a little bit of knowledge I have gained to other people, particularly family members, and really most of all to the children, my own grandchildren and other children. I've tried to interest them, the young generation in conservation matters, and natural history and natural things.*

(Julia, 2001)

Conclusions

The relatively small number of plants found in the ground flora of our woodlands, and the ease with which they can be identified, makes monitoring exercises such as this eminently suitable for adult education classes. Concern about changes to the countryside which they know and love provides the stimulus and context for serious engagement with unfamiliar concepts, and students learn about scientific investigation through participation in the process. They are, thus, better equipped to understand the environmental issues raised by global warming and to be convincing advocates for sustainable lifestyles.

Within the wider scientific community, the importance of this type of study that looks at the response of plants to changes in their natural environment *within* the context of the vegetation of which they are a part (first stressed by Pigott in 1982) is now widely recognised, especially for studies relating to the effect of climate change on plants and animals. However, the long-term nature of such studies makes them unattractive to researchers under pressure to produce publications for the next Research Assessment Exercise, and also most funding is tied to short-term, 3- to-5 year projects (Peterken, 2000, p. 12).

Kohler (2002) suggests that this was also the case in the late 1800s, when field-based studies became unpopular compared with lab-based studies because lab techniques were easy to learn, and quick to apply, leading to fast-track careers. Continuing education classes, on the other hand, can provide an opportunity for undertaking such long-term work.

Search for springtime

Phenology, the study of the timing of events such as flowering, is gaining in popularity as the long-term records of the first flowers of spring made by past naturalists are revealing that spring is arriving earlier now than it did a decade ago (e.g. Sparks *et al,* 1998). Such records are an easy way for CE students to learn about scientific recording, and again through local studies, to appreciate global issues. The second part of this chapter describes the complementary phenology study 'Search for springtime' in which participating students recorded the first appearance of key species in their local areas of Sussex on 'Search for springtime' sheets which they helped to design.

In the footsteps of Gilbert White

In Britain we have a wonderful tradition of natural history records going back to the eighteenth century. Gilbert White, who wrote about the parish of Selbourne in Hampshire (1789), is perhaps the best known of the early recorders, but as we shall see there are other very detailed records of the timing of events in the natural world. Students involved with the present study considered they were following in the footsteps of Gilbert White:

> If it wasn't for Gilbert White, starting somewhere, we wouldn't have a record. However modest our little record of the various surveys that we've done is, it may be of use in the future.

(Shirley, 2001)

This type of recording is also very suitable for use in schools, and, indeed, another of the well-known data sets was recorded by pupils and staff at Marlborough College under the direction of one of its masters, Thomas Preston, who founded the Marlborough College Natural History Society. These very detailed records covered a 20-year period (1875–1884) and included meteorological tables, which enabled Preston to produce a report in 1884 tabulating the earliest and latest dates for 127 plants, with weather statistics for each month in each of the 20 years (Clark, 1936). Clark (1936, p.

20) recalls a visit by Preston to his school natural history society in which he described 'the excitement with which their members, masters and boys, scoured the country for first records.' Here there were clearly links between the adults and the pupils who were jointly pursuing an activity and were learning together to identify plants and to recognise the habitats in which the different plants occurred. School pupils, with their sharper eye-sight, might excel in the search, and this sort of positive experience would stay with them for the rest of their lives. This seems to me to be a classic example of the type of *learning*, as opposed to *teaching*, which John Field (2000, p. 136) suggests that we need in our schools if we are truly to achieve the ideal of a learning society in which people are motivated by curiosity and excitement to learn in an explicit way throughout their lives. This type of excitement is sometimes engendered in family learning, and was given as an explanation of a lifelong interest in botany by a CE student when she was asked about her motivation for joining a certificate in field biology programme of study:

> *I've always enjoyed studying, and having seen, as I thought, a night school programme about the Field Biology Certificate it seemed to be offering everything that I was interested in. As a family we'd always been interested in gardening and natural flora, as a small child I can remember going on walks and trying to spot the different flowers before anybody else did. And there were very very few programmes that offered anything to do with botany, and I was delighted when I saw this offered, and it was really that that triggered me into deciding I would do the course.*
>
> (Shelagh, 2001)

Schooling which involved this type of activity would be one way of extending the 'social capital' (Field, 2000, p. 145) beyond those fortunate enough, like Shelagh, to have experienced this within their family. Experience with adult learners strongly suggests that the widening participation agenda has to start at school, since it is very difficult to reach people later in life who are not already interested in explicit learning activities.

Designing the sheet

Our quadrats in Hoe Wood were designed to detect early signs of a decline in bluebells which might be caused by warmer winters. Another related aspect of warmer winters which we could study at the same time was whether plants were coming into leaf and flower earlier in the year. In 1992 WATCH, the junior branch of the County Wildlife Trusts, produced a 'Search for springtime' survey form which asked for information about location and flowering date for horse chestnut, ox-eye daisy, wood anemone, hawthorn and foxglove. This idea was developed by the students to include leafing as well as flowering and to focus on the plants that were part of our woodland story.

We returned to our hypothesis that over the next fifty years there would be a decrease in the abundance of bluebells in local woods and an increase in the abundance of grass, and discussed the theory behind the predicted decline in bluebells. By looking at first-observation dates, we hoped to be able to detect changes in relative flowering or leafing of spring vernals like bluebell and wood anemone compared to warmth-demanding species like grass or cow parsley which might start to compete with these early flowerers following warmer winters. Students were asked to list all the habitats where their list of plants might occur and to consider the factors which might affect time of leafing or flowering. It was pointed out that plants, unlike animals, cannot move to another spot and so need to be able to cope with changing environmental factors. The habitat list included environmental factors such as whether the plant was growing in a sunny or shady location, or in a poor woodland soil or a rich garden soil, as well as differences between spring vernals such as bluebells and wood anemones, which are adapted to start growth during cold weather, and warmth-demanding species such as nettle, goosegrass and cow parsley, which have to wait for the weather to warm up before growth commences. It was also pointed out that some plants might be responding to increasing day length rather than temperature.

The final version of the sheet is given in the box overleaf. Garden locations were explicitly excluded, and nettle and goosegrass were to be recorded when they reached a competitive height (one foot – about 30 cm) rather than when they flowered. The sheet, which included date of leafing for the tree species likely to occur in the woodland canopy, covered nine species of tree and shrub and nine species of herb in addition to the nettle and goosegrass. For flowering we recorded the first flower with properly opened petals. This usually coincides with the shedding of pollen (Hepper, 2003, p. 2508) and is rapidly followed by other flowers opening, thus providing a good guide to the season.

Is spring getting earlier?

In practice some of the species on the 'Search for springtime' sheet gave more consistent results than others. A good species for survey purposes was one which was common in a wide range of habitats, could not be confused with closely related species, and which had a clearly defined point at which it could be said to have 'come into flower or leaf'. Pussy willow was one such plant. The white furry male flowers are familiar objects, having adorned many a nature table at primary school, and it is easy to see when these turn yellow with pollen. Thus, the presence of pollen should provide a consistent record for

Search for Springtime 2003

	Date	Location notes
Hazel catkins with pollen		
Dogs mercury leaves		
Dogs mercury flowers		
Cuckoo pint leaves		
Cuckoo pint flowers		
Celandine flowers		
Nettle shoots 1 ft. high		
Wood anemone leaves		
Wood anemone flowers		
Pussy willow with pollen		
Blackthorn flowers		
Primrose flowers		
Woodland hawthorn leaves		
Woodland hawthorn flowers		
Common hawthorn leaves		
Common hawthorn flowers		
Bluebell leaves		
Bluebell flowers		
Goosegrass shoots 1 ft.		
Cow parsley flowers		
Jack-in-the-hedge flowers		
Hornbeam leaves open		
Beech leaves open		
Oak leaves open		
Ash leaves open		
Ox-eye daisy flowers		
Foxglove flowers		

first flowering date for this species and give a good indication of an early or late spring. Blackthorn was less reliable because it can be confused with the earlier-flowering cherry plum, which is very common in our part of the country. Similarly, woodland hawthorn is sufficiently common in the Weald of Sussex to add confusion to the records for flowering and leafing of common hawthorn.

Over the eleven years of the 'Search for springtime' sheets, the first-flowering date for pussy willow varied by 80 days. The earliest date was in 1993 in late December and the next earliest date occurred in both 1994 and 2002. The most recent year, 2003, was a relatively late year. So there was no consistent trend towards spring arriving earlier. Eleven years is not a long enough timescale to show trends in climate change. This is an important point to establish, since many people will claim that spring gets earlier each year. The older learner will be interested to compare our data with earlier records, as recollections from childhood will suggest that on a timescale of, say, 50 years there has definitely been a change. Robert Marsham, a contemporary and correspondent of Gilbert White, kept records from 1736 which were continued by five generations of his family (Sparks and Carey, 1995, p. 322). From 1736, when records began, to 1947, when the records finished, wood anemone flowered earlier at an overall rate of 0.1 days per year (Sparks and Carey, 1995, p. 325). This works out at just 1.1 days over our eleven years, which would not be detectable with our method of recording – but over 50 years this would be a much more noticeable 5.5 days.

The first graph in Figure 3.1 shows the pattern of first-flowering date for pussy willow for the eleven years over which we have been recording. Our theory is that spring, as signalled by flowering pussy willow, arrives earlier following mild winters. But what do we mean by a 'mild winter'? Sometimes we have a mild December followed by a cold snap in January or February. Fitter *et al* (1995, p. 57) in a study of 243 plants recorded from one locality in southern central England from 1954 to 1989 showed that for most of the species February temperatures exerted the greatest influence on time of flowering. Does our data suggest the same picture? Mean monthly temperatures for England and Wales can be downloaded free from the Meteorological Society website, and in Figure 3.1 we compare the pattern for first flowering date for pussy willow with the mean monthly temperatures for the preceding December, January and February.

As expected, Figure 3.1 suggests a complex picture, but February temperatures are clearly important. Late flowering in pussy willow (peaks in 3.1a) coincide with low mean temperatures in the preceding February (troughs in 3.1b) and vice versa. The much larger data set used by Fitter *et al* showed many additional conflicting influences, with warmer temperatures in the two months before flowering leading to earlier flowering in 60 per cent of the

Figure 3.1(a) Pattern of first-flowering date for pussy willow (tens of days after 21 December of previous year), compared with (b) mean monthly temperature (degrees Centigrade) for preceding December, January and February in second graph. Late flowering in pussy willow (peaks in the first graph) coincides with low mean temperatures in the preceding February (troughs in the second graph) and vice versa.

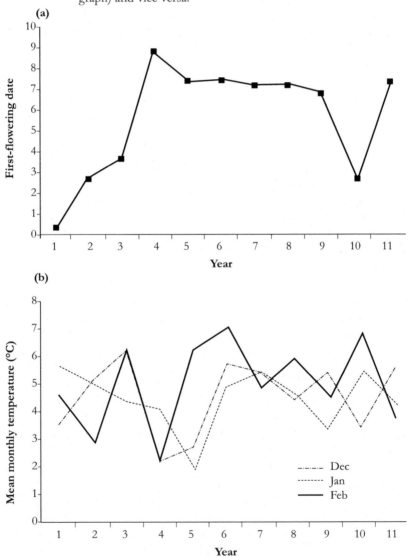

species flowering between January and April, but a warm late summer in the previous year (7–9 months prior to first flowering date) leading to a delay in flowering (1995, p. 59).

At the end of the first year of recording (1993), one class compared their data with records from Edith Holden's *Diary of an Edwardian Lady* (1979). They discovered that their first-flowering date for bluebell was 27 days earlier than the 1906 record from Warwickshire and for cow parsley 16 days earlier. Such a comparison of data from just two particular years needs to come with a very large warning about variation between one year and another, which subsequent students have been in a much better position to appreciate. From the vantage point of eleven years of data we can see the large variation both in time of flowering and winter temperatures. In this case, 1993 turned out to have the highest mean January temperature of the eleven years (year 1 in Figure 3.1) and we would expect this to result in early flowering. The Edwardian records were not just from an earlier period of time, but were also from further north, in Warwickshire, and recent results from the UK phenology network have demonstrated that spring arrives later the further north one goes (Collinson and Sparks, 2003, p. 230). Such discussions lead naturally into ideas about the complexity of the factors influencing the effect of climate change on plants and lead to an appreciation of uncertainty in relation to biological science.

Is there any evidence of change in relative timing of spring vernals and warmth-demanding species?

The primary aim of the 'Search for springtime' sheets was not to see if spring was arriving earlier each year, but to look at the relative timing of growth and flowering in spring vernals such as wood anemone and bluebell compared to warmth-demanding species such as cow parsley and grass. Our hypothesis was that over the next fifty years there would be a decrease in the abundance of bluebells in local woods and an increase in the abundance of grass. On our 'Search for springtime' sheets, cow parsley, which occurs with bluebells in our local woods, provided a reliable record for the first-flowering date of a warmth-demanding species which is also implicated in the decline-of-bluebells story (Plantlife, 1991).

If we follow the timing of the first flowers of wood anemone, bluebell and cow parsley over the eleven years of the 'Search for springtime' sheets (Figure 3.2) they all follow a very similar pattern, separated by about the same number of days each year with early and late years following the same overall pattern as pussy willow flowering. This suggests that although they are not dependent on warm temperatures in order to grow, nevertheless they still flower earlier

Figure 3.2. First-flower date (tens of days after 21 December of previous years) for cow parsley, wood anemone, bluebell and pussy willow over eleven years from 1993 to 2003.

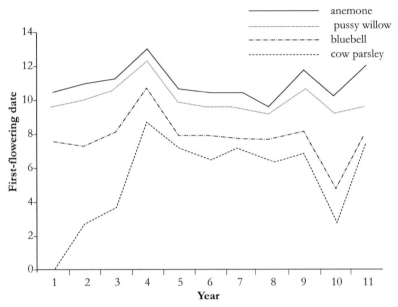

following milder winters. This gives some hope that they may keep pace with the cow parsley, which is predicted to flower earlier following warmer winters.

We can look at the relative trends for bluebell and cow parsley more easily if we plot first flowering day for each of these against the mean temperature in February. This is shown in Figure 3.3, with the two trend lines inserted. We can see that as the mean February temperature increases, the first-flowering date of both species gets earlier, but that this is happening slightly faster for cow parsley than for bluebell. The slope of the trend lines gives us a value for the number of days earlier resulting from a one degree rise in the mean February temperature. This is 4.4 days for cow parsley and 3.2 days for bluebell. It is tempting to extrapolate the trend lines and suggest that it would take a rise of 12.9 degrees in the mean February temperature for cow parsley to overtake bluebell and flower first, but this would be a gross simplification, which would only be true if everything else stayed the same. Such discussions again bring home to students the nature of the evidence being used in arguments and counter-arguments about climate change.

Another complexity which can be noted by students is the effect of genetic make up on flowering date. This is particularly obvious in pedunculate oak trees, where individual trees come into leaf and flower at slightly different times, so that in May the countryside contains a kaleidoscope of oak trees looking green, brown or yellow, a picture captured in John Clare's evocative

Figure 3.3. First-flower date (tens of days after 21 December of previous
year) for bluebell and cow parsley plotted against February mean
temperature, with trend lines inserted.

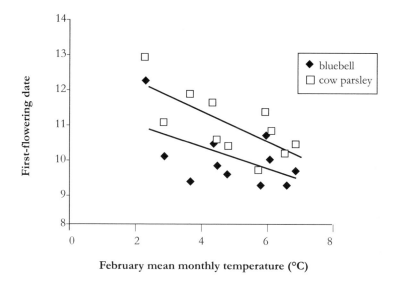

February mean monthly temperature (°C)

lines 'The oak trees budding into brown' (Clare, 1827; 1973, p. 50). Careful
observation will confirm that it is the same individual trees which leaf and
flower before their neighbours each year, but the extent of the separation
depends on the temperatures of a particular year. Plants are also sensitive to
day length and may not flower until a particular day length has been reached,
but the relative sensitivity of different plants to temperature and day length is
not known (Fitter *et al*, 1995, p. 55) and this is another complexity which adds
to the difficulty of predicting how the British vegetation will respond to
climate change.

Implications

In this chapter we have described some ways in which an interest in the natural
world can be developed into an understanding of the science behind nature
conservation and a resulting change to a more sustainable life style. In the next
chapter we explore the extent to which this was successful for participating
students. It is crucial that those of us who work in this field can demonstrate
how such learning for sustainable development can be achieved. To date there
has been very little action in spite of the 1993 Toyne report (HMSO) which
called for funding and the development of a strategy for delivering Education

for Sustainable Development (ESD). As we have seen in this chapter, ESD requires an understanding of the science behind issues like global warming. A subsequent review of progress towards implementation (Ali Khan, 1996) found that most institutions had ignored the recommendations, leaving the action mainly to organisations such as the World Wildlife Fund. There is plenty of interest in environmental issues amongst the general population of this country. Recent surveys in East Sussex conducted by the county council reveal a high and increasing concern for the environment among householders. In 1993, 83 per cent were worried about species and habitat loss and, in 1999, 87 per cent were worried about damage to the natural environment (Alex Tait, County Ecologist, personal communication). Here is the starting point for a more environmentally responsible citizenship, but our society is based on materialism and the perceived need for continually increasing consumption which runs counter to sustainable development. In frustration, environmental activists and anti-globalisation protestors resort to violence, but what is needed, John Field suggests, is a new vision in lifelong learning which will supplement the direct action of the activists with 'a global development strategy which is economically efficient, socially equitable, ecologically sustainable and politically democratic (Field, 2000, p. 155). For issues such as global warming, this needs to start with an understanding of environmental science and particularly the problem of uncertainty which prevents firm predictions. Such knowledge on the part of world citizens would enable them to integrate expert knowledge in this field of science with socially equitable, ecologically sustainable and politically democratic values. Economic efficiency, however, will depend on entering the full long-term cost of environmental degradation into the equation.

CHAPTER 4

Ecological citizens contributing to biodiversity conservation

...the best training for conservation work is still to do some, as a volunteer.

(Marren, 2002, p. 309).

In the last two chapters we have looked at some of the fieldwork designed to equip students to be ecological citizens and to take part in biodiversity conservation. In this chapter we explore, through the voices of some of the students, the extent to which this was achieved for them as individuals. Their voices were recorded during discussion sessions which took place in 2001 as part of a research project exploring ecological citizenship (Pilkington 2003b). But first, what do we mean by the term 'biodiversity'?

Biological diversity or biodiversity has entered our everyday language, but most people remain unsure about the meaning of these words:

We talked about biodiversity in class, and I really didn't understand it at the time

(Pam, 2001)

Hill *et al* (1996, p. 2) define biodiversity as the 'variety of life'. Concern about the variety of life came to the fore as a result of the United Nations Conference on the Environment and Development in Rio de Janeiro in 1992, when heads of state and governments signed two conventions, one of which was about conserving biodiversity. The definition given by the Convention on Biological Diversity spells out what scientists mean by the 'variety of life':

the variability among living organisms ... and the ecological complexes of which they are a part; this includes diversity within species, between species and of ecosystems

This is usually thought of in terms of genes, species and ecosystems corresponding to three fundamental levels of biological organisation (Heywood, 1995, p. xiii). The conference recognised that species are becoming extinct at an alarming rate, and that this can only be halted by conserving the whole range of world habitats and by preserving local geographic variation within species. To put this in perspective, the certified rate of extinction of birds and mammals, the best-known groups of animals, over the last 200 years is about 10,000 times the background level suggested by the fossil record (Hill *et al,* 1996, p. 3). The convention lists a series of objectives which include the conservation of rare species and habitats, but also the maintenance and enhancement of wildlife habitats and natural populations of species, and it sets out frameworks for national strategies and plans (Biodiversity Action Plans or BAPs) to achieve these objectives. The importance of increasing the awareness and involvement of people in this agenda is stressed. In fact, the agenda cannot be achieved without this public participation. At the most basic level, no matter how compelling the arguments advanced by ecologists and other scientists for conservation, people will not alter their lifestyles in order to conserve something which they do not value. At another level, there is an acute shortage of professional conservationists able to carry out the detailed survey work on which national strategies and local action plans depend. We have to identify what we have in terms of species and habitats, work out how to manage existing habitats to maintain and enhance their wildlife value, and monitor the chosen managements to ensure that they are in fact fulfilling our objectives. All this has to be done on a local, national and global scale: a truly enormous task. As a first step in the process we need to extend the notion of citizenship from the purely human confines of being a citizen of a community of people living in a particular area, Engel's democratic citizenship (1993, p. 199), to being a citizen of the ecological environment and the whole continuum of life in that area, Engel's ecological citizenship (1993, p. 199). Such ideas have led to transnational activism, since the effect of environmental issues such as pollution is felt beyond the boundaries of nation states (Moore 2003, p. 101). However, most people do not readily identify with being citizens of the world and need to belong to something more local. This was true for Shirley:

I don't feel I can contribute to the world, I feel much happier contributing to a given society in which I live.

(Shirley, 2001)

This suggests that ecological citizenship should start by focusing on the local, especially since positive local action will also have global consequences.

We turn now to the Ecological Citizenship Project and look at how well the fieldwork exercises described in the last two chapters prepared students for ecological citizenship.

The Ecological Citizenship Project – context and methodology

This project used a life-history approach to inform our understanding of the process whereby ordinary adults can be equipped to be ecological citizens.

Fourteen continuing education students took part: nine of them (two male and seven female) had attended natural history open-access courses which focused on interest and enjoyment, and the other five (one male and four female) had attended field biology and landscape studies courses which were part of structured programmes of study leading to HE qualifications (Certificate in Field Biology or part-time BA Landscape Studies degree). Most of them were also involved, as part of a research group, with an ecological experiment, the Meadow Management Experiment (see Chapter 5). The open-access natural history courses had a strong emphasis on project work in the field (Chapters 2 and 3 describe examples of the type of class projects undertaken) and, since fieldwork and identification skills were gradually acquired while learning about new habitats, the same students returned to the class for a number of years. The Certificate in Field Biology Course also had a strong emphasis on practical work in the field, but the programme was more tightly structured, with a more rigorous process of assessment and students were not able to return to a course in subsequent years.

Participants were sent questions in advance and then discussion sessions based on these questions were recorded on audio tape and transcribed. Three students who could not attend the discussion sessions were interviewed on a one to one basis. The findings are presented as the voices of individual students, chosen to convey the content of the discussions, and participants checked that their contributions were correctly portrayed.

I do not think that having me, their tutor, as the interviewer unduly inhibited the student contributions. They knew me well, having attended classes for a number of years (the majority for at least five years) and the tutor–student relationship was not predominant within the group, since, as discussed in Chapter 1, I embrace a Freirean pedagogy and try to stand alongside the students so that we discover together. The atmosphere within the sessions was relaxed.

Older learners – motivation for joining programme of study

Since the natural history and field biology courses were held in day time, they tended to attract retired people with leisure to attend classes during the working day. The discussion sessions also took place during the day. This would explain why, with the exception of one student in her mid twenties, these students fall into the over-50s age bracket of Carlton and Soulsby's 'Older Learner' (1999, p. 3). This is a good age-group on which to focus, given our concern with developing ecological citizenship, since many of the surveying and monitoring tasks which need doing are time-consuming and require the harnessing of daytime leisure if they are to be accomplished. There is a limit to what can be done at weekends, which are already extensively used for manual conservation tasks such as coppicing and bramble-clearing.

We start by exploring why these students chose to study these particular courses, since Carlton and Soulsby (1999, p. 76) suggest that 'Older people are learning predominantly in arts and crafts and humanities activities' and, within this, whether the assessment and credit attached to the courses acted as an incentive or had an inhibiting effect. These are important considerations, which we will need to bear in mind as we seek to widen participation to take in the older learner with leisure for conservation related activities. Some of the students had begun their study with me under the old liberal adult education programme, but at the time of the discussion sessions all the classes had carried credit for six years. Students attending the natural history open-access courses were not interested in collecting credit and gaining qualifications, but were happy to undertake accreditation work provided it contributed to the learning experience. This was also true of the four students on the Certificate in Field Biology. One student in her eighties had relished the assessment work associated with her open access course, so we should not be unduly worried about assessment provided it is clearly part of the learning associated with the course.

For all the students the principle motivation for joining courses was interest:

I thought it would be an extremely interesting thing to do after I retired. I have always had an interest in the natural history of the world so to speak, so I joined up. I have thoroughly enjoyed it.

(John, 2001)

Several were retired professionals who had spent their lives working indoors in offices and were keen to find an outdoor activity and to pursue an interest which perhaps they had had in their childhood, but which had been dormant during the years of professional life. Richard illustrates this for students enrolling on natural history courses and Bill and Shelagh for more structured Certificate in Field Biology courses:

I was first introduced to natural history when I was at school, so I have always been vaguely interested in it but never pursued it because of work pressures. I found myself having lived in Sussex for 18 years, having commuted to London every day, and I knew nothing about Sussex, so when I retired I decided that one of the things I wanted to do was to pursue my interest in local history and natural history. It is based on a real desire to learn and understand more about the natural environment, local history and indeed its development on the countryside over the centuries.

(Richard, 2001)

I'd been working in London, mainly in an office, and I wanted to do something that was out in the open, possibly something to do with nature and conservation, but in fairly vague terms …. a general interest in nature I suppose per se. I was born in the country and I lived in the country until I got an apprenticeship in the Midlands. I was a country person so it really has gone full circle in a way, back to the country.

(Bill, 2001)

At the time I joined the Field Biology Certificate, I was still working full time. We'd been through a very stressful time at work where we'd all been working lots of overtime and that petered out, and after about six months of not working at that level of pressure, I felt something was missing. And I've always enjoyed studying, and having seen, as I thought, a night school programme about the Field Biology Certificate it seemed to be offering everything that I was interested in. As a family we'd always been interested in gardening and natural flora, as a small child I can remember going on walks and trying to spot the different flowers before anybody else did. And there were very very few programmes that offered anything to do with botany and I was delighted when I saw this offered, and it was really that that triggered me into deciding I would do the course. And in fact I stopped working full time and just worked four days a week.

(Shelagh, 2001)

For Julia joining the class had been a way of getting to know people when she moved into a new location:

When I came down to Sussex I looked at the brochure, and thought that Margaret's natural history class in Crawley would be a marvellous start, and it's been the beginning of all sorts of things. Also it's been a way to get to know people with similar interests and to know something of the area I've moved to.

(Julia, 2001)

Janet too had been motivated by this. Recently widowed and having moved to Sussex, she was determined to make a new life for herself. She started with an open access course, Wealden Wildlife, but the Certificate in Field Biology was offered instead of this course in the following year and, somewhat reluctantly, Janet decided to make the change from open access to a programme of study leading to more formal HE qualifications. This led eventually to Janet doing a part-time degree:

I moved to Sussex in 1993. Well I had a whole new life to start. I was on my own and had a lot of time to kill so my first move was to start the Wealden Wildlife course, and then that turned into field biology, and I took a deep breath because at the time I thought do I want to get too involved in this? But I knew I was interested in the subject

... and I did enjoy the field biology, and found there were a lot of ways to go and interesting things to do. And then when that finished I wasn't one hundred per cent sure I wanted to do a degree, I mean I had no intention of doing a degree. And I had a year off then, didn't I? I had a pup and I couldn't possibly do a degree course and rear a young pup at the same time, and do both properly. And yes, it fills up a lot of time. I've thoroughly enjoyed doing it and it's opened up a lot of different areas, a new set of people to talk to and things to do.

(Janet, 2001)

Janet was not alone in following an educational pathway from Open Course to certificate to degree and this illustrates the importance of providing flexibility in provision with options for moving onto different types of course as an interest develops. Carlton and Soulsby (1999, p. 76) stress the importance of such flexibility particularly for the older learner.

Initially these students had joined their class simply to pursue an interest, but it became more than this:

It seems that everybody joined from self-interest to start with, but it became bigger than that once we were all joined together in a group, I think.

(Shirley, 2001)

I would agree with that entirely. Inevitably you do the things that you want to do, and it was an interest already and you pursued it. And if there are by-products, so to speak, then that's great all round.

(Josephine, 2001)

This small sample of older learners from open access and from more structured HE study courses illustrates a wide range of motivation for lifelong learning. As Carlton and Soulsby (1999, p. 2) suggest, continuing with learning after the age of 50 is important in keeping people active and healthy. Appropriate learning programmes should promote personal development and to utilise as fully as possible the potentially wasted resource represented by older people, as well as helping them to maintain a quality of life which is fulfilling and likely to lengthen independence (p. 21). None of these students joined classes with the idea of equipping themselves to be ecological citizens, but it is to be hoped that the classes will have enabled them to discover new ways in which to both fulfil their interests and contribute to their local communities.

Jo, in her mid twenties, was the only one of the group who joined with a career in mind. As we saw in Chapter 2, her degree in environmental science had not included fieldwork and so she did not feel equipped to pursue the type of career that she wanted. The Field Biology Certificate enabled her to develop fieldwork skills and subsequently she was able to use these skills, in her own research for a PhD.

So what can we learn from this? Field-based natural history classes are attractive to the older learner with a latent interest in the countryside and a desire to be outdoors, often following retirement from indoor office jobs. The older learner who has studied before may be actively looking for a class to fill a gap in their lives either on retirement or following bereavement. Either retirement or bereavement may lead to a move to a new part of the country, and field trips provide an excellent way of getting to know a new area as well as making new friends among people with similar interests:

> I am not a long-term resident of Sussex, I have been here for nine years, but, because a lot of our work has been outside with fieldwork, I have actually seen parts of Sussex which I am sure people who have lived here fifty years or longer maybe would not even know existed.
>
> (Pam, 2001)

> It has definitely very much increased my enjoyment and understanding of the countryside and the need for conservation. It's been marvellous for making new friends because I knew no-one down here, and that has been fantastic. I've made some very good friends.
>
> (Julia, 2001)

Course publicity could draw attention to these incidental benefits of participation while stressing the natural history interest. In this way more people in this age bracket might be encouraged to become ecological citizens. However, there is little evidence that we are widening participation through these courses in terms of reaching those with low income or little education. These students were certainly already reasonably well educated and most of them were not particularly poor, although the level of the fees charged for the certificate and degree courses was a cause of concern to several of the students. They fit Carlton and Soulsby's picture of 'already well-educated middle classes, eager for more' (1999, p. 10). For some, illustrated by Shelagh's voice, this process began as a child and, as we suggested in Chapter 3, we need to look at what is happening in our schools to engender this curiosity and excitement so that people who do not experience this within a family situation may be motivated to learn in an explicit way throughout their lives.

Changing perspectives: nature conservation and the environment

As adult educators, we hope that participation in our classes will lead to changed perceptions, but do we really know where our students are coming from? Looking at how student perspectives change in studies such as this will help us to design better courses. Here, the students talk about how their ideas about nature conservation changed and what ideas were new to them. Students from both the natural history and the field biology classes were surprised by the interdependence of the natural world:

> *The main thing that I think the class has brought home to me is the total interdependence of nature, that you can't alter one thing without its having an influence all the way down the line. And once you've got hold of that idea you realise that the effect of conserving one bit, may upset another bit, and obviously the more informed you are, the more sensibly you can think about it.*
>
> (Josephine, 2001)

It was not the way things were taught at school 50 or 60 years ago:

> *It was a comparatively new way of thinking to me, because when one was taught in school everything was compartmentalised and you didn't put the whole thing together. The first person that I came across that did was the landscape history man, WG Hoskins (The Making of the English Landscape, 1955). And because I had read that, and then found your class, I thought that fits in beautifully – you mentioned that book.*
>
> (Josephine, 2001)

> *This is part of the new science of ecology really isn't it, I mean traditionally we learnt it as individual things, you didn't have a book about the whole habitat you had a book about badgers or a book about birds or a book about something else.*
>
> (Janet, 2001)

Bill voiced similar ideas in more ecological terms:

> *It changed my ideas about nature conservation in the sense that there is so much interaction between species, between species and habitats at all levels, and between various habitats – which certainly I wasn't aware of.*
>
> (Bill, 2001)

He remembered a particular example which had stuck in his mind from an RSPB (Royal Society for the Protection of Birds) book, on woodland conservation for invertebrates. He had been surprised to read that if you wanted to increase the range of habitats for the conservation of invertebrates, you needed to cut down the young trees not the older trees because the old ones, were the ones that provided the habitats:

> *So, if you've got to make a choice because you've got to do some opening up, it's the young saplings that you thin out and you make sure you leave the old there. That really opened my eyes and that was a long time ago when I first started Field Biology, but it really opened my eyes to the whole area, because it's not what you'd expect initially.*

> (Bill, 2001)

This idea of the interconnectedness of the natural world is a very important ecological concept which we 'in the trade' tend to take for granted, but perhaps we should be more aware of how alien this idea may be to the 19.8 million people in the UK who are over the age of 50 (2001 census figure for 2002) and who will have attended school at the same time as these students.

Pam agreed with the others, and went on to talk about the difficulty of balancing two sides of the argument:

> *I think the thing that impressed me most over the years is the interdependence of one thing upon the other ... the business about the butterfly and the ant, I mean if you don't have the ants, you don't have the butterfly, so you need to keep the ant. And the other thing is, it does seem to me that there has to be two points to a lot of things, two arguments. For example as I was coming here I was listening to a programme on the radio about a pine forest in Cumbria that's quite old and there is a plan to fell it so that someone can replace it with a bog which was there before the pines. The idea is to bring back the bog plants. People were arguing for the forest and its creatures and plants. It's going to be totally changed if it becomes a bog instead and this may not be very effective anyway.*

> (Pam, 2001)

Shelagh used a similar example from nearer to home to explain how essential it was to have background knowledge in order to understand conservation arguments. Living on the edge of Ashdown Forest, an area of Lowland Heath, she was familiar with the work of the Forest Conservators in trying to maintain open heathland against invasion of birch scrub. As she explained, the removal of birch trees only made sense if you knew about the rare plants and animals which depend on the heathland habitat and understood the mechanics of heathland and woodland development:

I'm sure it's broadened my outlook. I understand far more of the background to conservation and the environment. There's still a long way to go but until you start studying any of these topics in depth and you look at particular sites and try and understand what is happening, you're in the position of the rest of the general public. On Ashdown Forest you drive through and you see people cutting down trees. Now if you are a member of the general public and you know that conservation is the buzz word, you wonder to yourself, well why are they cutting down trees? They are laying waste to vast expanses of ground and it looks as though you've got bare soil and they're cutting down the trees, and you cannot feel that this is conservation. It is only when you study how heathland has evolved, that you appreciate what it is that the Conservators are actually trying to do with the land. We don't want scrub, we want the heathland, because that's the important habitat there. So in aspects like that I think one understands more and perhaps because one is more informed, if you hear other people talking about it, you can perhaps enlighten them a little bit. But certainly it expands your own understanding.

(Shelagh, 2001)

Cutting down trees as part of management for wildlife is a particularly sensitive issue with the general public, and Parry (2002) suggests that appreciation of the argument is greatly aided by hands-on experience of nature conservation.

A large part of people's picture of nature conservation comes from the more passive activity of watching natural history programmes on television. These programmes regularly feature spectacular animals and plants in far away countries set against a backdrop of wild and haunting scenery giving the impression that there is nothing much of interest in our tamed and crowded island. This tends to engender a passive attitude to conservation: 'it's somebody else's responsibility, there's nothing I can do and it's all a long way from home'. In fact, our wildlife is equally fascinating, and we have the advantage of a long history of naturalists extending way back to Gilbert White and Charles Darwin so that our wildlife is among the best documented in the world (Marren, 2002, p. 16). This gives natural history teachers great scope for finding exciting projects and wildlife stories to interest students. If we are to motivate people to play an active part in conservation we need to engage them with the local. These students started with a passive attitude to conservation, but learning about the remarkable life histories of local butterflies such as the adonis blue *(Lysandra bellargus)*, which they had seen on the South Downs a few miles from home, had given a new scale of size and distance to the conservation agenda:

When I originally came to the class I think my concept of the environment or conservation, was to do with the more macro element of things like saving the

Amazon jungle or the Congo rainforest. I hadn't really thought of it in terms of the micro, the smaller elements, and it is these which have alerted me to what is important locally. I remember being very impressed by the story of a butterfly and its dependence on a type of ant, which I thought was quite remarkable and certainly that was all new information to me. That was something which impressed me a lot.

(Shirley B, 2001)

Shirley J agreed, and tied in this new perspective with the implications for local action:

Like Shirley B. my idea of nature conservation was big. A quote: 'large oaks from little acorns grow.' I hadn't realised that individual small group projects can actually be part of a big picture. I didn't really realise that amateurs such as me could make any difference, but obviously we can because enough people are doing it.

(Shirley J, 2001)

Shirley J had realised that if enough people were engaged in collecting data in their own areas, the patchwork would build up into an enormous whole. Mike too had come to realise that it was not enough just to learn about things, but the knowledge had to lead into action:

When I first joined the class I had no knowledge really of nature conservation or the environment, although I did have an understanding that each sector or part of nature intertwined with the other and depended on each other. But as I've kept going – for 10 years I think – my ideas have changed. I have travelled the world and seen some of the disasters that have taken place in various parts of the world and in this country as well – but I think my idea now is to try to get more involved and, not only to learn about it, but to become more involved and actually to try to do something about it, and not just sit there and listen to other people talking about it.

(Mike, 2001)

As well as changed perceptions about nature conservation, these students also had changed perceptions about themselves. The knowledge they had gained through participation in the classes had led to more self confidence.

Developing self confidence and a new way of seeing

In *Through the Joy of Learning* (Coare and Thomson, 1996), adult learners write about their initial lack of confidence, and describe how learning about their chosen subject created an enlarged view of self. Similarly, the students taking part in the ecological citizenship discussions talked about now having the confidence to do things, and related this to increased knowledge of the subject. For Julia, this started with confidence in her ability to make conservation judgements, but led on to action to conserve a species-rich area of countryside where she lived:

> The knowledge I have gained has given me a lot more confidence to make my own judgement and discuss matters of conservation with others, in a way I certainly wouldn't have been able to do before.

> My house and meadow is now due to be covered in houses, and I feel much more confident in being able to fight this development on the behalf of wildlife. I know the whole area involved, which is quite big, and I have been able to write to councillors and state what's there and what its status is, and why it's not a good place to build.
>
> (Julia, 2001)

Jo, who was trying to equip herself for a job in conservation, felt confident that she could now identify plants and animals in the countryside:

> It's given me an improved confidence in my ability to do this type of work and actually to be able to go out and identify things. And I've made quite a few new friends as well.
>
> (Jo, 2001)

Shirley had joined the management committee for her local nature reserve and Janet had become a Conservator, one of a small group of people responsible for the management of Ashdown Forest:

> It has actually given me the confidence to join the Steering Committee of The Friends of Blunts Wood and Paiges Meadows which I would never have dreamt of doing before, but after a few years in the class, I felt I could add something to their new Steering Committee.
>
> (Shirley J, 2001)

> If I hadn't done the Field Biology course and got the confidence in my knowledge that it gave me, I wouldn't have accepted the Conservator job.
>
> (Janet, 2001)

For Mike, a casual enquiry about whether there was any conservation work he could get involved in, had led to his local wood and eventually to him taking charge of its management:

> A few years ago Margaret introduced me to the people who ran the New England Wood Trust in Cuckfield and I have been working there for about seven or eight years. Five years ago I was formally made Chairman. Well I certainly didn't volunteer

for it, but now I have the confidence to proceed with a programme of conservation for New England Wood and I am certainly confident that I can manage and handle the task. A lot of people don't really understand the reason why we do certain things and I have the confidence now to tell them why we do these things and what I hope will be the result of what we do. But to me the main thing is confidence.

(Mike, 2001)

As well as increased confidence, the students talked about seeing with new eyes, and the empowerment of knowing how to use library and archive resources:

I look at things with a slightly more knowledgeable eye, and see things that I didn't notice before.

(Pam, 2001)

When I walk in the countryside now, I can look at the flora and fauna and the landscape and imagine how it might have been a hundred years ago or what was grown there, and so it has opened my perception of the countryside.

(John, 2001)

I don't walk anywhere now without looking at something, whether it's houses, buildings, countryside, even down to an insect or something. I take particular notice and question, why is that there? Or I wonder what was there before. So I think (participating in the class) has opened my eyes.

(Richard, 2001)

Like everybody else I think one of the great things that I got out of it is that I notice things much more. You walk around the countryside, and it doesn't just give you aesthetic pleasure, you also notice the details and hopefully you can name them and so on.

(Josephine, 2001)

It makes you much more aware of things as you walk around and look at things. You don't just go for a walk anymore.

(Fabae, 2001)

I have learned to use libraries and other forms of resources, that's been marvellous.

(Julia, 2001)

Ecological citizenship

We turn now to look at what the students thought ecological citizenship should embrace. It was about taking responsibility for their local area and 'trying to ensure that we pass on a good environment to future generations'. Very quickly in the discussion, sessions students started contrasting their ideas about active citizenship with the type of activism displayed by campaigning environmentalists. Yearly (1996, p. 177) distinguishes between two types of organisation concerned with the environment: 'conservation groups' which 'typically have a background in natural history', and a membership generally 'dominated by scientists and amateur naturalists' and 'environmental groups' which 'started off in the late 1960s and early 1970s as groups critical of contemporary Western society' with a different ethos. Both these groups would claim the ecological high ground for citizenship, but have very different approaches. As Yearly suggests the work of the environmental groups 'depends more on campaigning than surveying and management' (p. 180) in contrast to the conservation groups where campaigning may be seen as less important than the more scientific priorities of 'surveying, field observation and reserve management'. With their background in natural history and having pursued study of a scientific nature, it is not surprising that the students taking part in the discussion sessions tended to identify with the conservation group approach, which was what they thought of as 'Active Citizenship,' rather than the environmental group approach, which they called 'Activism'. An essential difference was the ability to argue your case. Activism was 'standing up and saying "I'm right and everyone else is wrong."' This was contrasted with acquiring knowledge and being 'able to put up your case for argument'.

In the south-east of England, where these students live, there is continual pressure on the countryside from housing development, and for several of them an important part of being an ecological citizen was trying to ensure that their local countryside was there for future generations to enjoy. Jen was trying to prevent houses being built on the open countryside to the west of the town where she lived. This involved preparing a report about the habitats and wildlife which would disappear under the housing and arguing her case. Here, she was using knowledge she had gained in the classes and extending techniques she had learnt to survey the areas under threat. The local council had bought up land to create a crescent-shaped area of countryside around the town, called the Green Crescent. Bedelands Farm Local Nature Reserve where the students had done a lot of survey work, was part of this. Already she had seen houses being built on part of the Green Crescent:

I think you have to take the responsibility for the area in which you live and you have to stand up for what you think is correct. I'm defying the amount of housing that's going to be in Burgess Hill. They want to build a town west of Burgess Hill that's going to go from Burgess Hill to the A23. That would destroy a tremendous amount, and they have already intruded into places in the Green Crescent. I feel this is where you've got to go and state your case and know what you're talking about. And really fight for what you think is right, whether or not you win.

(Jen, 2001)

Fabae agreed:

I agree with all of this: that you try and put in something to society; that we do try and stop things that we very much disagree with in the area; read the local paper; see what's going on; write to the Council if you very much disagree with what's going on; try to make things a bit better.

(Fabae, 2001)

As the following discussion illustrates, the students thought their approach was more dispassionate and less publicity orientated than an activist's, who might be just a professional protester:

I think we're more dispassionate about what we're doing. I think that some activists, not every activist but some, bend the facts to suit their argument.

(Bill, 2001)

I think they also attract people to their cause as activists – general activists – rather than being interested in a particular, like GM Crops. I think half the people who were protesting about GM crops were just almost like Rentamob. I think they were professional protesters.

(Shirley J, 2001)

They are there very much to get publicity.

(Bill, 2001)

But that has a role. Thinking back to the Brent Spar, most of us were totally unaware of the Brent Spar controversy until GreenPeace went in and then we all got thinking about it, reading about it.

(Shirley, 2001)

Although one of the students had been adamant that in the end Shell had been forced to do the wrong thing about the Brent Spar oil rig, everyone agreed that without GreenPeace the issue would not have come to public attention. So there could be a place for campaigning within their picture of ecological citizenship. Yearly (1996, p. 179) suggests that a similar dilemma is faced by professional conservationists:

> *The scientific ethos of conservation organisations may result in tasks which demand scientific expertise … taking precedence … even though … in many instances campaigning may be a more cost-effective approach to nature conservation than direct intervention*

In some situations, attracting public attention may be the only option left to prevent the loss of local habitats, as the protestors at Clayoquot Sound found after taking part in more than ten years of discussions about the clear-cut felling of the temperate rainforest on Vancouver Island, British Columbia. The logging continued throughout the discussion process and so in desperation the Friends of Clayoquot Sound blockaded a logging road in 1993, and 800 people were arrested. As Moore (2003) recounts, being arrested succeeded in attracting public attention to their cause in a spectacular way as 'comfortable Canada' discovered that friends had been arrested and gaoled. The publicity drew attention to the destructiveness of the logging practices more effectively than any educational programme could have done (Moore, 2003, p. 98).

Mike thought it was all too easy for people in this country to be critical of what was happening overseas while ignoring what was happening on their doorstep. He returned to the example of housing on greenfield sites:

> Somebody, I think it was Pamela, talked about Borneo where they're doing logging and Malaysia, but I think we tend to forget that we are just as guilty ourselves. In this country where we build houses on greenfield sites left, right and centre, without trying to restrict the amount of housing that we're building.
>
> (Mike, 2001)

Being ecological citizens might require altered lifestyles so that less housing was required. As Peter Marren records 'Despite a near static population, another 4.4 million "homes" are to be built over the next 20 years, at least half of them in the countryside. Apparently, this is because many people prefer to live on their own' (2002, p. 12).

For other students, being an ecological citizen meant being involved in the management of nature areas, such as the piece of countryside close to the area of housing in Newhaven where Jo lived. She was part of a group who were involved in practical nature conservation, looking after the site 'Because we don't want it to be lost or degraded. We want it preserved for other people in the future and improved, and also for people to get the benefit from it now.' For several of the students this sort of quiet ecological citizenship, getting on and doing it 'without making a great song and dance', was as important as the higher profile approach of going to meetings and getting press publicity. Shelagh compared this with the quiet, but nevertheless very active, democratic citizen who:

will initiate things, if they see something needs doing they will do it without necessarily getting involved in any formal groups. Somebody who would do something rather than pass it by and leave it for somebody else to do.

Her husband was a good example of this:

... he belonged to a group that did a lot of work with people that nobody ever heard about. They would visit people who were in need and would make sure that they were provided with chairs, cookers, or whatever else was needed. They raised lots of money and they did lots of individual things which were not shouted about and never put in the newspaper. Now I would say that somebody who does that is a very active citizen in a positive way and it doesn't have to be people who will go to meetings and talk in a loud voice.

(Shelagh, 2001)

Ecological citizenship could work in the same way like 'this friend of Jenny's who's got up a group to see if they can look at something that locally they feel needs conserving.' The group were looking after an area of flower-rich grassland beside a local road: Shelagh had been invited to help with the plant survey which would inform their management of the grass. Like the students taking part in the group discussions, Shelagh, who was interviewed individually, contrasted this approach favourably with the more publicity-seeking 'campaign and meetings' approach:

They're not making a great song and dance about it, but they are just getting a group together to do it. This is something that needs doing, so they're doing it, rather than people who only turn up to things where there's going to be something in the Press about it.

(Shelagh, 2001)

Interaction with others is part of building up a sense of community and will be important for both democratic citizenship and ecological citizenship. Bill thought this was particularly important in the countryside:

I think anything that involves groups of people, particularly in rural areas, working together helps the cohesiveness of the country – the whole fabric of rural society is under pressure with the way things are going generally.

(Bill, 2001)

Fieldwork activities had been important in engendering cohesiveness within the student group:

The Field Biology course was particularly good because so much of it was fieldwork and you were out in the field, and you were working as groups, and interacting and doing things together and each was giving some input, some degree of experience to the group – more so than you would in a course where you just sat in a lecture hall receiving lectures.

(Bill, 2001)

Adult educators frequently express concern about long-running classes which turn into clubs. It is argued that the learning stops, that people only come for the social interaction, and that an aura of exclusiveness develops which makes it difficult for new people to join the class. These are all dangers to watch out for, but surely if we are serious about developing citizenship, then we are trying to develop interaction that will lead on to other things. Perhaps the class will continue to meet as a group independently after the official course has ceased to exist, but this is only likely to happen with long-running class groups:

We continued your class, Margaret, the group still meets, although it is four years I should think since it finished, and we've kept going and we've got some quite knowledgeable people in the group and everyone really enjoys it and we walk and take a picnic and look at things.

(Julia, 2001)

This sharing of knowledge and working together is part of ecological citizenship. Jean, who was unable to attend the discussion sessions, wrote down her thoughts on how her participation in the class was of benefit to the countryside. First: 'It helps one to understand and so increases one's wish to protect the environment' and secondly 'One's interest and knowledge rubs off on others, they develop an interest, and sometimes get involved too.'

When one of the students who owned a farm decided to take a field out of production and to manage it for conservation, a group of her class-mates set up a research project to monitor the changes in the grassland vegetation. Ideally activities such as this should grow naturally out of natural history classes.

Participants talked about citizenship in terms of responsibilities: 'taking responsibility' for their local area. Pam approved of this emphasis, but suggested that in today's world there was much more emphasis on rights and that responsibilities tended to be forgotten about:

We all emphasise responsibility and I agree with that. When I was at school, we used to do this and that was 60 years ago. Rights and responsibilities was the phrase which we used to use. I think there has been an over-emphasis on rights and we ought to be emphasising the rights and responsibilities to our community.

(Pam, 2001)

Such an approach is in contrast to much of the writing about citizenship and the environment which has tended to focus on political issues and stressed the rights – environmental and ecological – of citizens (Lister, 1997; Apel and Franz-Balsen, 1998; Schemann, 2001). The contrasting attitude of these students bodes well for current attempts to fill the vacuum within practical nature conservation.

Ecological citizens contributing to biodiversity conservation

Students talked about the various ways in which they were now empowered to be ecological citizens and the activities in which their new learning had enabled them to engage. Belonging to organisations concerned with nature conservation was one way. Several of them had taken out membership of their local wildlife trust, two of them serving as committee members. Jan, who sent in written answers to the questions as she was unable to attend the discussion sessions, had become a member of Burgess Hill Town Council's Environmental Issues Forum which in turn had led to involvement in habitat surveys locally. She had also taken up membership of the county Wildlife Trust and RSPB. Other students had contributed to the management of local nature reserves by sitting on committees, giving talks, preparing management plans or contributing to practical conservation:

Joining the class really gave me the impetus that I needed and I have slightly gone into orbit on this. I have given 20 talks to various local people, groups of parents, groups of children, and I've also taken a walk related to the talks as well. I have done several photographic exhibitions to do with my work and I have written articles for the Bedelands Newsletter, put up display work every time we have our meetings at Bedelands, and I have also taken part in four children's safaris that we take every year ... this is what I enjoy doing, I enjoy being with people, talking to people and taking them on walks.

(Jen, 2001)

I'm now doing a Ph.D.. which I wouldn't have done if I hadn't done the course, and also quite a few local things. I'm on the management committee for a local nature reserve and sort of considered one of the plant people on the group and get consulted about everything because I've done a course and also because I have more knowledge now. There is another person who knows quite a lot of plants and us two are considered the plant people. We've been consulted and basically written the management plan. No-one does anything without asking us but I never would have had any of the knowledge or confidence without the course. Through this group, we've decided that there might be some other areas in Newhaven that we could look after – there's another wood that I'm interested in and there might be a chance we could do some work there.

(Jo, 2001)

Being on the management committee for a local nature reserve had led to Jo co-writing the management plan. John had also been responsible for writing the management plan for his local nature reserve. The class had contributed the ideas, but John had been the one to write it up into a suitable format paying

Being an ecological citizen means:

1 Taking responsibility for your local area – passing on a good environment to future generations.
2 Arguing your case based on scientific information.
3 Looking close to home rather than being critical about what is happening overseas.
4 Managing local areas for wildlife.
5 Getting on and doing rather than seeking publicity and going to meetings.
6 Being part of a community – interacting with others and working together
7 Focusing on responsibilities rather than rights.
8 Increasing your own and others knowledge about the environment.

particular attention to making it user-friendly and accessible to the Friends Group who carried out many of the management tasks. John was keen to point out the importance of the practical side of the management as well as the scientific data collection.

In the class itself we have been primarily responsible for collecting data, rather than actually doing anything, unlike the working party at Bedelands – you can stand back after the day and say look at what we have done

(John, 2001).

The two needed to go together or you could end up with a situation where amenity benefit became detrimental to the wildlife.

If you're removing all of the brambles, that might be good for the walkers, but not quite so good for the nightingales

(John, 2001).

Mike, who as chairman of the New England Woodland Trust was responsible for the direction of the practical management of New England Wood, had a similar conundrum to resolve.

There is the problem I have with New England Wood – it's partly an amenity for the residents of Cuckfield. They raised the money to purchase it, so why shouldn't they have the right to have access to it, to walk their dogs … and the other part is a duty to improve it as a nature reserve and an area of conservation for 'the birds, bees, flowers, trees, etc. that live there' – now if there's any dispute in my mind I always come down on the side of conservation. But there are a lot of people on the board of trustees who say…

(Mike, 2001).

New England Wood was purchased in 1981 by local residents in a successful bid to prevent the area being covered in houses, and has since been looked after by a trust. As Mike says (above), the objectives for management include a duty to manage it for the benefit of wildlife while at the same time managing it as an amenity for local residents. At times the two aims become incompatible, and this will increasingly become the case as pressure on the local countryside continues to increase as more people live in the area.

Dog-walking is also becoming more and more of a problem at nature conservation sites close to urban areas with many people now owning more than one dog. On visits to a local nature reserve one frequently counts more dogs than people and to be walking without a dog excites comment. The problem extends beyond the nuisance of dog-fouling (Shaw *et al*, 1995), particularly where there are ponds or streams; dogs break down the banks and stir up the water to the detriment of pond life and plants growing on the margins. At Bedelands Farm a series of species-rich wildlife ponds have been degraded over the last three years to species-poor mud pools. There is now talk of having to fence the ponds to keep dogs out.

Bedelands Farm, in contrast to New England Wood, is a Local Nature Reserve (LNR), owned and managed by the local district council under guidelines laid down by English Nature (English Nature, 1994b). Such reserves collectively cover a large amount of countryside (29,032 hectares in 1998), and occur mainly in densely populated areas (Marren 2002, p. 111), requiring a careful balance between amenity and nature conservation objectives. Quite rightly a key aim for LNRs, especially since the Earth Summit in Rio, has been to get the local population involved. In order to do this, councils try to set up two types of groups: Steering Groups and Friends Groups. A Steering Group has responsibility for approving management objectives, which are then carried out by the Friends Group or by contractors if the task is deemed to require specialist equipment or to be too great to be undertaken by volunteer labour. Both the Friends Group and the local council have a key aim of promoting public interest in and use of the nature reserve. This is admirable, but raises the question of how much pressure a site can take and still fulfil its nature conservation objectives. In the case of Bedelands Farm, the site, although right on the edge of a major conurbation, was relatively unknown and unused by local residents for the first five years of its life as a LNR. The Friends Group was established 10 years ago and now numbers 170 families. It is a showcase example of a successful group and the reserve now has a very high amenity value in terms of use by the local population. Unfortunately in some areas there has been a corresponding decrease in its value for wildlife.

Apart from continually balancing amenity objectives against wildlife objectives conflict of interest arises because it is not possible to manage a limited area for the benefit of all species. One of the problems of involving local people in management is that management objectives, often enshrined in a management plan which tends to be forgotten about, are continually modified to 'help' another aspect of wildlife. For example letting thistle go to seed in the meadows would undoubtedly benefit seed-eating birds, but is not compatible with management to enhance wildflower diversity in the grass. Since there is no shortage of seeding thistle in rough grassy areas outside the reserve it is possible in this case to argue that the rare species-rich grassland inside the reserve should be the priority here. Another difficulty with handing over management tasks to volunteers is encapsulated in the following quote from Peter Marren (2002, p. 313):

> *In Britain the historic link between land use and nature is so strong that to break it would spell disaster. Sites managed sustainably by skilled reedsmen and charcoal burners ...are better managed than by weekend volunteers, contractors and well-meaning idiots.*

Unfortunately, Peter Marren's quote about well-meaning idiots is all too often accurate, and the misdirected zeal of the conservation task group is capable of inflicting considerable damage, for example when rare and unrecognised shrubs are removed from a hedge during winter cutting-back operations. Clearly, input from knowledgeable ecological citizens would help here – it is crucial to have such people on the Steering and Friends Groups. There is also a tendency to manage for the benefit of the task force: interesting tasks are needed in order to keep the group viable. Coppicing of woodland is a number one favourite and this tends to get written into management plans with little consideration given to whether it is actually appropriate in this particular case. The recent move within professional conservation circles away from coppicing to non-intervention policies for certain types of woodland (English Nature, 2000) has yet to trickle down to the grassroots volunteer workers. Nevertheless it remains imperative that the local public are involved, if only because skilled reedsmen and charcoal burners are very thin on the ground. We will be returning to this theme in the next chapter.

In addition to nature reserves, gardens represent an important potential resource for wildlife, since, as Marren points out (2002, p. 210), they cover at least 485,000 hectares or 3 per cent of the land area of Britain and Wales. The way they are managed is crucial: the extensive use of pesticides and herbicides, not to mention peat-based compost and out-of-town garden centres, is going to have a negative impact on local wildlife, much of which was probably ousted from the area now occupied by the houses and gardens. This, then, is another important area of ecological citizenship. Several of the students mentioned changes to the way they managed their gardens as a result of their increased knowledge. For Shirley the new knowledge came as she was starting to develop a garden from scratch and so was particularly apposite:

When I started the class I was also at the start of developing a garden which was a totally new experience because I never had a garden before, and I had a blank canvas on which to work. And I think the class reinforced ideas that the garden could become part of the background of natural life in that particular environment and how you worked your garden could contribute to plants and insects and birds and making that a part of your surrounding natural environment. I have become aware of the effect of chemicals and therefore I have more or less eliminated the use of chemicals in the garden and I have seen a great increase in insect life by doing that.

(Shirley B, 2001)

The knowledge and skills developed in the classes were particularly associated with vegetation survey work. Most of the students talked about surveys which they had done either by themselves or in small groups or with other people. These included national surveys such as the CPRE (Council for the Protection of Rural England) Hedgerow Survey (five students mentioned that they had done at least one) and the Plantlife Cowslip Survey (one student mentioned this). Three students had been part of different groups doing a Phase One Habitat Survey which produces 'a snapshot of the local natural environment presented as a coloured map of local habitats' (Philips and Wilson, 1995, p. 4). Perhaps most exciting was the group from one of the natural history classes who for four years had been recording changes in the vegetation of an agriculturally improved field which had been taken out of cultivation and was being managed for conservation purposes. Shelagh also had plans to take part in vegetation surveying:

I have agreed to help somebody out at Staplefield. When I went on the holiday to the Orkneys with the archaeological group, I met someone who is part of a very small group that is trying to record the flora of the grass verge in Staplefield. And when she heard that I'd done all this field biology I was pounced upon and I have agreed to go two or three times a year with them to do it.

(Shelagh, 2001)

Bill, living in the High Weald AONB (Area of Outstanding Natural Beauty), was able to use his new knowledge and skills to assist in conserving the very special countryside found here. He was particularly involved with the conservation of wildflower meadows, of which a number remain in this part of the country:

I finished the course and joined the High Weald Group and I found that everything I had learned I was able to apply, certainly in relation to grasslands and plants. The group is trying to take an overview of the High Weald as an area, not only in the narrow area of just biodiversity and conservation, but looking at the whole structure of the weald, the people there, trying to keep traditional skills, trying to keep people in employment that sort of thing – it covers a very wide spectrum. The part I was involved in was very specific, meadows, trying to improve their biodiversity.

I was able to get involved with landowners and persuade them on conservation, and I got involved in Countryside Stewardship, getting new grants. It's important particularly in Sussex where the farming community is not in a good state. There's a lot of criticism of farmers, but they're caught in structures that are not of their making. They've got to live. And they don't get an awful lot of help in practical terms. They get all these people who come down and visit them but they don't necessarily get a lot of people with hands-on. Whereas the people that I work with on FWAG (Farming and Wildlife Advisory Group) they are hands-on people. I found that they reacted quite positively once you got them involved and they saw that you were there to help and advise rather than impose rules and regulations on them. Even some of the most hard-nosed commercial farmers: I found that you can at least move them along further than they had moved before. Maybe you shouldn't be too idealistic. If you can offer them the money for it there's another factor in it – it's not a lot of money, they can't make a profit out of it, you get some money for doing things.

(Bill, 2001)

While he was with the Meadows Group they introduced a new system for collecting wildflower seed from species-rich meadows without damaging the donor meadow and using it to seed new conservation meadows. As well as increasing the area of species-rich meadows, the system provides some financial return for farmers who are maintaining these meadows rather than going for the greater financial returns of agricultural improvement:

We ran the system for collecting wildflower seed from various meadows and selling it, and while I was there we helped set up a similar system in the Shetlands. They've got a lot of species-rich meadows and we helped them fix up systems, how to go about it, mechanics of collecting, preparing seed and drying it and how to go about it.

(Bill, 2001)

Bill also found himself involved in teaching, which he greatly enjoyed. This was hands-on teaching in the field and very much part of ecological citizenship:

I've done courses for the High Weald Group. They run two-day courses on grassland management and creation and conservation. I found it was particularly good because you had quite a spectrum of people there. Some of them had never done it before, some of them had done it and forgotten it, and some had got a little bit of information. So when you got them out in the field the ones who had done it, it was like drawing the curtains back for them, they were off. They picked it up so quickly and immediately you got the interaction going with those who hadn't. It wasn't as difficult as it would appear on paper. You're trying to teach people how to survey, why to survey, how to identify, all in a couple of two hour sessions during the course of two days. It wasn't as bad as it sounds. People would be saying we haven't done this for 20 years and they were off again. And again there were people like Jo who were highly qualified, but had never done a field trip in their life.

(Bill, 2001)

Janet had also done some teaching as a demonstrator helping the next cohort of Certificate Field Biology students with fieldwork. Here she talks about a different aspect of citizenship as a Conservator of Ashdown Forest:

There are various committees that decide what's going to happen on the Forest. I am on the Conservation Committe ... you are looking at what is going on and what is being proposed. What will be done and what won't be done.

(Janet, 2001)

Julia talked first about recycling and 'doing your very best to use less energy' because she was anxious not to appear to concentrate on her own backyard, but since the meadow and large pond which she owned and had spent a number of years developing as a haven for wildlife were now scheduled to be covered with houses, this was her major concern:

I have got very depressed about my meadow because it is hatched in for a development. I had actually made arrangements, as far as I could, that it would be kept after my death, and that was in a way my little project, but if the area is developed, obviously even if the meadow is left, which I possibly could get, sitting in a sea of concrete with the pond being filled with old cars and bicycles and bedsteads – I would rather it was built over almost. No, it would be doing no good.

I am doing my bit to save it and the whole area. The fact that I've got to move house, well I mean that's of little importance to me compared to losing a very very nice piece of land which is being fairly lightly farmed and is teeming with wildlife and wonderful hedgerows. The whole area that I'm talking about is quite a few acres because the development is 2,500 houses. So I am fighting very hard for it because it is very nice and it is very much appreciated. One can see from the meetings we've had, there were hundreds of people, the big theatre full of people and everyone loves that area and they are very very angry about it.

(Julia, 2001)

Jo had found that her new knowledge was useful in making a case for conservation to the local council:

Before (the course) I walked into a wood and thought this is a nice wood. Now I walk into a wood ... Is it old? Is it ancient? And that has actually helped in our local wood, because we've found some things that are interesting and looking on old maps there is a possibility that some of it already had trees on it, which we wouldn't have known about before. Now it's something we can throw back at the Council and say, well it could be old, so look after it.

(Jo, 2001)

Implications

This chapter has used student voices to show how ordinary adults with an interest in the countryside can be equipped to become ecological citizens and participate in biodiversity conservation as ecological citizens. The students in this study were predominantly retired and so had leisure to take part in time-consuming conservation activities. We have seen the various ways in which they have contributed to looking after the natural environment in their local areas. This illustrates the importance of education for ecological citizenship rather than just education for career which tends to concentrate on a younger age group. This type of education can be rigorous, but we need to encourage students to return to the class for a number of years as it takes time to acquire the necessary fieldwork and identification skills. We do not necessarily want them to acquire credit and move on out of the class, as happens with certificate and degree programmes. At the moment, as we have demonstrated, it is still possible for university adult education institutions to put on such courses, but government thinking and funding needs to be directed in a more explicit way towards this sort of education for citizenship.

The students in this study were able to afford class fees and were already reasonably well educated, but there is huge potential for widening participation to include poorer and less educated older people. A modest level of funding would enable retired people without generous pension provisions to access such courses. It has been suggested (Oosthuizen, 2002, p. 155) that this would actually lead to economic benefits in terms of the health of older students, and the present study shows that there would be continuing benefits in terms of improved local environments through the unpaid efforts of these new ecological citizens.

At the moment the emphasis in nature conservation seems to be in the wrong place. At the end of the day, setting up nature reserves, writing management plans, involving the public in steering groups and producing glossy documents about local biodiversity will not benefit nature conservation. What is needed is ecological citizens working in and enjoying their local wildlife areas. These student voices represent a celebration of what can be achieved and hopefully an inspiration to other would-be conservationists to become involved too.

CHAPTER 5

Achieving biodiversity action plan (BAP) targets: managing habitats for nature conservation

In a world dominated by human action, the fate of biodiversity will be determined by what we know about it and how we choose to value it

(Engel, 1993, p. 188).

In Chapter 4 we looked at how ordinary adults with an interest in the countryside could be equipped to become ecological citizens and participate in biodiversity conservation. We have seen the various ways in which these ecological citizens have contributed to looking after the natural environment in their local areas. This is a good beginning, but as well as equipping adults with the necessary knowledge and field work skills to participate, a university should also be providing a focal point or lead in taking forward the agenda for biodiversity conservation and in educating the wider public. In our crowded island, and increasingly throughout the world, this requires understanding of the natural world and putting people in touch with nature so that they value it and as a consequence are prepared to alter their lifestyles. Here, engagement with local issues leads to changes at both the local and the global level. In this chapter, an innovative community project, the 'Meadow Management Experiment', is used as an example to show how a university CE department, working in collaboration with a local council, can contribute to the understanding of a threatened habitat and the achievement of local targets. Continuing Education students have been involved throughout from the initial planning stages through setting up the experiment to the ongoing annual scientific monitoring. They talk about how they see their contribution in terms of ecological citizenship and the overall objectives of the project. Their voices were recorded during discussion sessions about ecological citizenship described in the previous chapter. Participation in the project also enabled them to extend their learning beyond the more formal learning of their part-time courses. Their voices explore the nature of this learning and how it was mediated.

Biodiversity Action Plans

Why should the countryside be conserved? Bryn Green suggests that 'It is the pleasure wildlife and wild country give that is a large part of the reason why we want to maintain them' (1981, p. 12). The rational arguments advanced may be to do with material benefits and scientific ideas about ecological balance, but if we are to involve the general public successfully in countryside conservation we will need to engage their feelings. Following the United Nations Conference on the Environment and Development at Rio de Janeiro in 1992, the UK government published its Action Plan (1994) identifying how the UK would contribute to the global conservation of biodiversity over the next twenty years. The steering group established to take this UKBAP forward published its report in 1995 and the government responded in 1996 (DETR, 1997). It was agreed that an evaluation of progress towards implementing the UKBAP would be made every five years. The first of these reports, the Millennium Biodiversity Report (EntecUK Ltd, 2001), is based on the responses to questionnaires sent out to individuals and organisations involved in nature conservation. A key finding was that much more needed to be done to raise public awareness and that 'Awareness should be linked to biodiversity targets – awareness with a purpose.' This is one of the objectives of the Meadow Management Experiment. Another major finding of the Millennium Report was that there was a lack of resources for data collection and that surveying and monitoring were widely seen as 'something of a luxury given the limited resources available for biodiversity work and the many other priorities.' It was suggested that the public could be involved in data collection. Again the Meadow Management Experiment aims to address these issues.

The UKBAP has led to a proliferation of documents: 391 Species Action Plans (SAPs) for individual species and 45 Habitat Action Plans for habitats. There are also County Biodiversity Action Plans. The Millennium Biodiversity Report (EntekUK, 2001), endorsed the clear direction of this Action Plan approach, but amongst practising ecologists there is scepticism about the practical effect of this mountain of paper. 'The documents of the conservation industry… tell us what ought to happen and what they would like to happen, but all too often do not tell us what actually happened. The emphasis tends to be on the means – plans, strategies, partnerships – rather than the ends' (Marren, 2002, p. 10). The Millennium Biodiversity Report shows that very little monitoring is being done to see how effective are the individual action plans because of lack of resources. Where monitoring has taken place, the picture is not very reassuring. Recovery is only happening in rare species which are limited to a very few sites, while widespread species continue to decline because most of our countryside is still intensively farmed and inimical to wildlife. It looks as though Species Action Plans alone will not be enough and that we will need initiatives that address far wider countryside issues. And this again will require the understanding and support of ordinary people.

The Meadow Management Experiment is concerned with that most widespread of habitats, grassland, and in particular that widely distributed grassland habitat which occurs in the lowlands on moist mineral soils which are neither very acidic nor very calcareous. For centuries such grassland was full of wild flowers such as meadow buttercups and ox-eye daisies, which thrived in the stable conditions produced by an annual hay cut followed by grazing of the aftermath. However, 95 per cent of these wildflower meadows have been lost since the 1940s (Nature Conservancy Council, 1984, p. 50). This is more than any other habitat in Britain, but you could be forgiven for not noticing the loss, since the fields still look grassy. In fact, these fields now contain very little apart from grass, having been ploughed up and re-seeded with agriculturally improved, vigorously-growing grass. Fertiliser is applied regularly to produce a fast growing crop of grass which is harvested as silage several times a year. Such grassland, maintained by the application of fertiliser, and by ploughing and reseeding every three or four years, lacks wildflowers and so, in turn, lacks the butterflies and bumblebees which relied on the wildflower nectar. In addition, many of our butterflies are now scarce because the food-plants used by their caterpillars have disappeared along with the meadows.

Wildflower meadows continue to be lost from the farming sector (Pilkington, 1999 Sussex survey, unpublished) because the remaining meadows tend to be in the hands of aging farmers on small farms which get bought up by larger agricultural enterprises when the farmer dies. Once a meadow has been improved by the addition of fertiliser, it is very difficult to turn the clock back. Recent research (Smith *et al,* 2000) has shown that, even with seed sowing and the application of traditional management, such agriculturally-improved swards do not readily return to the species composition of the old meadows. This means that the achievement of biodiversity targets for this type of grassland will depend on finding practical ways of managing all the existing areas identified under local habitat surveys (Philips and Wilson, 1995). Many of these are in small scattered patches (Sussex Wildlife Trust, 1995), often within urban areas and often managed by councils who lack specialist knowledge about conservation. Appropriate management can only be introduced if council officials and the general public using the site appreciate the benefits. The Meadow Management Experiment was set up in 1997 with a Royal Society COPUS (Committee on the Public Understanding of Science) grant to find out how best to manage some wildflower meadows on the edge of what has been billed the 'fastest growing town in Britain'. Here, as with many of these sites, we have an 'island of former countryside' (Marren 2002,

p. 201) caught up within an expanding urban area. Such sites represent an enormous opportunity for putting people in touch with wildlife and linking public awareness of conservation issues to the achievement of biodiversity targets.

The Meadow Management Experiment

The experiment was set up at Bedelands Farm, a Local Nature Reserve (LNR) of approximately 33 hectares which lies in the middle of Sussex in the south of England (National Grid TQ 319204) on the outskirts of the conurbation of Burgess Hill. The site, which is managed by the local district council and extensively used by dog-walkers, is old-style farmland on heavy clay soil and consists of a series of moderately species-rich meadows separated by overgrown hedges and areas of ancient woodland. The meadows contain more than 50 species of native grass and wildflowers including common knapweed and meadow vetchling, with some crested dogstail (Figure 5.1), an attractive native grass which is not very common in this sort of grassland in Sussex. According to the National Vegetation Classification (NVC), this type of grassland is known as crested dogstail – common knapweed grassland of the meadow vetchling sub-community (MG5a, Rodwell, 1992). The site was bought by Mid Sussex District Council in 1989 and became a Local Nature Reserve in 1991.

In the experiment two fields are divided up into areas which have different management regimes applied to them, including cutting at different times over the summer and grazing the aftermath with sheep. A simple experimental design has been used, so that visitors to the site can see for themselves the effect of different management treatments on the wildflowers in the meadows, and the local council can apply the treatments in the same way as they would for the whole site. Since future management of the site will be governed by the results of the experiment, changes in the vegetation are also being monitored as rigorously as possible. Scientific monitoring is being carried out by the Meadows Research Group, a group of continuing education students from the University of Sussex.

Ecologists studying changes in the composition of vegetation such as meadow grassland often use square samples (called quadrats); within each square they estimate by eye the amount of the square which is covered by each species in turn. Since vegetation is made up of layers of plants, the overall cover for any one square will come to more than 100 per cent. Site managers monitoring the effect of the management regime they have introduced usually use marked quadrats (so called permanent quadrats) to which they can return each year, and this is what was done in the meadow experiment. Quadrats (of

Figure 5.1 Wildflowers from the meadows at Bedelands Farm: from left to right, meadow vetchling, grass vetchling, common knapweed and crested dogstail grass and, at the bottom of the figure, birdsfoot trefoil. Grass vetchling has bright red flowers, but grass-like leaves, which are very difficult to find in the sward when it is not flowering. (Drawing by Peggy Alves.)

2 m by 2 m size) were laid out at regular intervals on transects across the meadows from a base-line marked by posts at the edge of the meadow. This is an extension of the principle which we used in Chapter 3 to set out quadrats in Hoe Wood. Before the treatments commenced, percentage cover was recorded for all the plant species in all the quadrats in mid-summer and this is being compared with data collected in the same way in subsequent years.

Objectives of the experiment – the student perspective

The overall aims of the experiment from my perspective are set out in the box.

Objectives of the Meadow Management Experiment

- Contributing to the understanding of a threatened habitat – Chapter 7.
- Achievement of BAP targets for a threatened habitat – Chapter 5:
  1. training of site managers – local and national BAP targets;
  2. getting local people to value wildlife and care for their local environment – local target;
  3. living exhibition to demonstrate effect of habitat management to landowners – regional and national targets;
  4. training of biological monitors – learning through fieldwork – applicable internationally.

Did the students share this vision of what they were doing? Many of the students taking part in the discussion sessions had been part of the original group which set up the experiment and thought that the aim was to find out the best management for the meadows, with 'best' being defined in terms of biodiversity and aesthetic appeal. Pam put it like this:

... to study how best to manage Bedelands Farm both from the point of view of biodiversity and to re-create an environment attractive to the people who use it. This we defined as more wildflowers.

(Pam, 2001)

Or as John put it: 'establishing the needs of this type of habitat.'

(John, 2001)

This, they thought, was part of ecological citizenship because the Bedelands meadows are a biodiverse habitat of the kind which is disappearing from the countryside, and without appropriate management the meadows would turn into ordinary grassy fields. Working towards ensuring that the meadows remained flower-rich, was:

> trying to ensure that we pass on a good environment to future generations' because 'you've got the diversity there
>
> (Mike, 2001).

Bedelands Farm was seen as being:

> no different to a listed building. It's part of the history and heritage of the country'
>
> (Bill, 2001),

but was:

> much easier to spoil. I mean in the sense that there it lies and it's asking to have houses built all over it.'
>
> (John, 2001).

Nature reserves were seen in this light by the founding Wild Life Conservation Special Committee in 1947 who recognised 'their culture value and compared them with ancient monuments and national museums, that is artefacts of the human spirit as well as a means to a desired end' (Marren, 2002, p. 108). Such notions also embrace the need to raise public awareness of the issues. For Mike the most important thing was:

> ... increasing our knowledge and at the same time making it widely known that there is a need to preserve this type of habitat or type of countryside.
>
> (Mike, 2001)

It was important to the students that they were working in their 'local patch':

> I do think you've got to do something about your local patch, and if everybody did their own local patch, it would build up into a huge patchwork really. I think every little helps.
>
> (Shirley, 2001)

But the closeness of the 'local patch' to where they lived varied. Most of the students lived within a few miles of Bedelands, and it could rightly be considered their local patch, but some of those coming from more than 10 miles away still considered Bedelands to be their patch, perhaps because they had been involved with the site over a large number of years. Others, with a shorter history of involvement, saw the project primarily as an opportunity to improve their identification skills and participate in research, and did not think of Bedelands in terms of citizenship. This was reserved for their involvement in other 'local patches' nearer to home.

> I don't feel so involved at Bedelands because it is not somewhere where I tend to go other than for research.
>
> (Jo, 2001)

Not just for me, but also for the students, the aim of the experiment was inextricably bound up with public awareness at many levels. Students talked about the number of people who had been involved with the project over the years. Some of these had remained on the periphery, coming along to some of the monitoring sessions, but not becoming part of the core. Others had joined the group for a while and then had taken the skills they had learned and put them to other uses. A good example of this was Melanie, who had been part of the original group, but whose new job had prevented her from continuing. Since then she had organised a series of very successful annual children's safaris at Bedelands, the particular success of which the students attributed to her participation in the Bedelands research. Then there were members of the general public who saw us working in the meadows and came to ask questions. And children saw us at work too:

> *I think it's quite a good example for the younger generation. I mean Melanie's safaris encourage children to go on the reserve and they see us sitting down in a field of grass, and that's quite a good example for them to follow if they're interested. I mean we won't be here in 50 years time but they will be and hopefully they'll be doing the same sort of thing, maybe not at Bedelands but somewhere else.*
>
> (Shirley J, 2001)

> *And there's another level where even the children that aren't interested do actually see that someone is interested.*
>
> (Janet, 2001)

But also there was a wider significance to what they were doing. Bill remembered that the experiment had been used as a 'Living Exhibition' at an information day on the management of wildflower meadows.

> *There are people outside the local patch who visited it last year when there was a nature day there and people from quite a big area came to that, certainly beyond the local patch, so it does have a wider significance in that sense.*
>
> (Bill, 2001)

The day had been organised by FWAG (the Farming and Wildlife Advisory Group) in conjunction with the High Weald Meadows Group, and about 60 farmers and landowners had attended. A morning of talks had been followed by a walk across the reserve to look at the Experiment in one of the meadows. Standing at the side of the field and looking across at the two halves, one of which had been grazed and the other not, delegates were impressed by the clear display of more wild flowers in the grazed half. A few weeks later a meeting of the East and West Sussex County Council Biodiversity Group was held at Bedelands Farm so that representatives from this group could see the experiment.

Finally, the students saw their work as contributing to a wide body of scientific knowledge:

I think that what we learn goes into the general body of knowledge on managing grassland habitats – this type of neutral grassland.

(Bill, 2001)

This would require the writing of a scientific paper.

It requires someone like you to write a learned paper on it. The general principles of the experiment that we have been doing are I believe understood by most people who are in your sort of profession, but you might find out something about it which would really need to be publicised.

(John, 2001)

This aspect of the research is discussed further in Chapter 7.

Students saw the objectives of the experiment in a very similar way to me, except that they didn't explicitly see themselves as being trained to be biological recorders. However, as we shall see, the skills that they wanted to acquire are exactly those needed to be a biological recorder.

Learning to be biological recorders

An acute shortage and using the older learner

Both the British Ecological Society (Doberski, 2002, p. 20) and local Wildlife Trusts report a current lack of biological recorders. Full time undergraduate courses have moved away from fieldwork (Tilling, 2001) and many graduates with degrees in ecology and environmental science lack basic identification and fieldwork skills (Doberski, 2002, p. 20). People taking up posts in environmental consultancy advising farmers and landowners frequently have to learn these skills on the job and, as we have seen, the Certificate in Field Biology has catered for the needs of such people.

Quite rightly, a major focus for effort to address this problem is directed towards schools and the school curriculum. However, we have a shortage of recorders now and we can't afford to wait for these schoolchildren to grow up. Adults in full-time employment may not have the space in their lives for time consuming monitoring activities, but more and more people (and especially professional people who form the bulk of CE classes) are taking early retirement and are still active. Many of these, as detailed in the previous chapter, have an interest in natural history and may be actively seeking appropriate courses to further this interest. If we can convert this passive interest into the knowledge and skills required for biological monitoring, CE classes could harness this resource. Listening to the voices of students who have made this transition talking about how they learned the necessary skills and what motivated them to spend the large amount of time necessary to achieve this, may help to inform wildlife trusts and government agencies involved in the vital task of training biological recorders. It is also hoped that these voices will reach the many people interested in natural history who have never thought of being biological recorders and will inspire them to start now.

The skills needed to be a biological recorder require a considerable amount of perseverance on the part of the learner and plenty of practice particularly in identification of difficult plants such as grasses and mosses. It is difficult to acquire the necessary practice within the confines of a short course, so projects such as the Meadow Management Experiment are needed to provide a stimulating and supportive environment in which this can happen. Questionnaires completed at the end of each summer's data collection for the Experiment reveal that even new recruits joining after one 20–hour course find the experience rewarding:

I have really enjoyed the experience and feel more confident about identifying species.
(New recruit, questionnaire feedback summer 2003)

An invitation to take part in the experiment was extended to all students who joined natural history or field biology classes. In practice, only those who were available for daytime fieldwork were able to accept, but this is the group that we want to target, since biological monitoring is of necessity a daytime activity. Many were retired professionals like Julia, a retired occupational therapist.

I've always been interested in natural history but with job and family commitments I've not been able to pursue it. I am a country person and I had been living in London a long time but retirement in Sussex got me going. I've always attended evening classes in something – well, for over 30 years – and when I came down to Sussex I looked at the brochure, and thought that Margaret's natural history class in Crawley would be a marvellous start. And it's been the beginning of all sorts of things.
(Julia, 2001)

Students participating in the experiment did not have to be experts, but a serious commitment to attend for a morning or an afternoon once a week from mid May to mid July was required. This is a major commitment – what did they expect to get out of the large amount of time which they were putting into this activity? Most students hoped to improve their identification skills, particularly of grasses. This was 'part of an innate wish to learn. I'm not an academic, but I like to learn and I want to increase my knowledge about natural history' (Mike, 2001). Richard Jefferies, a naturalist writing in the latter half of the 19th century, describes this drive to know:

The first conscious thought about wild flowers was to find out their names…and then I began to see so many that I had not previously noticed. Once you wish to identify them there is nothing that escapes, down to the little white chickweed of the path and the moss of the wall.

(Jefferies 1979, p. 6).

It was a picture in a wildflower book that got Jefferies started: and it was to be a lifelong journey of discovery:

The birds-foot lotus was the first…I sat on the sward of the sheltered slope, and instantly recognised the orange-red claws of the flower beside me. That was the first; and this very morning, I dread to consider how many years afterwards, I found a plant on a wall which I do not know… So many years and still only at the beginning

(Jefferies, 1979, p. 7–8).

Identification was not always as easy as that first birdsfoot trefoil (Figure 5.1), and Jefferies writes movingly about the difficulty of being sure about identification based on pictures in books (p. 11). The students, too, had found learning from books to be slow and at times frustrating. Books were only really useful once you knew the identity of the plant from hands-on experience.

I don't think you can substitute books for hands-on. You could read all the books in the world and it still isn't necessarily clear until you look at an actual specimen of say the grass that is being described and then it is obvious.

(Shirley, 2001).

The experiment, though, was not just an exercise to improve students' identification skills and to extend what they had learnt in class: it had the added advantage that they would be participating in research and contributing to biodiversity conservation.

Well having got interested in all aspects of the things I've done with Margaret, it seemed a natural thing to continue and increase my knowledge. Particularly as I'm very interested in botany and identifying all those grasses was interesting and it's something I wanted to do. And it was nice to keep in touch with some of the people I'd come across during the studies before. And I felt I might be making a small contribution to scientific research in a subject which I feel passionately about.

(Julia, 2001)

When it was suggested to me by Margaret, my first thought was, I really have forgotten an awful lot of my botany, and if I go into this fieldwork I will get to grips with identification and I will understand far more about quadrat work and about the flora that we were looking at. The next point was that it was research work, which was interesting, we could find out what was going on and it was in a good cause as well, but I must admit it was selfish reasons to start off with.

(Shelagh, 2001)

The fact that these students have returned in subsequent years is, I believe, due to this extra research dimension. Bill talked about the benefit of more extended activity than was possible in time-limited class sessions:.

In a way, Bedelands is just a longer field trip. Which is good because, when we did Field Biology, field trips were never long enough were they? Also, it is a chance to be involved in something that goes on over a period of time. You don't get many studies that go on for more than four or five years.

(Bill, 2001)

It is clear from the voices of these students that some older learners do have the interest and time to devote to time-consuming vegetation monitoring activities, but how do we convert an interested adult learner into a trained biological monitor so that we can utilise this potential resource? As well as interest it will require a high degree of perseverance on the part of the learners to carry them through the great length of time required to acquire the practical skills of identification and fieldwork needed to become a proficient biological recorder. They will also need knowledge about what has to be done and why. To some extent we can do this by providing appropriate identification and recording classes, but it is difficult to build enough practice into such courses. There is a danger that practice without an overall objective becomes a rather sterile exercise. A research project that students can identify with and contribute to, while at the same time getting lots of practice in biological identification and monitoring, is ideal. A similar approach is used to train practical archaeologists: new students work alongside professionals and contribute to a major piece of excavation while at the same time acquiring necessary skills. This is explored further in Chapter 7. As well as developing skills, the experiment has the added advantage that it is at the same time contributing to the local conservation agenda and to building up knowledge about a particular habitat.

Learning through fieldwork: acquiring the skills required for biological monitoring

In the Meadow Management Experiment, continuing education students were responsible for monitoring the meadow vegetation in the different treatment areas each summer. So the skills learned were exactly those required for monitoring this sort of habitat and could be relatively easily extended to other vegetation monitoring. A careful exploration of how these students learned can shed light on the process and so help us to understand how to apply the principles in other situations. During interview-based learning in the workplace, Eraut *et al* (1998) found that people were able to talk more explicitly about their knowledge if they were given some mediating object such as a picture or drawing that they were used to discussing. A similar approach was used during discussions about the role of learning in fieldwork situations, with photographs and plant specimens being used to evoke the learning situations.

1. Identification skills

For these students the skill which they most wanted to acquire was plant identification and particularly grass identification, which was universally perceived as being difficult. In this they were not alone, Darwin too was challenged by grasses:

> *I have just made out my first grass, hurrah! hurrah! I must confess that fortune favours the bold, for, as good luck would have it, it was the easy* Anthoxanthum odoratum: *nevertheless it is a great discovery; I never expected to make out a grass in all my life, so hurrah! It has done my stomach surprising good…*
>
> (Darwin, 1889, p. 418, in letter to J.D. Hooker June 5th, 1855)

Bill wanted to be able to identify grasses 'without having to refer to books when doing it out in the field somewhere'. In order to do this, he had to learn the key features of the different grasses and to know how to recognise them in different specimens. Even with books, identification depends on being able to recognise key features:

> *The knowledge of key features is invaluable as a maxim for the identification of specimens, but like all maxims it is useful only to those who possess the art of applying it .*
>
> (Polanyi, 1962, p. 351)

And, as Darwin discovered, it is easier if the grass has distinctive features that are easy to see.

Students paced themselves and learnt in steps starting with the more distinctive species and moving on to new species when they were ready to. It was easier when the grasses were in flower, but at the beginning of the monitoring season many of the species were not yet in flower and they had to learn to identify from vegetative characters too. John and Janet explain:

> *Personally I think you learn in a series of steps. I mean as far as I'm concerned the easy grass to identify is something like* Holcus lanatus *(Yorkshire fog) – because it's*

pretty unique isn't it? I mean it's everywhere soft, particularly soft on the leaf, and you also gave us the clue about striped pyjamas (a reference to the maroon-coloured stripes on the base of the leaf sheath in this species) – but after that the next thing is the flower head isn't it? Trying to identify grasses when you can't see any flower-heads is infinitely more difficult to me.

(John, 2001)

I think that you learn one particular grass like the Holcus lanatus, *yes. I mean I'd be happy with* Holcus lanatus, *but every spring I go back and beyond* Holcus lanatus *I've got to start all over again, and you gradually remember features.*

(Janet, 2001)

These students having learnt on the job tended to use botanical names and were quite comfortable with these. It may be that introducing plants by common names to start with, which one tends to do, may lead to confusion. Students worked in groups, usually of three or four, so they learned from each other. As Janet and Bill explained this was not necessarily from someone who was more experienced than the rest of the group, but someone who knew the particular species they were puzzling over. They were reminding each other.

You're reminding each other and anybody could have remembered a particular thing that points you again, but it all comes from learning one or two and adding to it.

(Janet, 2001)

Different people learn to identify the different grasses at different rates. If you've got three or four of you round a quadrat, you've all got the same level of knowledge, but the detail of the knowledge is going to be different.

(Bill, 2001)

It was also easier when there was continuity of location. The same species could look very different on different sites. One student remarked that he found it easier to identify grasses at Bedelands than in his own garden. Another student remembered his surprise at finding bent grass five feet high when carrying out monitoring in another, wetter, nature reserve.

A number of the students were concerned that it took them longer to learn these days than it had when they were younger. As Pam explained:

Learning, and more importantly recall, takes more effort as one ages. In my own case it is necessary to continually look things up again and again until eventually the information sinks in.

(Pam, 2001)

The repetitive nature of the monitoring, where students moved across the meadow identifying all the plants present in a series of sample areas (quadrats), was clearly important. And was repeated in subsequent weeks with minor variations as the grasses grew and came into flower.

> *Constant repetition as far as I was concerned from one week to the next, week after week after week, it eventually sank in.*
>
> (Mike, 2001)

2. Using identification books and field guides
Students were keen to learn to identify most species without needing to refer to a book, but they also agreed that identification books were an essential tool and were used in a number of situations:

- when there was a dispute;
- as an *aide-memoire*;
- for explaining points to newcomers;
- when a species new to the group was found.

With two or three students working together round a quadrat there were frequent occasions when there was disagreement about the identification of particular specimens. Sometimes these were referred to me, but mostly these were resolved within the group using identification books such as Hubbard (1954, 1984) for grasses.

> *If there is a dispute then that's when books really come in. If two people disagree then you laboriously go through every single characteristic of that blade of grass.*
>
> (Shirley, 2001)

> *I think as a back up they're essential.*
>
> (Bill, 2001)

> *I think also when you've got someone who's joined who's relatively new and doesn't know too much – Nick came this year – the book is useful because the book backs up what you're telling that person if they ask what the characteristics are, and sometimes the book shows the characteristic that you were trying to describe.*
>
> (Bill, 2001)

> *And it gives you something to go back to at a future date. I wouldn't go anywhere, really, without the book because I know that what's in my head is sometimes difficult to raise, whereas what's in the book – I know it's going to be there.*
>
> (Janet, 2001)

What sort of guides did they find most useful? Many of the students used the recommended identification guides from the courses which they had started on. This was Rose (1981, 1991) for general plant identification apart from grasses, and sedges, Hubbard (1984) for grasses and Watson (1995) for mosses and liverworts. Some of the students had been brought up on McClintock and Fitter (1956, 1961) and found this a very useful book as the specific characteristics of species which are difficult to separate are clearly brought out in the descriptions and it covers grasses and sedges as well as forbs (wild flowers) in the same book. It is a pity that this book is out of print, as other students frequently express interest in it, and it is still held up by professionals as the standard towards which field guides should aim (Akeroyd, 1991). The starting point for grasses was usually the Field Studies Council key (1988), followed up by Hubbard (1984), although Hubbard's descriptions, where everything is qualified (eg 'slender to somewhat stout'; 'flaccid or firm'; 'rough or almost smooth'), caused a lot of frustration.

> the other thing I argue with, you know when you read Hubbard and it says more or less hairy, more or less this, perhaps this, perhaps that...'
>
> (Janet, 2001)

However, Hubbard's line drawings were found to be very useful. A key feature in grass identification, which the students talk about in the following quotes, is the ligule: a small outgrowth at the base of the leaf blade where the stem emerges from the leaf sheath.

> From the overall appearance I think it's easier just to glance at the Field Studies sheet initially, if you don't know what it is, and you can see well it's not that one, it's not that one, it might be that, it might be that. So then you go into more detail.
>
> (Mike, 2001)

> I think there're two levels of 'book': a sort of field guide like the sheets that the Field Studies Council do which are purely visual. They're ideal for people who are starting because you can look at what a ligule looks like and the picture is worth a thousand words. If you're still not sure, you then go back to a book and read the description. You can then say well yes that does or doesn't match. And also, different authors take things in different ways and I think that you need more than one book. I find that I look at Hubbard and then go and look at another book and if they correspond then I'm satisfied.
>
> (Bill, 2001)

Students also constructed their own worksheets and diagrams to help them sort out the different species they were encountering:

Quite often I will sketch the ligule in my book where I've identified it. I think one's own drawing is better than someone else's.

(Bill, 2001)

John, as a recently retired engineer, used an engineer's approach:

I'm trying to create a worksheet with all these different sorts of grasses and their ligules. That you see I would describe as a 2D ligule and that would be a 1D ligule, because that gives some correlation between the diameter of the stem and the length of the ligule.

(John, 2001)

These students were plainly making a new field of study their own in the best tradition of Freire's re-creation metaphor (1996). They were also learning from each other, as a new-comer joining the group in summer 2003 wrote 'I have gained a lot by being with more experienced people who helped me with identification.' (questionnaire, Summer 2003). At the end of the day 'probably the best guide of all is still a knowledgeable field biologist' (Akeroyd, 1991, p. 216).

3. Using keys

All the students had been introduced to keys on the courses they had attended, and from time to time keys were used during the monitoring. However, as identification skills within the group improved they were used a lot less, and this made the monitoring exercise easier to fit into the time available. Hubbard's short key for the identification of grasses in turf (p. 437) was a useful starting point and an abbreviated version of his key for the more common grasses using vegetative characters (p. 387) was frequently used in the early days. In this version, species that we were unlikely to encounter had been removed by one of the Field Biology students and the key had been set out with alternatives following each other. I drew up a 'synoptic' key based on the characters used by Hubbard where all the common grass species could be seen on a single page and arrows directed you through the diagram from the distinguishing characters to the species. Again this was used in the early days, and replies to questionnaires handed out at the end of the 2003 summer monitoring indicated that new people joining the group had used this key. It has the advantage over traditionally laid out keys that your eye can go straight to the part of the key that you need – for example which are the species in which the young leaf blade is rolled rather than folded. For mosses, Watson's excellent 'Field Key to the commonest and most conspicuous species of mosses and liverworts' (regrettably absent from the latest edition of the book) was always used.

In the discussion it was clear that the students felt that keys were something that everybody else used and that we should have used them more. I think keys were seen as the magic answer to a difficult identification problem, and that with more practice they would be able to run things down quickly and easily. In practice, they had found them cumbersome and time-consuming, and difficult to do in the field.

> *If I'm stuck and I take something home, then I will sit down – you seem to need to sit down and have your hand-lens – and go through it. It's not something that's easy to do in the field ... It's very time-consuming, and if there are two of you it's easier, because somebody reads it and you say yes or no and you go on. But to actually put the paper down and pick up the thing – it's awkward and it's easier to do at home.*
>
> (Janet, 2001)

When unfamiliar or difficult specimens of moss were found, the specimen was called 'Species 1' in the record and the fieldwork continued. The moss was looked up later at home by one or other of the core students who had done the Field Biology Certificate and so were good at identifying mosses. Watson's field key was the preferred one:

> *Well, the key that I use is the field one that came out in Watson's book. I use it because you haven't got to start right from the very beginning, so you can put the moss into a group fairly quickly. And if you get lost or if you can't find it, you know that it's something a bit unusual perhaps.*
>
> (Janet, 2001)

Several of the students had found that sometimes they could not make a key work and this they attributed to their own inexperience. They needed to learn how to use the key. We agreed that you needed to know the vocabulary in order to make the key work, but there was something more than this. Although the idea that some illustrations and descriptions given in books were better than others was generally accepted, the idea that some keys might be better constructed than others and might be using more reliable characters, was not so readily received. Like learning about the limitations of science through doing science, getting students to construct their own keys, which I have done on occasions, would be a good way of getting students to appreciate the limitations of keys. In future, too, I intend to put more emphasis on using keys so that students build up a picture of which keys are useful. Keys may be one of the major stumbling blocks preventing people who are working on their own from making progress in biological identification.

4. Being able to pick out everything that is in the quadrat

As well as being able to accurately identify the species in their sample, students needed to be able to spot all the plants that were present. In the Bedelands meadows some unusual species caused particular difficulty, such as grass vetchling, which has grass-like leaves (Figure 5.1), and adder's tongue fern, a tiny primitive fern with a single oval-shaped leaf similar to one leaf on a common sorrel plant (Figure 5.2).

Figure 5.2 Adder's tongue fern, a tiny primitive fern about 2 centimetres high found in the meadows at Bedelands Farm. The single oval-shaped leaf can be very difficult to spot in grassland. Fertile specimens, like the one photographed, are easier and shed clouds of yellow spores from the tongue-like structure. (Photograph by John Pilkington.)

Once one specimen had been found, the group could usually find more.

> *And once you've seen one though you can see more. Once you've actually seen a vetchling – then you spot half a dozen. But that doesn't necessarily hold on does it? I mean the next week you'll probably be just as slow spotting the first one because it was slightly different.*
>
> (Shirley, 2001)

However it wasn't just the unusual species. As Bill pointed out it was easy to overlook common, familiar plants when they were scattered through the sample at a low frequency:

> *But even common plants, you may not see them in a quadrat. You see one, then you see another and another. Anything with a low frequency is difficult to pick up initially. It could be a quite common plant really.*
>
> (Bill, 2001)

This 'getting their eye in' happened anew each week, with students starting off slowly and speeding up as the day wore on (Figure 5.3). Speed of identification also increased as the day progressed. Bill had found that when he joined the group just for the afternoon he was much slower than those who had been present for the morning shift.

> *Speed of identification is another factor which comes in and increases week by week, and as the day goes on. I usually find coming in the afternoon – for the first quadrat I am really lagging. Whoever I am with has been there in the morning and is up to speed – has got a rhythm going.*
>
> (Bill, 2001)

We also tend to speed up each year as the weeks progress. At the start we work slowly and I wonder whether we will finish the monitoring programme in the time available, but we get quicker with practice and so far have always managed to finish in time.

5. Estimating percentage cover of the species in the quadrats

A very important aspect of the monitoring fieldwork is estimating the percentage cover of each plant species in the samples so that we can see whether this is increasing or decreasing in the different parts of the experiment. Percentage cover is estimated by eye: if you mentally take away all the other species in the sample how much of the total area is covered by the plant whose cover you are estimating? This is notoriously difficult to do accurately with professional ecologists recognising that their estimations vary

Figure 5.3 John and Shirley finding plant species in a permanent quadrat in the Meadow Management Experiment at Bedelands Farm. This 'getting their eye in' happened anew each week with students starting off slow, and speeding up as the day wore on. (Photograph John Pilkington.)

as the day goes on as well as varying between one worker and the next (Nilsson, 1992). Perhaps by looking at how these students learnt this difficult skill we can make recommendations about the training of conservation professionals. But first we need to consider how accurate the end result was.

There is no reason, of course, why ordinary adults should not be as good at doing this as trained ecologists, who have probably had very little fieldwork practice amongst all the theory of sampling technique which they will have received in lectures. However, this was one of the features of the experiment that most worried me, and in the early years we spent the first monitoring session of each year on a group exercise to try to standardise the estimations. Students worked in groups of four, and each quadrat was done by two groups in turn, who then compared their estimations of percentage cover. I was surprised by the good agreement which we obtained for most species: the exceptions being species of grass such as the different species of bent grass which were difficult to separate within the sward without looking at ligules on individual specimens. This problem was solved when we discovered hybrids and decided to lump all the bent grass species together in our records.

Students used all the usual tricks of the trade, like dividing the sample up into quarters and building up mental pictures of what 15 per cent might look like. They were aware of special difficulties like overestimation of species with eye-catching flowers. However, most important both to the learning process and to accuracy was the interaction which went on within the small groups. This is illustrated by the following discussion:

> *Because you're in a group one person not being sure doesn't matter because somebody else fills in that space and then if you're not sure you look at what they're doing and if you agree with it, fine, and if you don't you suddenly see why you don't agree with it.*
>
> (Shirley, 2001)

[So sometimes you step back and just watch what's going on until you feel confident?]

> *You get more confident and you throw out a figure, and then everybody else says no, whereas if you're a real beginner you're not even going to say 15 percent, and you wait. But if you say well I'll go in at 15 per cent and someone else says 40 per cent – well this is fine – it opens up a conversation.*
>
> (Shirley, 2001)

Through these discussions, and through working with different people each week amongst quite a large group of perhaps 15 to 20 people, a consensus technique developed which students felt gave accurate results, although they recognised that as individuals they tended to make different estimations (Figure 5.4). They also felt that they learned and improved with practice in the context of the group.

> *It's a technique that we developed – maybe not consciously – but because we were all working together we have developed a consensus technique which has improved the accuracy of what we do. [...] If there are more than two of you in the group, you often get one who is low and one who is high, and if you are the last in you would tend to bring them together – take an average. And after a while one begins to know how different people estimate. Now I know I always underestimate and I know there are others who tend to overestimate.*
>
> (Bill, 2001)

> *But then, with Margaret circulating amongst the groups, you do reassess on an ongoing basis.*
>
> (Shirley, 2001)

Grasses remained difficult. If they were in flower how much vegetative growth was there below the conspicuous flower heads? And if they weren't in flower, how did one manage to pick out one grass species from another in a generally grassy sward? Actually this was relatively easy to do for grasses with a distinctive colour like Yorkshire fog or cocksfoot, but very difficult for crested dogstail or meadow foxtail. At the beginning of a season, before one got one's eye in again, one tended to have the feeling that for these grasses percentage cover could not really be done without looking at every blade of grass in the sample! We all found this to some extent, but it was a particular problem for new students.

The assigning of a percentage cover I found a lot easier on the more obvious plants, particularly the herbs, rather than the grasses which I found extraordinarily difficult. If we were to do grasses properly we would have to look at every blade.

(John, 2001)

Figure 5.4 Pam and Julia estimating percentage cover of a plant species in a permanent quadrat in the Meadow Management Experiment at Bedelands Farm. Through discussion, and through working with different people each week a consensus technique developed, which students felt gave accurate results. (Photograph John Pilkington.)

6. Making an accurate and efficient record of the data

All fieldwork requires data to be recorded accurately and efficiently. Often recording takes place under less than ideal conditions. It may be wet or windy, or you may end up balancing on a slippery slope or in a pool of water following a cloud-burst. Under these conditions the ability to make an intelligible record using the minimum amount of writing is crucial. For the experienced students who took part in the discussion, the making of such records was automatic and they could not remember how they learned the skill. Indeed it was so automatic that they were doubtful about whether it was really a skill. As a tutor, though, one remembers early efforts when some of these students wrote out a separate list of species for each quadrat and collation of class data at the end of the session was a nightmare. In early class sessions beginners are usually given a record sheet set out with columns into which they write their data, but they should be encouraged to design their own data collecting sheets as soon as possible. Where beginners work with more experienced students they quickly learn from each other, and the value of getting this right becomes apparent early on when classes regularly collate data from different quadrats at the end of sessions. Collation of data is much quicker if species lists are ordered alphabetically or in some other logical order which has been adopted by all participants (such as the most common species first). At Bedelands, newcomers were given a species list, but not a record sheet. On the whole, most students dealt with grass species all together, either before or after non-grass species (forbs). Some students preferred to deal with the forbs in their quadrats first, coming onto the more difficult grasses all together at the end. Others preferred to deal with the grasses first, as it is perhaps easier to assign percentage cover values to grasses while the vegetation remains erect and untrammelled by searching for species through the sward. As long as species were arranged alphabetically, collation was easily effected from data sheets set out either with forbs and grasses in two separate lists, or with forbs and grasses together in one list. Some biological recorders start by listing the species present in their quadrat before going on to assign cover values to the species. We found that this was much more time-consuming than assigning values directly to the species as they were noted, and during the Bedelands monitoring the direct method was always used.

7. Setting out permanent quadrats and locating them again in subsequent years –
   surveying skills

Conservation monitoring is usually long term and requires quadrats to be set out in such a way that those doing the monitoring can return to the same samples in future years. Sometimes the position of such quadrats, known as permanent quadrats, is marked with posts, but meadows which are going to be cut using standard farm equipment need to be free of obstructions. Metal rods can sunk in the ground and then re-located using a metal detector. This sounds foolproof, but had proved unreliable at two other sites in Sussex. One was a wet meadow where it is possible that the rods went on sinking into the wet ground and ended up beyond the range of the detector. The other was a meadow in the High Weald where apparent quadrat markers were detected everywhere. Eventually it was discovered that a Spitfire had come down there during the last war! Another requirement for long-term monitoring, which has been found in woodland studies is a simple quadrat layout, such as a transect, so that quadrats can be relocated at dates sufficiently far into the future to become long-term (Peterken, 2000, p. 13). In the Meadow Management Experiment, quadrats were set out on orthogonally-directed transects from a baseline which had been set up using a sighting compass and correcting for magnetic deviation (Figure 5.5).

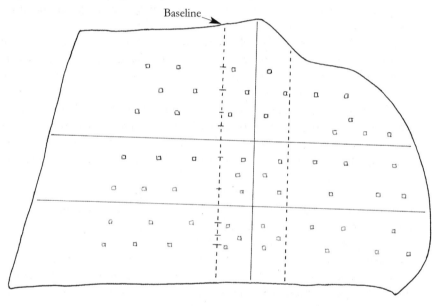

Figure 5.5 Diagram of experimental meadow (Old Arable) showing arrangement of quadrats. Quadrats were set out, on orthogonally-directed transects from a baseline, in a regular pattern across the different treatment areas. Care was taken to avoid paths and other discontinuities, and unfertilised quadrats were placed well away from the central fertilised strip. (See Figure 7.2 for diagram showing treatment areas.)

Initially, transects, at appropriate distances along the baseline, were set out at right angles to the baseline, using the sighting compass, but subsequently triangulation (in which two tapes are placed equidistantly from the point of origin on the baseline and then are brought together to make an equilateral triangle) proved to be much quicker and more accurate (Figures 5.6a and 5.6b)

By triangulating on both sides of the baseline it was possible to check accuracy by seeing how well the two triangulated points lined up with the point of origin on the baseline. Towards the end of the monitoring season the tapes tend to become caught up on tall plants in the sward, resulting in curved rather than straight lines, and it sometimes required more than one go to make the points line up. Quadrat positions were marked on a map and located by measuring given distances along each transect. Setting out the experiment at the beginning required considerable surveying skills. Some students found the compass very difficult to use:

> Well, I remember when I first started, it was, I found the compass extremely difficult, I had no confidence in my ability to use it.
>
> (Shirley, 2001)

> I think triangulation is quicker, because there's enough of us for the tapes and we can triangulate quite quickly.
>
> (Shirley, 2001)

Everyone became proficient at triangulation and could set out the next transect and locate the position of the quadrat on it. I would recommend this as a simple and convenient way of setting out permanent quadrats in public spaces (Figure 5.7).

Figure 5.6a Setting out a transect at right angles to the baseline using triangulation. Two tapes, placed equidistantly from the point of origin on the baseline, are being brought together to make an equilateral or isosceles triangle. (Photograph John Prodger.)

Figure 5.6b Setting out a transect at right angles to the baseline using triangulation. The tapes have been brought together at the point of the isosceles triangle and the surveying pole is being inserted. This should line up with the point of origin on the baseline and the triangulation on the other side of the baseline. (Photograph John Prodger.)

Figure 5.7 Recording plant species in permanent quadrats set out along a transect in the Meadow Management Experiment (photograph Jen Fernee).

Implications

The use of visual clues definitely helped the discussions about learning in fieldwork situations, with students picking up pieces of grass or referring to the books and photographs to make their points. However, this may have channelled discussion in particular ways and it would be nice to take recordings in the field of the team actually at work, perhaps concentrating on new students as they were going through the process of learning. Care would have to be taken not to compromise the learning situation.

These student voices demonstrate that a latent interest in natural history can be converted into the knowledge and skills required for biological monitoring and they tell us from their own experience how this can be done. Their learning can be used as a model by other institutions or by individual or groups of interested adults to follow. Many lay people are involved with sites, and it is hoped that they will feel able to set up their own monitoring programmes. If we succeed in doing this on a sufficiently wide scale we could solve the problem of lack of biological monitors. A lack of biological recorders is a problem throughout the developed world and in fact Britain has been one of the best equipped countries in this respect, with a very well documented wildlife (Marren, 2002, p. 16), and is only just starting to feel the effect of the shortage now. In the past, we have taken the lead and have exported our expertise:

> *Our 60-odd butterflies are nothing on the world stage, but the expertise acquired in studying them has been exported worldwide. British bittern experts are in demand internationally, though we have only a handful of bitterns.*
>
> (Marren, 2002, p. 16).

In a similar way, we could take the lead in demonstrating a way forward in which this type of lifelong learning leads into community-based biological conservation projects.

Learning through collaboration: the site managers

At the beginning of the chapter we emphasised the need to conserve all remaining areas of this type of flower-rich grassland, and that much of this was managed by local councils. These councils may be keen to acquire green credentials, but may have little appreciation of what nature conservation means in practical terms. The council involved in the Meadow Management Experiment, Mid Sussex District Council, was probably more sympathetic to such ideas than most. They were key players in the three year Mid Sussex Greenspace Project set up in 1993 with the Sussex Wildlife Trust, and in 1997 they produced the Mid Sussex Greenspace Directory, and took on the task of updating it. In October 2001 they produced a landscape and biodiversity strategy for Mid Sussex called 'Our Green Heritage.' They have had an active policy of buying up farmland to create green areas around major conurbations and have made several of these into Local Nature Reserves. However, they do not employ a full-time conservation officer and have little idea about how to manage their conservation areas. As Marren (2002, p. 110) observed: 'Acquiring a nature reserve looks like an achievement, but it will come to naught unless the place is looked after properly'. How can such councils be educated in the practical measures needed to deliver on their biodiversity aspirations? The Meadow Management Experiment demonstrates one way in which this can be achieved. Here the council, as one of the stakeholders, is learning through doing in a similar way to the students. Problems of grazing are dealt with on a small scale in the experiment and, having seen the benefits of the aftermath grazing for themselves, they are now prepared to graze more of the meadows. Hopefully this will go beyond the local area because, as Bill explained, they might spread the word to other councils:

> *They (the Council) are putting grazing into the management for the whole reserve. I would have thought that that had a wider significance, coming back to the wider significance of the project, because there are a lot of locations around the country where councils as well as various other bodies have these sorts of areas and they are very loathe to graze. [...] I would have thought that Mid Sussex District Council will spread that information to other councils. I am sure the councils themselves have a network. Nobody wants to be first do they, just in case it's an absolute disaster? If someone can say well we've done it....*
>
> (Bill, 2001)

Potentially this could be very important because in 1998 there were 598 Local Nature Reserves covering 20,032 hectares, mostly in densely populated areas and managed as public amenities (Marren 2002, p. 111).

Learning to be 'Citizens of the local ecosystem': site users

For the first few years after Bedelands Farm was bought by the council it remained almost unknown, hidden by the wood that bounded the houses and the football pitch. Gradually, local residents became aware of the site, largely through the efforts of a very active 'Friends of Bedelands Farm' group who organised open days, talks and walks, and a newsletter as well as conservation work parties. One hundred and seventy families are now members and the site is very heavily used by dog-walkers and birdwatchers, family groups, and gangs of children and youths. It has changed from rural idyll into an urban greenspace, complete with inherent vandalism and dog problems, but with this change has come great potential for putting people in touch with nature. A key function of nature reserves, as Marren (2002, p. 131) suggests, is to 'promote wildlife conservation ... by inspiring wonder and compassion for wildlife in a more involving way than television.' This happened for Judith Thompson when she took part in the peace camp at Clayoquot Sound in Canada, and she learned about the temperate rainforest by just going into the forest and experiencing what it was like to be part of it:

> *...to go into the [...] forest and just learn about nature and learn how things interact and to be part of that*
>
> (Judith Thompson in Moore 2003, p. 92).

This ideal of putting people in touch with nature poses a real dilemma for site managers in Britain today. Wildlife would certainly do better in the absence of dogs, and it has been argued that we need places in our crowded island where the interests of nature are paramount and are put before people (Marren 2002,

p. 207). But if people have no experience of the natural world they are unlikely to value nature and we will be unable to be effective in conserving biodiversity. As Hamilton recognised as long ago as the 1970s, the biggest threat to world biodiversity is 'a needless consumerism (particularly in the developed world) and the unmitigated faith in the ability of science and technology to provide ever increasing levels of consumption' (Hamilton, 1993, p. 3). We need a new kind of public myth to replace the dominant myth of perpetual progress through economic growth (Engel, 1993, p. 201) which will result in altered attitudes and behaviours. Engel goes on to suggest that citizenship could be the unifying theme needed to make this effective: a citizenship which linked people not just to a human community, but to a local ecosystem. Nature reserves like Bedelands, which are contiguous with urban areas, offer the opportunity for this to become a reality, but as well as experiencing the wildlife habitats, the general public need to understand what sustains the environments they are enjoying.

Many of the dog-walkers and local residents who use the site for recreation will be unaware of the need for conservation management. They will view the meadows as essentially unchanging without realising that the grassland will revert to scrub and woodland if left to itself. They will appreciate the beauty of the meadows in full flower in summer, but will not realise that it is necessary to cut at the right time of year and to graze the aftermath to maintain this cornucopia of flowers. They will enjoy the butterflies, but not realise how crucial it is to have the caterpillar food plants present in the grassland. They may be unhappy at the prospect of fences being erected to contain grazing animals and may feel that having sheep on the site even for a few weeks is an infringement of their rights to allow their dogs freedom of movement in an unrestricted space. As citizens of Burgess Hill this is their green space and they will have strong feelings about any changes which are made. A key aim of the experiment was to harness these feelings by taking site users into the plan, so that they could be citizens of this their local ecosystem. Display boards in the two experimental meadows show how the field has been divided up, so that people can look for themselves and see the effect of the different management treatments. Equally important has been the weekly sight, come rain or shine, of the research group recording from the quadrats and the opportunity that this affords of talking to us about what we are finding out.

It is clear that although we may need some sites just for nature, this is not the prime function of Local Nature Reserves in urban areas. Here, putting people in touch with nature is more important – and this includes the dog-walkers. And as well as experiencing nature, people need to be educated about how things interact and the ecology behind conservation management.

CHAPTER 6

Hands-on science in the countryside

...science's considerable success has been purchased by its self-chosen limitation of the scope of its enquiry. Science can only consider impersonal experience, reality encountered as an object that we can manipulate and put to the experimental test....its official discourse deals with measurements and not with values .

(Polkinghorne, 2002, p. 44).

This quotation from Polkinghorne states the crux of the matter and explains why citizens need to understand about science. It is at the interface between the objective world of scientific experimentation and the subjective, but no less important, world of ethical values that the problems lie. The issues involved are too important to leave to a small section of society: they are properly the concern of every citizen. However, citizens will not be able to exercise this right if they are unable to separate the science from the values. Traditionally, science teaching has emphasised the importance of developing a knowledge base made up of many pieces of individual information and building this up in a hierarchical way to form a complete picture. There has also been considerable emphasis on learning through doing, with large amounts of laboratory time being seen as an essential component of science courses. However, the amount of time available for each exercise is comparatively short and leads, rather like multiple-answer question papers, to the idea that there is a single correct answer (Knapper and Cropley, 2000, p. 75). In order to understand the strengths and limitations of science we need a new approach to science teaching – one which emphasises the learning rather than the teaching and is based on open-ended exercises which do not have right or wrong answers. In this chapter, CE student voices are used to illustrate the practice of science learning through hands-on, open-ended exercises in the countryside. Their voices were recorded during discussion sessions which took place in 2001 as part of the research project exploring ecological citizenship, discussed in Chapter 4.

Public ignorance or arrogant scientists?

The 'public understanding of science' is a much contested issue. From a scientist's point of view it is clear to me that science and technology alone cannot solve urgent world problems such as malnutrition and environmental degradation, and that the democratic process requires a better understanding of how science operates on the part of all citizens. This view was encapsulated in the Royal Society report *Public Understanding of Science* (Royal Society, 1985), which suggested that a better understanding of science by the general public would promote national prosperity, improve decision making at both the private and public level, and enrich the lives of individuals; and in 1986 the joint Committee on the Public Understanding of Science (COPUS) was established in partnership with the British Association to further these objectives. However, non-scientists, particularly social scientists, have argued that this approach is patronising and elitist, and that the problem lies with the operation of science itself and not with lack of understanding on the part of the general public. For example Irwin and Wynne (1996, p. 6):

> *There is an apparent assumption of 'public ignorance' in matters of science and technology... According to these, the general public often lacks a basic understanding of scientific facts, theories and methodologies. Public controversy over technical issues is created by inadequate public understandings rather than the operation of science itself. This projection of a 'public ignorance' model also serves to problematise the general public rather than the operation of scientists and scientific institutions.*

Irwin and Wynne (1996, p. 7) go on to suggest that we need to rethink the public understanding of science issue beginning with 'our notion of science' because research into the sociology of scientific knowledge over the last twenty years has shown 'the *socially negotiated* nature of science.' Science is not the 'unified, cleanly bounded, and clear body of knowledge and method' that is usually presented (Irwin and Wynne, 1996, p. 7). I would accept that the things which science investigates are socially conditioned as is the use to which scientific knowledge is put, but would maintain that the operation of science itself is objective. We need to keep Polkinghorne's words, quoted at the start of this chapter, in mind and to separate very clearly the objective results of scientific investigations from the rest of reality. The 'self-chosen limitation' of scientific enquiry is both a strength and a weakness, and for me the issue of public understanding of science is bound up with getting people to understand the limits of science as well as its 'considerable success'. Science by itself cannot solve world problems such as loss of biodiversity: we need public understanding of the issues involved and we also, as Engel (1993, p. 198) suggests, need to motivate people:

We must overcome the gap separating the technical-scientific world knowledge regime (environmental scientists, natural resource managers, policy specialists and development experts) from the creators and transmitters of cultural symbols, values and myths (artists, writers, educators, humanists, social scientists, religious and moral leaders)

It is true that some lectures given in the name of public understanding of science, reinforce the elitist view, with lecturers revelling in their own cleverness and making no attempt to connect with where the people in their audience are coming from. However, such apparent elitism is often driven by a belief on the part of individual scientists that what they have discovered is so beautiful that it needs sharing with the world.

As Michael Mayne recounts (2001, p. 98):

In early 1953, I was at Cambridge, living in college lodgings in Bene't Street just above the Eagle *pub. Round the corner, in the Cavendish Laboratory, Francis Crick and James Watson were working on what was to be one of the most revolutionary and far-reaching discoveries of the century: the structure of DNA. One day at lunchtime Francis Crick arrived in the* Eagle *to tell everyone within hearing that he and Watson had found the secret of life. Not long afterwards, Watson was invited to address the Hardy Club. Crick was present and describes how the Club's practice was to ply the speaker with a fair amount of drink before the lecture. He recalls that an unsteady Watson did well for a while 'but when he came to sum up he was quite overcome and at a loss for words. He gazed at the model, slightly bleary-eyed. All he could manage to say was 'it's all so beautiful you see, so beautiful!' 'But then, of course,' adds Crick, 'it was'.*

Sometimes, caught up in enthusiasm for the beauty of one's subject, it can be difficult to keep a hold on the balance between the detail and the wider picture.

In contrast museums putting on science exhibitions may be so keen to make science accessible through using simple language and through presenting the science within familiar contexts that they end up saying very little that is new to their audience, and, as one study concluded, the 'science' proper is 'still moved elsewhere, still out of the public's grasp' (McDonald, 1996, pp. 167–8). As a result, participants do not come away with a better understanding of science or more empowered to deal with it. In a similar way, nature conservation societies such as the Wildlife Trusts no longer cover any ecological science in their interpretation boards and reserve guides. The idea is to use simple language and appeal to people's emotions, rather than to attempt to give any real information. The result is very bland and frustrating for the many people who already know something about wildlife and would like to know more about specific sites and conservation challenges, but is designed, like the museum science, to be non-intimidating and to appeal to those not already interested in nature conservation.

Neither the big lecture approach nor the simplistic everyday-science approach enables the public to be scientifically literate and to exercise their democratic rights to shape the society they live in. In order to do this they need to understand how science works and what the limitations of science are, so that important issues, such as genetic modification of crops or control of greenhouse gases, are not left to a few scientists to handle. This requires that the public *practice* science, not just hear or read about it. Far from making science elitist this puts scientific knowledge in its appropriate place as part of the overall equation and allows a proper debate to take place about the use to which it should be put. There is clearly a role for continuing education here, but we have a difficult task on our hands because much of science *is* intrinsically quite difficult to understand, requiring a certain amount of dedication to the effort of understanding on the part of would be students, and also because of the negative press arising from recent controversies. As Irwin and Wynne (1996, p. 220) emphasise:

> *It is important for scientific institutions to recognise that science is often seen by public groups as a resource for the powerful in society – and against the everyday interests of the weak....science should ...not simply resort to the arrogance of a supposed 'higher rationality'. Such a worldview only serves to reinforce current attitudes of ambivalence, hostility, and indifference.*

Perhaps not surprisingly in view of this, the proportion of people entering HE to study science and mathematics has continued to fall since the 1960s (Millar, 1991, Nicholson, 2002). At Sussex, the falling number of applicants to mathematics is leading to drastic cuts in the department, and this at a time when the AUT is claiming that all present maths undergraduates need to go into teaching if the shortage of maths teachers is to be avoided ('The pm Programme', BBC Radio, 21 April 2003). Bad teaching in schools is going to exacerbate the negative trend. Continuing education provides a second opportunity for studying science for adults who missed out on a science education at school and, for some of the students taking part in the discussion sessions, this had been the case:

> When I was a child I was interested in science but I went to a very typical old-fashioned girls' school and science was taught extremely badly. And being, I think, a slightly awkward child who always asked why to everything, and even to staff at school, I would always ask why on the awkward questions. And I got slapped down so often, that in the end I gave up on science. I felt if nobody was prepared to explain it to me, I wasn't prepared to do it. And so fact I only did Arts subjects for my A levels, I did History and English. I had always been interested in science subjects and later

on, well much later on, I did do the Foundation year for the Open University in the Science Foundation course, which I found absolutely fascinating.

(Shelagh, 2001)

But, as Carlton (2001, p. 13) reports in a major survey of science teaching in continuing education, many adults share a negative image of science and scientists with school leavers.

For many people scientists continue to be seen as mad, bad and dangerous to know boffins who can function only in laboratories and cannot relate to the everyday concerns of the rest of us.

The well-educated person is seen to be arts-based in less applied but seemingly more cultured subjects like history, humanities, languages or the law.

Memories of science at school are often bad, and, in addition, the fear of failure and the lack of confidence which many adult learners experience is particularly marked when the subject is science, since science is perceived as being abstract, difficult, and needing good mathematical ability.

However, adult learners in practice are likely to be good at studying science, since they tend to be more able to study in a multidisciplinary way and are better at lateral thinking and problem-solving than school leavers (Carlton, 2001, p. 21). In order to capitalise on this potential, we need to find a popular and non-threatening way into science.

Natural history as a route into science

Here, it is worth emphasising, we are interested in developing an understanding of how science operates, of its strengths and limitations, so that we can break down the barriers between scientists and 'ordinary citizens'. This will involve becoming familiar with the knowledge base of some aspect of scientific endeavour, but this need not be the most mathematical and abstract aspect. As a practicing ecologist I have very little knowledge of astrophysics or even of molecular biology, but understand how science works. Indeed, for science to be understood it needs to be practised, and since we will not have access to expensive equipment and laboratory space, molecular biology would not be a good choice. We would be wise to choose a science subject that we can study in the field using easy to understand equipment and methods of measurement. Natural history is an ideal choice. It is popular with a large section of the adult population and leads naturally into making measurements in the field: that is to practising science. In continuing education, natural history and other field-based courses are almost alone among science courses in still recruiting sufficient students to run. Student voices recorded during the Ecological Citizenship Project (Chapter 4) demonstrated that it was an interest in natural history rather than science which led to their enrolment on the course, and that most of them had not associated natural history with science. The following voices are typical of their comments:

I had always been interested in natural history and happened to see this class advertised and an additional bonus was that a lot of it was going to be in the open air – and it would be fun to get out. And it did indeed prove very enjoyable indeed.

(Josephine, 2001)

I had no education or knowledge of science at school and I suppose in a way I was totally naïve about the subject and thought that science was something that was only carried on by academics. It surprised me really, like Richard and maybe John, that science can be applied to natural history and conservation and the environment.

(Mike, 2001)

Natural history classes, then, can provide a popular and non-threatening route into science. There will always be some students who join such classes simply to enjoy the beauty of wild flowers or butterflies, and whose exposure to science may be brief, like the student on a recent 'identifying and recording your local flora' course who told me she wanted to paint pictures of pretty flowers rather than make lists of those present in the grassland being studied. Making lists was science and she didn't have a scientific mind. I think that we have to recognise that just as not everyone is interested in classical music or Latin, not everyone will want to approach the natural world from a scientific perspective. It may not be possible to accommodate all within the same class. However, other students who had continued to come to the class had also found the scientific approach alien to start with:

I had no scientific knowledge at all and I found that a great problem, because I found it very difficult to relate to a scientific approach and it really hasn't quite sunk in yet. I think I'm still struggling with it because it somehow doesn't fit into my sort of pattern of thinking. It's so totally foreign. It hasn't really gelled and come together. I mean I can understand what we do in limited exercises and I can see the practicalities but it doesn't sort of knit together, where we're going with it. I found it very difficult to relate to the science. You know I think if you're not scientific, then you tend to think in terms of interpretation, you look at things and you interpret them, like an emotional process.

(Shirley B, 2001)

Shirley was still finding it difficult to fit science into the bigger picture, but in the context of the class surveys she could see where we were going, and her way of looking at the world in terms of interpretation was probably nearer to a scientific way of looking at things than she realised. For science, too. this is the first step, which then leads into formulating questions which can be tested:

> *Our vision of reality, to which our sense of scientific beauty responds, must suggest to us the kind of questions that it should be reasonable and interesting to explore...In fact, without a scale of interest and plausibility based on a vision of reality, nothing can be discovered that is of value to science; and only our grasp of scientific beauty, responding to the evidence of our senses, can evoke this vision*
>
> (Polanyi, 1962, p. 135).

The idea that science is somehow separated from common sense and creativity is a common misapprehension and, as Jean Barr (1999, p. 151) found in her study of women and science, makes it particularly difficult for women to engage with science. The difficulty here, though, is not with science, but with people's perceptions of it.

Most of my students had found the science hard to start with, but it had got easier with time:

> *It became more enjoyable as time went on. When I started I had no idea and it was really hard work for me. But gradually it became fun. Hard work and enjoyable, and then really enjoyable.*
>
> (Pam, 2001)

> *It became more satisfying than something that is easier and becomes boring.*
>
> (Josephine, 2001)

> *I had very little knowledge or ideas about science before I joined the class. At times I found it quite a challenge. I realised that I needed to get my mind back into thinking academically rather than just superficially.*
>
> (Jen, 2001)

For one student it was the fieldwork, rather than the theoretical science that she could read about, which was difficult to start with. Not having done any laboratory science at school she had felt at a disadvantage during her Open University science foundation course. Pieces of equipment had arrived in the post and she had had to conduct chemistry experiments in her kitchen by herself. As an Open University tutor for this course for ten years I can remember many students finding these 'kitchen' experiments difficult, but in my experience students usually found the more extended laboratory work during the week-long summer school enjoyable with fellow students and tutors on hand to help. Sufficient help had not been at hand in this case and the bad experience had cast a long shadow which extended over the first few fieldwork sessions later on when she was doing field biology:

> *The little bit of practical work we did for the Open University frightened me to death. I hated it. It was the one bit of the Open University course I absolutely loathed. I hated doing the bits that were sent to me at home, and I hated having to do it on the summer school. I had done no lab work at school at all, and everybody else knew how to use microscopes, knew how to use all the chemistry equipment and everything else, and I hadn't got a clue and they didn't have time to really show you and I felt totally at sea and I couldn't understand what it was I was trying to do. So when I got to the Field Biology (Certificate courses), perhaps not registering the field part of the biology so much when I signed up to the course, I enjoyed the lectures and the first few field trips we went on frightened the living daylights out of me as well. I was very very nervous about going out and actually doing something. I wasn't sure I knew what I was trying to do, and being a bit of a perfectionist I find it very difficult not knowing. But after the first two or three field trips I think I relaxed a bit and then I began to enjoy it. So the participation in the Field Biology, the actual practical biology, has made me much more comfortable with that side of science and I do feel that it is very important. It's by seeing things and understanding things in the field that the rest of theory makes sense and now I feel quite strongly if anybody asked me, yes people ought to do work in the field because it has much more impact on you, you remember things better and I think that you understand things better.*
>
> (Shelagh, 2001)

Fortunately, Shelagh had been able to relax and enjoy the fieldwork after a few sessions, and looking back was able to appreciate the value of the hands-on experience. In the next section we look at an approach to science teaching which puts hands-on fieldwork centre stage.

Learning science through doing fieldwork

My approach to science teaching as an adult educator has been to underline the importance of hands-on, of *doing* science, and I have seen the countryside as the ideal laboratory since genuinely open-ended exercises abound and I can come alongside my students and learn with them. I have watched with dismay the demise of fieldwork in full-time undergraduate programmes: in a recent study of graduate biologists training to be teachers, less than one third had significant experience of fieldwork and a further third had no experience of fieldwork at all (Tilling, 2001). And I have applauded the current drive within the British Ecological Society to re-state the value of fieldwork which emerged under the leadership of the 2002 President John Grace 'For all science the important thing is to do it, not just to read about it' (Grace, 2002) and here scientific fieldwork can be particularly helpful because it 'helps to link theory with observation' (Barker, Slingsby and Tilling, 2002, p. 4). In the adult education context, fieldwork is particularly good as it encourages interaction between students and peer-teaching within the groups, as Bill remembered:

> *I think the Field Biology course was particularly good because so much of it was fieldwork and you were working in groups interacting and doing things together and each of us was giving some input, some degree of experience, to the group.*
>
> (Bill, 2001)

One of the students, who already had a good theoretical knowledge of science gained through doing an Open University science degree, had found that the fieldwork sessions in the natural history class had given her a different sort of knowledge and it was this new knowledge which she was going to be able to use.

> *I had a superficial wide scientific knowledge from the Open University before I started the class. I was bowled over by the huge amount of wide science that I had learnt with the OU, but I thought it was quite superficial. I thought the class was in part much deeper about specific subjects which I knew nothing about really. A superficial knowledge of quantum mechanics is not going to enable me to input into that world at all, but perhaps individually I can make a contribution to my local small world, whereas I can't in quantum mechanics and astrophysics.*
>
> (Shirley J, 2001)

As well as being absolutely committed to a proper scientific approach, I have been equally committed to engendering a love and appreciation of the natural world. Course publicity has stressed the beauty of the local countryside and the practical nature of the classes: a voyage of discovery about the natural world. This is very different from the perceived view of science subjects which came out of the Carlton survey (Carlton, 2001, p. 13), where science subjects were seen as being 'hierarchical, concentrating on teaching a systematic body of knowledge of structures and techniques, rather than conveying a more holistic view of how the world works and how different aspects inter-relate.' A scientific approach is not incompatible with aesthetic appreciation, and the voyage of discovery can be linked to the posing of questions and the taking of measurements to try to answer them. Such an approach was appropriate in the pre-accreditation world of liberal adult education, and has transferred easily to today's world of credit-based courses because this type of teaching produces material which demonstrates student learning. Such general interest courses can provide pathways into part-time certificate and degree courses, but can also be extended into long-running workshop courses to which students return year after year and gradually acquire fieldwork and identification skills. Such a dualistic approach is essential if we are to satisfy both the career aspirations of many of our younger students and the quite different aspirations of our older learners, for whom learning for a useful and fulfilling retirement is more important than acquiring qualifications. In the latter case, although there is no problem with assessment of student learning, the awarding of credit may be inappropriate since students go on amassing credit without wanting to use it to gain paper qualifications. Non-credit-bearing courses would look more appropriate, but at the moment institutions are preferentially funded for credit-bearing courses. Carlton (2001, p. 56) advocates a review of institutional funding mechanisms to encourage wider participation in non-qualification bearing science subjects and experience from Sweden (Rubenson, 2002, p. 212) suggests that adequate funding will be essential if we are to be successful on a wide enough scale.

So there is much to commend a fieldwork approach to science education, but does it work? What did the students think they had learned about science as a result of participation in these classes? Pam, with little previous experience of science felt that she now understood how to record in a scientific way and that it was important to record in this way so that her records could be understood by other researchers:

> *My science education ended at 16 and I have had no real input since then at all ... I think I have a wider knowledge about how science works – the method, the way in which you study, the ways in which you record what it is that you are looking at, so that when you want to use that material you've got something concrete. You've got something that is recorded in a manner that other people will understand as well, so that they could use our results ... in future because they will recognise that the method is a proper scientific method.*
>
> (Pam, 2001)

Josephine remembered her school science, but had not expected to be able to apply it to studying plants in the countryside:

> *I had done a couple of 'O' levels at school, physics and biology, and somehow associated that very much with pottering around in a laboratory and it was interesting to see that you could in fact broaden the system, you took the same sort of method, the same ways of thinking, and you could apply it perfectly well to something totally different.*
>
> (Josephine, 2001)

Similarly John, a retired engineer, had not expected there to be much science in the study of natural history:

> As an engineer (retired) I don't think I had appreciated that natural history was a subject about which one could apply an awful lot of science.
>
> (John, 2001)

His idea of science, developed over a lifetime of working with a very precise branch of science, was rather different:

> In the science that I think of, the answer is a figure to three decimal places which is very different from the sort of science we're talking about here.
>
> (John, 2001)

John went on to explain the essential difference between his type of science and the ecological science we had been doing in class:

> I think the science that we've been doing in the class relates to the correlation of interdependencies, trying to establish that, and there are always grey areas within this.
>
> (John, 2001)

Bill, another retired engineer, had also found that biological science was very different to engineering. To start with, his ideas about the precision of science had undergone a radical change.

> A lot of the things that you are analysing in biology you are looking at probabilities. Very little of it you can say with a hundred per cent certainty that this is right, or this is going to happen. The uncertainty is far greater in biology than it might have been in engineering. The sort of degree of variability in biology was completely foreign to me. I was horrified at the degree of variability you get when you collect data in biology – compared to what you get in engineering. Now I have an understanding of the greater degree of uncertainty and it doesn't surprise me. For example the idea that global warming could increase temperatures by 0.5 to 2.5 degrees Centigrade – this range horrified me five years ago, now I can see that it is pretty good.
>
> (Bill, 2001)

Then he had been surprised to find that scientific research progresses in a series of steps and that knowledge at any one point in time was simply the 'best theory to date'. It might be overturned by new evidence that came to light. This was very different from the way engineering operated:

> The other thing about science that was new to me was that one's knowledge of science isn't necessary fixed, it is the knowledge at this point in time. All ideas that underpin areas of science can be swept away almost overnight by some new discovery. When I was doing engineering it was more like evolution in its continuous

phase, things evolved and things fell off the back end and you didn't use it any more. Computers came in. Where as science is much more about a sort of punctuated equilibrium. It kicks along nicely and then something happens and the whole.....! – which is great. That was new to me. That really opened my eyes.

(Bill, 2001)

All the students had found that the scientific discipline had enabled them to think through issues more clearly. This was first articulated by Mike, but Richard and the other students agreed:

Well, what it comes down to is training the mind to think along specific lines and follow those specific lines ... you may have some sort of position from the beginning, but at least it enables you to think upon the roots.

(Mike, 2001)

I would like to echo that because I think it has trained the discipline in thought processes.

(Richard, 2001)

They had also learnt how time-consuming collecting data was, and this had surprised them:

I don't think I ever appreciated before the enormous amount of repetitive work that's necessary to establish one single fact.

(Josephine, 2001)

I think I've been made aware of how extremely accurate you've got to be and how well everything has to be recorded and how slow it is in a way before you really say you've come to a conclusion, what extremely hard work it is.

(Julia, 2001)

Julia was used to making scientific assessments and making accurate records in her job as a medical occupational therapist, but this type of science was new to her:

I had a certain amount of science in my training, because I'm a medical (not social service) occupational therapist. I'm used to making assessments – a different sort of science, completely different – but you still have to make proper assessments and record properly, so it's not completely new to me.

(Julia, 2001)

Josephine chose to comment on an aspect of accreditation which she had enjoyed, but which she knew most of her fellow students had not been keen on. This was writing up field trips as practical reports:

> But the other thing that I personally got out of it was the thing that most people grumble about most, which was the homework and having to write up accounts of maybe an expedition to Chailey Common or something like that, and my absolute delight at the end of it, to find that at my great age I can still do it. That gave me tremendous satisfaction.
>
> (Josephine, 2001)

This is something which we must not lose sight of in our zeal for non-qualification bearing courses, and to which Carlton and Soulsby (1999, p. 76) draw our attention: 'There are some older people for whom some evidence of progress in learning and certification of their achievements will be extremely important. In some instances ... there can be a direct task-related purpose to achieve.'

Bill had also found that he had learned a lot through writing practical reports, and in particular that this had led to an increased understanding of how science operates:

> Through having to do assignments in the form of a scientific paper, and learning the rigour of having to go back and do your checking of past papers, you realise that you're building on a foundation that has been laid by an awful lot of people over a long period of time. I certainly wasn't aware of that aspect of science. [...] It was new to me because I'd been in engineering. Engineering and technology represent a different sort of avenue to science. You're tending to use scientific information but not enter into researches of this sort. You're using it for a different objective – as far as I was concerned it didn't generate scientific papers or technical papers, it generated business and profit hopefully!
>
> (Bill, 2001)

This is not something that I had expected students to learn from written assignments.

Science literacy and national debates

A major theme of Sheila Carlton's recent book on science and lifelong learning (2001) is the need to provide adult-friendly science learning so that everyone is able to understand and participate in current debates on important issues such as global climate change. The ability to understand and participate in such debates can be thought of as science literacy, as it enables democratic participation in a similar way to being able to read and write. The student voices that we have been listening to in this chapter suggest that the hands-on science which they experienced in the field was adult-friendly and enjoyable. It had enabled them to acquire an understanding of scientific methods of data collection and measurement in ecology, but had it equipped them to take part in national debates from a position of knowledge and understanding? In the Ecological Citizenship Project, I tried to find out about this by inviting the students to discuss a piece of popular writing about genetic modification of plants, a subject which they had referred to in earlier discussions. In the extract chosen (from the October 2001 edition of *The Countryman Newsletter*) the editor suggests that a newly developed, genetically modified version of the English Elm, resistant to Dutch elm disease, was 'posing a moral dilemma for those of us who have so far been opposed to GM experiments.' The setting for the debate was thus rather different from supermarkets and multinational companies, and I hoped would be of particular interest to students interested in the countryside. It also proved quite topical with one student turning up to the discussion session with a newspaper article which he had found on the same subject.

Students were quick to point out the lack of sustained argument in the article and the readiness with which the writer came to unsubstantiated conclusions. As Bill explained:

> *I thought this was a classic case of a little knowledge being a dangerous thing. I don't know who the editor is and whether he's a qualified biologist or not, but it doesn't read that way. It looks as if he's just cherry picked bits of information out and I think the worst thing he's done is to come to a conclusion on the basis of this, rather than saying 'should we do this': 'should we do that.' He says the good seems to outweigh the dangers and then at the end he brings in this business of Chinese super-rice.*
>
> (Bill, 2001)

The article was a bit disingenuous, going into details about how the DNA was transferred into the English elm chromosomes, but neglecting to mention the all important matter of where the transferred DNA came from. The natural history classes had not covered details of DNA and chromosomes, much less the mechanics of genetic modification. The nearest we had come to this was in discussions about asexual and sexual stages in life cycles and the way in which reduction division within the sexual process leads to genetic variation within populations. However, two of the students taking part in the discussions had more detailed knowledge from their Open University courses and were able to point out which key bits of information were missing from the article:

I do think people understand about breeding which farmers have been doing for years. They pick characteristics that they want and interbreed and it takes hundreds of years. It can now be done virtually overnight and I think people understand when it is within the same species. I think the very difficult thing about genetics is when you transfer genes from one species to another. I would be very very wary of it. The article sounds reasonable, but it doesn't bring out the transgenic part of the argument, which I think we should be very wary of.

(Shirley, 2001)

He doesn't come to the core of what's been done. He has no idea! He doesn't even attempt to summarise how they've done it.

(Bill, 2001)

Even without this detailed knowledge, the students in general felt that they were now more able to critically evaluate what people wrote about science:

When you read reports, scientific reports, I can now think 'Well why did they do that?' or 'That doesn't make sense, they're not giving us the information'; 'You can't say that from that': which wouldn't have crossed my mind before.

(Janet, 2001)

For Bill, this meant not taking someone else's word for it. It meant going back to the original paper and checking that the correct interpretation had been put on what the researcher was saying.

I find that I am much more wary now when I read something on science, and I will go and read something else to see whether it gives the same view and the same opinion. Perhaps there's a paper in Nature and you track it down and read it and think well yes but they've not necessarily interpreted it correctly.

(Bill, 2001)

This raises another issue in the public understanding of science debate and that is the role played by the science communicator. There is usually a layer between the general public and the science, with science communicators acting as 'authors of the science for the public' (McDonald,1996, p. 152). As the polarisation between scientists and the public increases, this role becomes increasingly important. Media conventions encourage the presentation of issues as a balanced debate between two sides even when only one side commands widespread respect within the general scientific community (Yearly, 1996, p. 184). This has been dramatically demonstrated in America, where in high profile environmental debates, the media have been able to focus public attention on sensational, but minority views (Yearly, 1996, p. 187). Concern about the increasing demands being put on journalists and broadcasters, often arising from new European policies being pushed through by the European Commission as part of their 'Science and Society Action Plan', but also by individual national governments, has led to the development of courses designed to train scientists and communication professionals to deal more effectively with the complex situation that exists between society and science (ENSCOT, European Network of Science Communication Teachers, 1999, Project Summary). A set of modules and workshops has been developed from best practice (ENSCOT, 2002) taken from France, Germany, Ireland, Spain and the UK. This is to help scientists to communicate and to be involved in public dialogue and debate, which is not something which has been traditionally covered by university science courses. The courses are also designed to help journalists and broadcasters who are expected to be both more supportive of science and at the same time more critical. These approaches are needed to stand alongside initiatives which increase science literacy within the general population and this is surely another area which should be addressed in our lifelong learning agenda. Professional development courses at postgraduate level would be most appropriate.

It is not just journalists and broadcasters, lawyers too exacerbate the problems between scientists and the general public. The adversarial system means that they have to try to undermine scientific judgement, and this can make it difficult for the general public to differentiate between scientific fact and opinion. This is particularly true in the USA where it is very common for official action to be subjected to adversarial legal processes (Yearly, 1996, p. 185). Again, we come back to this problem of the limits of scientific knowledge and the general lack of understanding of the context in which science operates. The students understood this and could talk about the difficulty of getting the message across to the general public.

> *The trouble is that the general public view an expert like a scientific god: he/she knows the answer to everything. But in fact they know the answers based on what they understand and what the current knowledge is and also coloured by their own personal views. [...] Because you're an expert, therefore you must know. In many ways the idea of an expert is a bad thing. When you get an inquest where you decide things by expert witness and they are diametrically opposed, it's making a nonsense of the term expert in a way.*

> (Bill, 2001)

Janet agreed. Public faith in science tended to:

> *fall down the hole between two experts because, if he says that and he says that and they are both experts, how am I to know?'*

As well as the unhelpful idea of an 'expert', the students felt that the legal system was making it more difficult for the public to understand risk and uncertainty in science.

> *The other big problem of science is this concept of risk. How do you put across to the public the concept of risk? It's a very very difficult thing, made worse by the legal scenarios going on now. The legal profession doesn't assume risk, it assumes that everything that happens is somebody's fault. There is an element of risk in whatever you do. You can minimise it but you can never get rid of it. [...] There is the element of risk that what you are proposing is right or wrong. There's a probability on the evidence that you've got at that time, but it isn't one hundred per cent. I think that this is where statistics comes in – for a lot of the things that you are analysing in biology you are looking at probabilities. Very little of it you can say with a hundred per cent certainty that this is right, or this is going to happen. This uncertainty is far greater in biology than in engineering. [...] A lot of the uncertainty is because there are so many interactive areas. You're closing it down. Knowledge is slowly getting better but you're trying to predict and forecast aren't you?*
>
> (Bill, 2001)

These students have come a long way. Here is Bill the precise engineer talking about uncertainty and feeling quite at home in the very different field of environmental science. This feeling of a changed way of looking at the world was common to many of the students:

> *There are nine of us sitting round the table, together with Margaret, and more than half of us have had basically no science background or a very limited one and what is amazing is that we are able to sit here and discuss about how science has changed us, and actually from the things we've said it seems to have changed our lives a fantastic amount.*
>
> (Pam, 2001)

Implications

The student voices demonstrate that a hands-on approach to teaching science using the countryside as the laboratory can lead to the enhancement of the relationship between citizens and science. Here the science is presented in a more holistic way than is usual in science teaching, with an emphasis on how different aspects inter-relate rather than concentrating on building up a body of knowledge, and this, as Carlton (2001, p. 13) suggests, is likely to appeal to adult learners. The student voices again demonstrate that this is the case. So here we have an alternative approach to the science shops advocated by Irwin and Wynne (1996, p. 220) for establishing progressive relationships between expert knowledge and citizenship, including an improvement in scientific literacy in an appropriate context, and a more inclusive alternative to Jean Barr's feminist approach to developing 'really useful knowledge' (1999, p. 151).

And finally we return again to the mismatch, so clearly articulated by John Field (2000) between education *policy* which is driven by economic considerations resulting in measures designed to improve the skills and flexibility of the workforce, and education *needs*, particularly for ecological citizenship. A price tag cannot be put on 'new intangible areas of social capital, cultural change and citizenship' and so, in spite of government rhetoric, adult education remains neglected (p 29). This is particularly pertinent given our need to find answers to pressing environmental questions. Scientists need to be up-front about the limits of scientific knowledge and to explain clearly when they are dealing with uncertainty in scientific data, but we also need the participation of a scientifically literate population able to engage democratically in debates on environmental issues. Unfortunately, recent moves in continuing education in which most 'extra-mural' programmes have been absorbed into subject-based university departments, coupled with the focus on recruiting a younger age group (Carlton and Soulsby, 1999, p. 46), have moved the agenda further away from the sort of science education we are talking about here. Such an agenda needs to be restated and applied to all levels of science education.

CHAPTER 7

Ecological research for nature conservation: proactive conservation monitoring in Bedelands meadows

Research grows out of and draws on the work of people who have engaged with the subject previously, and offers the opportunity to add to the knowledge about any particular area of inquiry. Like joining a conversation, it is crucial that we listen and try to understand what has been said before, that we attempt to make our contribution clear and to offer something that moves the conversation forward, allowing others to join in too.

(Anne Bellis in Coare and Johnston, 2003, p. xiv)

In Chapter 5 we saw how the plant identification and fieldwork skills required for vegetation monitoring and surveying can be acquired through participation in nature conservation projects such as the Meadow Management Experiment. We turn now to explore this participation from the point of view of learning about scientific research. Were the students taking part just learning skills or were they genuinely participating in the research? In the quotation at the head of this chapter, research is likened to joining in a conversation. How far were the students able to join in the Bedelands meadows conversation? Again, the student voices heard in this chapter were recorded during the discussion sessions about ecological citizenship described in Chapter 3. We then turn our attention to the research itself. What sort of research is needed for nature conservation objectives to be achieved and how does this sort of research fit within current trends in ecological research? What can we learn from other field-based disciplines such as archaeology?

Participative research

A large amount of research into the natural history of plants and animals has been conducted by knowledgeable amateurs, motivated by curiosity, who have tried to answer questions about puzzling events such as 'Where do swifts go in the winter?' by making detailed observations. Others simply chronicled daily events, but each little record has added to the picture of our natural heritage. Marren (2002, p. 16) suggests that British wildlife is the best documented in the world, and, as we saw in Chapter 2, the resurgence of interest in phenology (the study of the timing of natural events such as spring flowering) in connection with climate-change scenarios has made use of this resource. However, there is an essential difference between collecting data which may subsequently be of use in research, and collecting data to answer a specific question. In participative research the amateurs working with the professionals are motivated by curiosity. They are collecting data to answer questions that they themselves have framed, and the outcome of the research will be as important to them as the activity of collecting the data. This is not what happens in most national surveys, where volunteers are essential for data collection, but are not part of the research process itself. For example, bird-ringing is a labour intensive activity in which volunteers work alongside professionals to collect data that contribute to research. A recent book on the movement of birds in Britain and Ireland (Wernham *et al*, 2002) represents 'the culmination of more than 90 years of investigation involving 10,000 people and about 30,000,000 birds' (Mead, 2003, p. 313). This is a truly massive data -set requiring a very large input of people time, which could not have been collected without non-professional volunteers. Most of the volunteer bird-ringers, however, are mere data collectors and are not engaged in participative research. As Chris Mead (2003, p. 319) explains 'Ringing plays a fundamental role in ornithological research and it is essential that the ringers realise that they are practising a technique which enables the real research to be carried out. It is therefore their duty to do the best they can to ring safely and record accurately as many data as are required of them.' It would be very difficult to conduct this sort of research in any other way, and indeed even the professionals involved did not always know how the data would be used: they were 'ringing for the future' in addition to 'results-orientated immediate ringing' (Mead, 2003, p. 319). This is very different to the objectives of participative research, where everyone is engaging with the whole process of the research, rather than just one part of it, the data collection. The Meadow Management Experiment was to be a corporate effort between the amateurs and the professionals, so that the amateurs would get a real understanding of how this type of research is conducted and would be able to apply this knowledge to new situations in the future.

Participative research, then, implies a collegiate effort. The tutor does not stand apart from the students, and the students are more than 'unpaid data-collectors' (Knight, 1995). One person, acting as project manager, will have responsibility for the overall direction of the project, but the other participants will have a say in what that direction should be.

The objectives of this type of research are that all participants should:

1. understand what the questions are which the research is addressing;
2. understand how data are to be collected to answer the questions;

3. understand how the data collected are to be analysed;

4. understand how far the data analysis goes towards answering the questions.

Apart from undertaking their own piece of individual research, it is only by participating in this way that students can appreciate what scientific research is all about. This is important both from the 'understanding of science' perspective and for the learning process that will enable them to set up their own conservation monitoring programmes in the future. This is something that, I believe, short courses in monitoring singularly fail to do. In the Meadow Management Experiment adult students were involved from the very beginning. In 1996 they took part in a vegetation survey of all the meadows at Bedelands Farm, the Local Nature Reserve near the venue for one of the natural history classes. During the following winter they analysed and discussed the data they had collected, and planned the experiment.

Planning the Meadow Management Experiment

The meadows, on heavy clay soil, contained more than 50 species of native grass and wildflowers including common knapweed, meadow vetchling, sweet vernal grass and crested dogstail. Using the National Vegetation Classification (NVC) system the students concluded that the grass in all the meadows belonged to crested dogstail – common knapweed grassland of the meadow vetchling sub-community (MG5a, Rodwell, 1992). There were considerable differences between the meadows, though, some of which reflected different landscape histories. Four of the meadows had been carved out of the prevailing woodland ('assarted') about 700 years ago, while the other three meadows in the north of the reserve had been part of the grazed commonland of Valebridge Common for centuries until it was enclosed in 1828 (see map in Figure 7.1).

Students were concerned that these rather fine meadows were being managed on an *ad hoc* basis by the local council, which was likely to be detrimental in the long term, and decided to set up a Living Exhibition to demonstrate the effect of different management options on the meadow flowers. As Pam explained:

The original aim as I understood it was to study how best to manage Bedelands Farm, both from the point of view of biodiversity and to re-create an environment attractive to the people who use it. This we defined as more wildflowers.

(Pam, 2001)

Bedelands Farm Local Nature Reserve

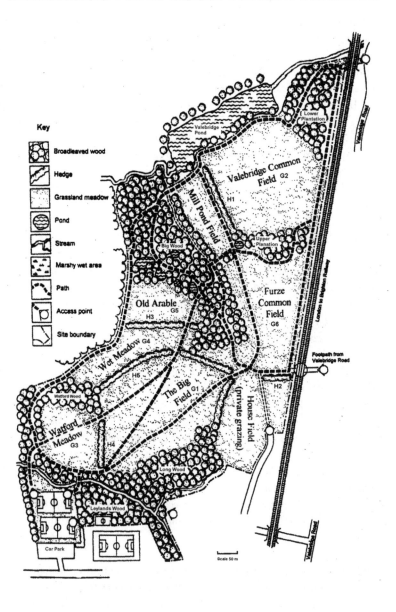

Figure 7.1 Map of Bedelands Farm Local Nature Reserve showing the series of wildflower meadows (Mid Sussex District Council).

The management options were to be based on traditional farming practices, which over the centuries had led to the development of these flower-rich meadows. The historians in the group interviewed the last farmer of Bedelands who had moved to Dorset and was then in his 80s. They were given photographs from the 1950s of haymaking in one of the assarted meadows, Big Meadow, and of cattle grazing in one of the meadows on Valebridge Common. A search of the literature revealed that, traditionally hay meadows were cut once a year and the aftermath was grazed in the autumn or winter (Rodwell, 1992). No additional fertiliser was applied, apart from manuring by the stock. In the lowlands, hay meadows were left ungrazed from February or March and were cut for hay between June and August (Sutherland and Hill, 1995). The exact cutting time depended on particular weather conditions in any one year (Smith and Jones, 1991), but a late cut would allow late-flowering species to set seed and might be crucial for the continued presence of certain species in the sward. In a community setting such as on our site there might be good financial or logistic reasons for cutting early rather than late, so we would need a clear demonstration of any benefits from a late cut. Grazing provision was going to be difficult so we consulted widely: with the local county council, who grazed sheep on a nearby piece of common land; the local wildlife trust; and English Nature. We were advised that cattle grazing would be difficult because the site as it existed now did not have a good supply of water. Sheep require less water and were also less likely to cause damage to the ground in wet weather by their trampling, an important consideration on this wet clay site. Electric fences would be an appropriate way of containing the sheep. We also needed to demonstrate the effect of applying fertiliser because the local farmer, who had been cutting the meadows and taking the hay crop in lieu of payment, wanted to increase his crop of hay by applying fertiliser. He proposed to use organic fertiliser, which he maintained would be 'good for the wildflowers'. So the demonstration in the hay meadow would compare: grazing with no grazing; a mid-July, mid-August and mid-September hay cut; and the application of organic fertiliser compared with no additional fertiliser beyond manuring by the sheep. In contrast, the meadows on Valebridge Common would have been extensively grazed for centuries as part of an open common. Here the experiment would simply compare the effect of grazing with no grazing and an annual hay cut.

The Meadow Management Experiment would be a 'Living Exhibition' with a simple experimental design so that anyone looking at the meadow would be able to see and understand the results. This was important because we would not be able to introduce appropriate management on this public and much-used site without the approval of the local people who were using the site on a regular basis. It was likely that they would view the site as essentially unchanging and would not understand the dynamics of conservation or the need for active management. Also, because we were trying to find out the best method of managing this type of site, it was important that the management treatments we were testing could be applied by the district council officials responsible for its management. However, because the results of the experiment were going to inform future management of the site, it was also important for the vegetation to be monitored scientifically and the results subjected to as rigorous an analysis as possible.

These considerations meant that the experimental design consisted of a simple division of the field into areas to which different treatments were applied, and the setting up within each treatment area of sufficient 2 m by 2 m permanent quadrats (see Chapter 5) to give a reasonable sample of the vegetation in each. Thus, one of the hay meadows was divided up into three strips with different cutting times and, orthogonally to these strips, half the meadow was grazed in the autumn leaving the other half ungrazed (Figure 7.2). A central band had organic fertiliser applied to it. On Valebridge Common we compared grazing with no grazing by dividing the selected meadow into two halves. This simple experimental design required a relatively uniform meadow, so the data from the vegetation survey was sorted using a computer programme called TWINSPAN which separates out similar samples from dissimilar samples. Old Arable turned out to be a relatively uniform hay meadow with most of its vegetation samples arriving at the same end point in the sorting process; and Valebridge Common Field was the most uniform of the fields on the old Valebridge Common (see map Figure 7.1). Before the treatments commenced, percentage cover was recorded for all the plant species in all the quadrats in June and this would be compared with data collected in the same way in subsequent years.

Discussions took place with officials from the local district council, who agreed to collaborate, and a successful grant application was made to the Royal Society (Committee on the Public Understanding of Science) for equipment to set up the demonstration. The experimental meadows were then marked out using a sighting compass and the divisions marked with posts on the meadow boundaries. Display boards were erected in the two meadows explaining the conservation value of the meadows, the traditional management on which the experiment was based, and the experimental layout.

'Unveiling reality': collecting the experimental data

> *All science is rooted in observation of the real world, leading to questions, hypotheses, predictions and experiments. Biological fieldwork provides one of the few places in a science curriculum where students quite literally observe the real world and use it as a basis for scientific enquiry*

(Barker *et al*, 2002, p. 5).

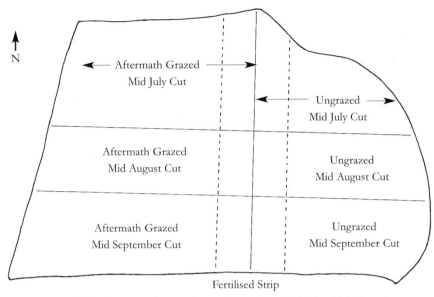

N

Figure 7.2 Sketch map of experimental meadow (Old Arable) showing layout of management treatments.

In the Meadow Management Experiment, numerical data are collected in an open-ended manner which brings surprises for both me and the students. We are working together 'in the task of unveiling reality' (Freire, 1996, p. 51). This is not pseudo-participation, but genuine involvement in the process of research, enabling students to get a real appreciation of what scientific research is about. It was not simplified in any way, and after several summers collecting data, the students understood the value of hard-won data.

> *I don't think I ever appreciated before the enormous amount of repetitive work that's necessary to establish one single fact.*
>
> (Josephine, 2001)

> *I think I've been made aware of how extremely accurate you've got to be and how well everything has to be recorded and how slow it is in a way before you can really say you've come to a conclusion. What extremely hard work it is. Also it's very time-consuming.*
>
> (Julia, 2001)

There were particular problems with trying to do this sort of science. One wanted things to be as controlled as possible and yet one was relying on other people. For example, it was often difficult to get the hay cut at the right time because we were relying on the farming sector. The mid-July cut was the easiest as the hay was attractive and the weather usually reasonably dry. The mid-September cut was almost always a nightmare. The hay was not agriculturally attractive and usually had to be disposed of rather than used, and on the days when the weather was dry enough to cut, the farmer or contractor was busy with other more urgent tasks. Julia, who was trying to manage a meadow of her own, understood the difficulties well:

I have learnt how extremely difficult it is to make the scientific assessments and it's just not so cut and dried and yet being a science it has to be. I've had similar sorts of problems myself with my own meadow, getting farmers to cut it when you want it cut and they've obviously got a living to make, and they've got very hard times at the moment, and it's very difficult for them, and often they're not totally cooperative in being involved in our project, and I think everybody has these sorts of problems, even I do, although I'm on a farm and the farmer is basically there.

(Julia, 2001)

Analysing the data

The third objective of participatory research is that the students should understand the data analysis. In the Meadow Management Experiment this was much less easy than involving them in the data collection, because the statistical methods required for this type of data were quite difficult and required access to specialist computer software. A few sessions were organised each winter to take the students through the processes using a laptop computer and data projector. Not all the students wanted to take part, but most sessions had 8 to 10 students in attendance. The other students were kept informed about the results through brief reports and information put on the website. Students came with a desire to know what the results might show and some of them found the sessions very interesting. Shirley enjoyed seeing how their contribution was part of a wider story:

I think you're also fitting our small detail into a much larger pattern because other people were using the same hypothesis, and that made you feel a bit useful as opposed to every week just doing a tiny bit.

(Shirley, 2001)

However, it was not hands-on. I was choosing the statistical methods and there was no opportunity for the students to play with the data by themselves. As Shirley remembered:

You chose the different sorts of analysis, didn't you? We weren't skilled enough to. We had to be pointed in the right direction to do that. We just didn't know enough to use these things on our own.

(Shirley, 2001)

The two retired engineers in the group found this unsatisfactory.

I hate the idea of putting numbers into a black box and accepting what comes out. I like to understand what we can do.

(John, 2001)

It would have been nice to have been able to play around with SPSS – I mean up front before we actually had the session. Of course the problem is it's the most user un-friendly programme going. It's the most powerful, everybody uses it, but it's just impenetrable.

(Bill, 2001)

Many of the students found the computer-mediated statistics very difficult, but it did enable them to see what the experiment had achieved, as Pam explains:

I had no idea when these sessions started and to begin with I felt completely out of the picture. I don't feel I have ever really contributed to these sessions, but the formal presentation and discussion of the data has helped to put the visual evidence which I have 'into context'.

(Pam, 2001)

This understanding, albeit limited, of how the statistical procedures had been applied to their data did enable them to follow the results of the analyses. At the last of these sessions at the end of the fourth year a decision had to be taken about the future direction of the experiment, and the group came to a decision that was not the decision that I would have made or the decision that I was expecting us to make.

Where do we go from here?

We had clear-cut results for the effect of grazing and the application of fertiliser, but no significant difference between the different cutting times. One of the students suggested that this might be because the beneficial effect of more seed set in the late cut also required grazing to enable the seed to reach the surface of the soil and germinate. In our data analysis, we had not been able to separate out the grazed late cut from the ungrazed late cut because we only had six quadrats in each area. Instead, when analysing the effect of cutting time, we had treated all the late cut, grazed and ungrazed, together. The student's suggestions seemed very plausible, but we couldn't just increase the number of samples we were recording as we were already coping with as many as we could in the time available. I suggested that we might divide the meadow into two rather than three cutting times and just go for an early and a late cut. However, the group disagreed, because as John put it:

> I can suggest a reason against dividing the field into two because you're really starting the experiment again, in some respects and that might not be a good thing to do.
>
> (John, 2001)

Instead it was suggested that we should abandon the fertilised strip as Bill remembered:

> We cut out the fertiliser because we knew the effect of the fertiliser and we'd shown it ... having taken that out we had x number of quadrats spare that we could put in without overloading ourselves with more quadrats.
>
> (Bill, 2001)

I was delighted to find that the students were now able to take a lead in driving the future direction of the experiment, demonstrating that they had understood both the questions that we were trying to answer and how far we had got with answering them. We are now collecting data from the new quadrats instead of from the quadrats in the fertilised strip, and are looking forward to analysing the results with the grazed separated out from the ungrazed.

There is another important aspect to participative research which needs to be emphasised. Although, as an educationalist, I was keen to have students participating fully in the research project, I would not have been able to undertake the project without their help. It would have been impossible for me to collect the data by myself in the time available, and I believe the data would have been less robust. As discussed in Chapter 5, the accuracy of the estimation of the amount of the different plants present in the quadrats was improved by the consensus of the group. Working with the students I found my estimations also needed to be brought into line with the group estimations from time to time. Granted that I needed their help, they could have been simply data collectors, but I do not believe the same sort of loyalty and interest in the project, which has sustained the group through many miserable wet days in the field, would have been displayed without ownership of the project. For Shirley the context of the research project provided the rationale for the data collection.

I think it's seeing the results of the data that we collect. It's not just for us. But it's going to be used in a bigger way.

So the partnership worked. Together we were able to undertake a project which would not have been possible for one person, and at the same time students were learning about research, and, as we saw in Chapter 5, learning the skills required to be biological monitors. A group of these students have already taken this learning and have set up their own monitoring programme on another local farm. Here they are using their biological recording skills, but they are doing more than this, because it is their own project. They are conducting their own piece of research into the changes that are taking place in a meadow that has been taken out of agricultural production and is being managed for conservation. The result of their study will inform further conservation on this site.

Archaeological digs

In the Meadow Management Experiment enthusiastic amateurs are working alongside a professional. We turn our attention now to another discipline, archaeology, where this happens too, and look at the similarities between participation in practical archaeological research and the meadow research. Most archaeology courses at HE level require students to take part in practical work at an excavation site, but as well as these students, archaeological excavation relies on enthusiastic amateurs who turn out weekend after weekend in the summer to scrape away at the ground and reveal the past. An exciting excavation is currently under way at Barcombe in East Sussex (Rudling, 2003), where a Roman villa of some substance stood in a commanding position on a slight elevation above a bend in the River Ouse. Volunteers working at the site were all spurred on by the excitement of finds, a piece of tessellated pavement or pottery beaker, but most of them were also motivated by a desire to be useful, and by the pleasure of physical outdoor exercise in the company of like-minded people. *'It beats lying on the beach'*, and it was relaxing after a week working in the office. For a few, the activity went little beyond this, but for most of the volunteers the overall picture that the research was revealing was of great interest and they were very knowledgeable about what had already been found on the site over the two years of the excavation and about what the current season's excavation was revealing. Most had a long-standing interest in archaeology, but many had been turned off history at school where it had been presented in a theoretical way with great emphasis on dates and facts. Through engagement with the practical, they had come to a new appreciation of the historical. Cutting-edge research was much more exciting than documented accounts.

This is all very reminiscent of the natural history student voices, but there are important differences too. Most of the digging is very mechanical. You have your area of ground to trowel away at and until something is found you can chat away to the person working next to you. By contrast, the quadrat work at Bedelands requires intense mental effort most of the time as the plants found have to be identified and a percentage cover value assigned to each. Meticulous records have to be kept by each participant. Meticulous records are also kept at the archaeological site, but this is not the responsibility of each digger. Finds are put in a tray for subsequent cleaning, analysis and recording. The archaeological work is physically more demanding, especially when new areas are being prepared with mattocks, but the volunteers put in a longer day than the Bedelands students, perhaps because it is less demanding mentally. Many of the volunteers are very knowledgeable about the pottery that is being found and in some cases this is their particular interest. At this point the activity becomes more closely allied to quadrat work. Very detailed field notebooks are kept by these volunteers, with drawings and notes about the pottery found and the significance of the finds to the overall site. Other volunteers kept no records at all.

All volunteers undergo a week's training before they are allowed to take part in an excavation. During the weekend sessions they are continuing to learn about site excavation techniques, but not particularly about how the archaeological research is being conducted, and most of them would not have an overview of the process of this particular piece of research. The research, anyway, is rather different from the Bedelands Experiment, because it is not trying to answer specific questions. It is more akin to bird-ringing research, where information is being gathered which will subsequently answer questions, either about bird migration or about life in Roman Britain. There is, thus, less to be learned about how research is conducted from taking part and what is being learnt is at the same level as the techniques of putting out quadrats and recording vegetation in the Bedelands Experiment, which is not at the level of participative research. The volunteers were definitely learning, though: about excavation techniques; about surveying; about dating pottery; about life in Roman Britain. And just like the Bedelands students, who wanted to find out how to identify grasses, the desire to learn was a major motivating force.

Amateur astronomers

Astronomy is another discipline whose foundations lie in the careful observations of amateurs and which continues today to use data collected by non-professionals. The most famous example is Copernicus who in 1543 turned the universe inside-out by putting the sun, instead of earth, at the centre of the known universe. Amateur astronomers today continue to make new discoveries, particularly of bright objects such as novae, spurred on by the excitement of the discovery in a similar way to the amateur archaeologist trowelling away in the hope of finding a Roman coin or the student at Bedelands wondering what will be in the next quadrat.

Both natural history and astronomy are based directly on careful observation of the natural world. As with bird-ringing, or hunting for hazel nuts opened by dormice, amateur astronomers have a particular contribution to make because of their numbers. They represent many hours of observing which can not be matched by the relatively small band of professional astronomers. Ferris (2002, p. 56) estimates that there are perhaps ten times as many experienced amateurs as professional astronomers. In addition, the high-tech equipment used by professional astronomers actually cuts down on the amount of looking that they can do. A more powerful telescope means that a smaller area is being scanned and, because they are trying to record very distant and therefore faint objects, longer exposures are needed and only a few photographs can be taken in any one night. This means that they miss much of what goes on in the night sky. Amateurs, on the other hand, are looking all over the place. Also, because there are lots of them all round the world they, collectively, are looking all of the time.

Discoveries can be posted on the internet and the image viewed anywhere in the world in minutes. Professionals and amateurs alike are thus quickly alerted to any new developments in the night sky. Professionals are needed to provide the knowledge that enables amateurs to know what to look for. This cooperation has led to the establishment of global networks which link professional and amateur observers around common interests and can lead into collaborative research programmes akin to the Great Nut Hunt of the biological recorders. A research programme based on a network of amateur observatories that enabled the night sky to be observed continuously, led to the discovery of the 23 hour period of the star V803 Centauri (Ferris, 2002, p. 52).

But amateur astronomers also go off and do things by themselves, and here it is the time factor which enables them to make discoveries. Professionals do not have sufficient telescope time for long-term projects. This is why most of the brighter novae have been discovered by amateurs: discovering a nova can take five to six hundred hours of observing (Ferris, 2002, p. 56).

Astronomy, then, is another science discipline in which careful observation and measurement, as much as theoretical background, contribute to original research giving possibilities for hands-on learning about science. Recently, general interest astronomy courses, put on by our department in various centres across Sussex, have become very popular: they could be developed in this way.

Rigour versus realism in ecological research

We turn now to the relationship between ecological research and nature conservation action. In our crowded island, nature has to co-exist with people, and there has been a long history of pastoral land-use, leading to species-rich habitats such as the semi-natural grassland we have been discussing. The research needed to underpin conservation action, therefore, has to embrace realism. We need to find answers to questions about how to manage whole habitats for nature conservation in the context in which they occur, not isolated in a laboratory. It is recognised that 'successful ecological management will become one of the most pressing necessities of our time' (Osmerod and Watkinson, 2000, p. 2) and yet very little of the ecological research that goes on in universities is directed at finding the answers needed for conservation management. Academics are interested in discovering general principles through controlled experiments with few variables and random replication, enabling standard statistical methods to be applied leading to a high degree of statistical certainty. Other academics understand the methods used, leading to acceptance by the peer-reviewers and publication in reputable academic journals. At a recent meeting of ecologists from Britain and America, a gloomy picture of present ecological research was painted:

> *Numerous highly replicated but simplified experimental studies of limited originality and information pass swiftly through the review processes of journals and fill their pages. In contrast, urgently needed studies at larger scales and embracing greater complexity and realism may not be attempted because it is correctly anticipated that they will fail to meet the exacting statistical criteria developed and applied to highly reductionist experiments!'*
> (Grime, 2000, p. 16)

The article went on to suggest that the balance between rigour and realism in ecological studies and publishing should be reversed. There is some indication that this may already be happening. In a recent edition of the *Journal of Applied Ecology* (2001), which featured grazing and biodiversity of grasslands, the editors drew attention to the need to raise the profile of the issues involved and 'to improve our understanding of the applied ecology required for successful management' (Watkinson and Osmerod, 2001, p. 233); particularly as pressures on grasslands intensify 'in the face of climate change and growing demands for agricultural productivity.'

Pro-active conservation monitoring in the Meadow Management Experiment

In the Meadow Management Experiment we wanted to find out answers to practical questions about how some flower-rich meadows on a public site should be managed and in so doing to also shed light on the management of similar meadows in other parts of the country. We needed to involve the site managers and site users, and to demonstrate that the proposed management regime was practical under the constraints imposed by the situation of the meadows in an urban green space. We were attempting to grapple with the complexities of a real-life situation. This was very different from a typical ecological experiment, which might look at the effect of cutting on sown plots of one or two species, or even a field trial where a mixture of species might be used, but the plots receiving different treatments would be scattered at random across the field. Such an arrangement of plots is necessary in order to say unambiguously that any differences recorded in the vegetation are due to the treatments. In our experiment each treatment was applied to a single area of the meadow, so differences in the vegetation in one part of the field might not be due to the treatment, but instead might be due to some unrelated event which just happened to be taking place in that location. This is not ideal, since a golden rule of scientific experiments is to try to ensure that all conditions are controlled except the variables that are being studied – in our case the grazing, fertilising and cutting. However, research (Tow and Lazenby, 2001) has shown that small plots also bring in uncontrolled factors such as edge effects; that they cannot encompass the range of variability that occurs in a pasture field; and that grazing cannot be adequately simulated by cutting techniques. 'Long-lived grasslands almost always contain a range of plant species, so short term experiments on annual crops grown in monoculture or simple two–species mixtures, many of them cut rather than grazed, are of limited use in predicting long-term ecological outcomes in botanical composition of grassland communities' (Tow and Lazenby, 2001, p. 305).

So it is a case of juggling difficulties and coming up with a rational way of proceeding. Site managers will be more interested in the questions that our experiment is designed to answer than in the sort of questions posed in more tightly controlled experiments that relate much less directly to actual situations on their sites. They will be used to the idea of conservation monitoring to check whether the management that has been introduced on the site is having the desired effect. For instance, if grazing had been introduced in an amenity meadow, they might check that the percentage cover of the wildflowers was not decreasing under that management. Targets would be set, usually degradation thresholds below which abundance should not fall. In our Meadow Management Experiment we have extended this idea to look at more than one management treatment. In a sense this is proactive conservation monitoring because we have introduced different management options and are following the effect that they have on the vegetation. This allows us to assess the effect of different treatments within the context of the actual site and the practicalities of a particular situation.

I would suggest that this is a good way for site managers to proceed in other situations where a range of possible management options needs to be explored. In this way we can build up a body of data relating to real sites rather than relying on extrapolation from simplified situations. Our research at Bedelands will enable us to implement appropriate management for the meadows on this reserve, but can this sort of exercise be considered an experiment?

What is an 'experiment'?

Our Meadow Management Experiment lacks the controls of a laboratory experiment and when talking to academic ecologists should perhaps be called a demonstration or a field trial, rather than an experiment. On the other hand, non-academic conservationists and laymen would probably regard any endeavour which instigates a change and follows what happens subsequently as an experiment. This was clear from a recent conversation I had with a member of the Bedelands conservation group about leaving the margins of one of the meadows uncut to provide butterfly habitat. As he put it, 'We want to have our own little experiment'. By this he meant, 'We want to leave an area uncut and see if more butterflies are recorded on this part of the reserve next year'. Archaeologists also talk about experiments: indeed the Centre for Continuing Education at the University of Sussex runs a course called 'Archaeology by Experiment', which is part of the Certificate in Practical Archaeology. Students might for example build coracles and try them out on the moat at Michelham Priory. All of these would fall within the definition of 'experiment' given in the *Concise Oxford Dictionary* (Allen, 1990): 'a procedure adopted on the chance of its succeeding, for testing a hypothesis etc, or to demonstrate a known fact'. Within this definition we might do an experiment when cooking a casserole. We might add extra ingredients to a standard recipe and decide whether the result tasted better. However, when we are dealing with science we are imposing extra limitations on the scope of the enquiry in order to arrive at an objective view of reality. The physicist John Polkinghorne (2002, p. 44) writes: '…science's considerable success has been purchased by its self-chosen limitation of the scope of its enquiry. Science can only consider impersonal experience, reality encountered as an object that we can manipulate and put to the experimental test.…its official discourse deals with measurements and not with values.' So, returning to the cookery experiment we would need some objective way of determining whether the result tasted better – and for the butterflies some objective way of counting butterflies before and after leaving the margin uncut. And then some unambiguous way to link any change in butterfly count to the 'experimental manipulation'.

Archaeology experiments

The best known examples of archaeological experiments are those conducted at the Butser Iron-Age Farm in Hampshire, which was set up as a 'Living Historical Museum' (Reynolds, 1979, p. 94). From excavations at a large number of sites pictures have been built up of how Iron-Age people lived. At Butser Farm, these pictures are lived out and the constructs tested under a range of conditions. For example, on a large number of excavated sites hundreds of pits have been found, which, it has been assumed, from their size and shape, were used for storing grain. So here is the hypothesis:

Pits of a certain size and shape, occurring in large numbers on Iron-Age sites could have been used for storing grain.

Implicit in this is the notion that the pits were an effective way of storing grain. At Butser, pits of the same size and shape were constructed and their storage properties investigated under a range of conditions. The experimenters determined the conditions under which the grain decomposed and the mechanism that operated in successful pits to prevent spoilage. Most pits were successful, in these the grain did not require drying before storage, and loss of germination was less than in most modern systems, so that the grain could be used as seed as well as for food. These experiments, which eventually spanned a period of 15 consecutive years (Reynolds, 1999, p. 36), have demonstrated a presumed (rather than 'known') fact as well as testing a hypothesis. The tests were based on measurements rather than value judgements. Another type of experiment was more like an ecological experiment. Specially constructed pottery sherds, which could be located with a magnetometer, were placed on a grid within a large field. The field was then ploughed and the subsequent positions of the sherds mapped. It was found that, contrary to accepted ideas, 90 per cent of the sherds remained within 2 m of their start point (Reynolds 1999, p. 40). Here the experimenter has manipulated the environment by ploughing and measured the subsequent movement of the sherds. This is akin to an ecological experiment.

Ecological experiments

Hurlbert (1984) provides a useful framework for thinking about what we mean by an ecological 'experiment'. He distinguishes two types of experiment, mensurative and manipulative. 'Mensurative experiments involve only the making of measurements at one or more points in space or time: space or time is the only 'experimental' variable or 'treatment'…Mensurate experiments usually do not involve the imposition by the experimenter of some external factor(s) on the experimental units.' This is in contrast to a manipulative experiment, which 'always involves two or more treatments, and has as its goal the making of one or more comparisons. The defining feature of a manipulative experiment is that the different experimental units receive different treatments.' The archaeological experiment looking at the movement of sherds under ploughing is mensurative, as is most conservation monitoring. Although the experimenter has manipulated the system by applying ploughing or a particular management treatment, and is taking measurements to see how the system is responding, different treatments have not been applied and no comparisons are being made except a comparison in time. Both the wildlife manager and the archaeologist are following changes that are taking place over time. In the Meadow Management Experiment, comparisons are being made between several different treatments: grazed and ungrazed; fertilised and unfertilised; July cut, August cut and September cut; so using Hurlbert's definitions this would be a manipulative experiment. However, we have not replicated: each treatment is in only one area of the meadow and the samples taken within each area make our picture of that area more complete, but do not enable us to say that the different pictures that we get in the different areas are unambiguously due to the treatments applied to each area. We have to use our common sense to make the connection. Hurlbert (1984) recognised that replication of treatments was often impossible in field ecology experiments and that, where gross effects of the treatment were anticipated, experiments using unreplicated treatments might be the best option, with common sense being used to draw conclusions.

Analysing non-replicated ecological experiments
We have gone to a lot of trouble to collect data from a series of samples in each of the treatment areas. What extra information has this given us, to enable us to be more objective than simply looking and making the judgement that there are more wildflowers in the grazed half of the meadow? For the exercise to be an experiment we need to measure something. The measurement that relates to this observation is total percentage cover of wildflowers. This would be impossible for us to measure or estimate for the whole of the grazed and the ungrazed area. So we have sampled. We have recorded percentage cover from 18 quadrats that have been grazed and 18 quadrats that have not. From this we can work out an average percentage cover of the wildflowers in a grazed and an ungrazed quadrat, but that will not take account of how much variation there is between quadrats within each area. As we were recording these values in the field we often noticed that some quadrats

were much more exciting than others. For example in the grazed half some quadrats were full of the colourful annual yellow rattle (see Figure 7.3), while other quadrats quite close by lacked this species. How do we take account of this sort of variation when we are trying to assess the difference between quadrats from the two areas? Analysis of Variance (ANOVA) is a mathematical procedure which takes into account this variation and decides how big these differences are compared to the differences between quadrats from the two areas. If the differences within an area are small compared with the differences between the two areas, we say that the difference between the two areas is significant. In the Meadow Management Experiment the differences between the grazed and ungrazed areas, and between the fertilised and unfertilised areas were statistically significant ($F_{1,7}$ = 14.86, p = 0.000 for grazed areas and $F_{1,7}$ = 15.42, p = 0.000 for fertilised areas), but differences between July-cut, August-cut and September-cut areas were not significant ($F_{1,7}$ = 0.87, p = 0.424). Notice that we are being very careful to talk about areas and not treatments; at the end of the day we are relying on common sense to make this connection.

Figure 7.3   Yellow rattle, a colourful annual typical of hay meadows which is totally dependent on seed production each year for regeneration, resulting in a patchy distribution (Drawing by Peggy Alves).

Outcomes of the Meadow Management Experiment

Before the Meadow Management Experiment was set up, the meadows were designated as farmland by the local Council and assigned a low budget compared with playing fields. An annual hay cut was taken some time between the end of June and the beginning of July by a local farmer. The aftermath was not grazed and because the hay crop was in lieu of payment, the management was becoming increasingly driven by economic farming considerations rather than conservation objectives. For example, the farmer had seen his yield of hay decrease over the years and was keen to reverse this by applying fertiliser. He was of the opinion that organic fertiliser would be good for the wildflowers, whereas there is a substantial body of research showing that fertiliser, organic or inorganic, leads to an increase in grass (leading to an increase in yield of hay), but to a decrease in wildflowers. The timing of the hay cut was also likely to be too early for conservation objectives. The experiment demonstrated that the application of fertiliser did indeed result in a sward with a significantly lower overall percentage cover of wildflowers and that, conversely, grazing of the aftermath led to an increase in the percentage cover of wildflowers. The council have now accepted that fertiliser should not be applied and there are plans to extend the aftermath grazing to the other meadows on the reserve.

In the experiment in the hay meadow, the sward is cut at three different times over the summer: mid July, mid August and mid September. It was expected that the early cut would be before some of the later flowering plants (such as greater birdsfoot trefoil and common knapweed) had set seed. Although most grassland plants are perennial and do not rely on seed set each year in order to maintain their presence in the sward, they will not survive indefinitely without regeneration from seed. In the long term it is likely that these species will disappear from the sward if it is consistently cut before they have set seed. This is a long-term effect, so it is perhaps not surprising that over the first three years of the experiment we have not been able to demonstrate any difference between the percentage cover of wildflowers in swards cut at different times. However, there is another possibility, which is that any beneficial effect of the late cut is being outweighed by detrimental effects that result from trying to cut hay in September when the weather is likely to be wetter. On one occasion the hay was left rotting on the surface of the sward for several weeks before the heavy farm machinery of today's farming industry was able to get on to the waterlogged site to remove it. As the experiment continues we hope to be able to demonstrate which cutting time will result in the most wildflowers under the conditions that pertain to the practical situation of this site.

The experiment in Valebridge Common Field is also proving to be more long term than the initial three years. At the start of the experiment, this field had a much less grassy sward than Old Arable and already had a high percentage cover of wildflowers. Consequently, the difference between the grazed and ungrazed areas is not so obvious and the experiment is continuing beyond the initial three years.

As we have already emphasised, management options can be introduced only with public approval. This is particularly true for grazing, which requires the erection of fences. This can be seen as a curtailment of people's right of access, and there is increased responsibility on the part of dog-owners because dogs must be kept away from the grazing animals, in this case sheep, and this may mean curtailing the freedom of movement of their pets. In order to convince this audience of the need for grazing there will need to be an effect on the sward, which they can see by looking at the meadow, for instance a more colourful display of wildflowers in the part of the meadow that has been grazed. The grazing in Old Arable had a dramatic effect very quickly and the grazed half was clearly distinguished in this way as early as the second year of the experiment. However, as well as the summer display of wildflowers we also need to ensure that the grazing in the autumn is as practicable as possible.

Both the County Wildlife Trust and the County Council use sheep for conservation grazing on sites open to the public and have successfully used electric fences to contain the sheep. When we consulted with experts at the planning stage of the experiment, the biggest worry expressed, apart from dogs attacking the sheep, was the possibility that the battery might be stolen. This seemed quite likely given the level of vandalism at Bedelands. However, although electric fences were used for the first 2 years of the experiment, the batteries remained safely on site. The system was not without its problems though. On one occasion the electric fence was severed using the flame from a cigarette lighter and the posts removed and left bundled up in the hedgerow, and on several occasions dogs ran into them and broke the wires. This resulted in unhappy dog-owners and many expensive staff hours spent chasing lost sheep. Since then the council have used a post and stock-proof wire fence, which has proved to be much more satisfactory in spite of the higher initial cost because there have been no instances of sheep escaping, and this type of fence is more acceptable to dog-walkers. There is now public approval for progressive fencing and grazing of the other meadows.

Another problem, particularly where there is public access, is finding someone prepared to put their grazing animals on the site. Ideally the grazier is local and interested in conservation. The Grazing Animals Project (GAP) was set up to facilitate links between managers of conservation sites which required grazing and local farmers. There are some inspiring examples of how this can work to mutual benefit (for example, Grayson, 2000), but our experience at Bedelands is that it is very hard to set up this sort of arrangement. At the start of the experiment, a distant conservation grazier was employed and his excellent service was used again in a subsequent year when other options fell through at the last minute. However, such a service is too expensive to be sustained by a council dependent on taxpayers' money. Last year, seven years after the experiment was set up, a satisfactory local grazier was found for the first time and it is hoped that his services will be used again in subsequent years. The local Wildlife Trust has just set up a 'Flying Flock' of sheep which will be used on their sites as well as other conservation sites within the county, and this may offer the possibility of future partnership.

Academic research and wildlife management: towards a common vision

Another difficulty with applying research to management issues of this sort is the lack of a common agenda between university research scientists and wildlife managers. This was addressed in an inspiring speech by John Rodwell to a recent FACT (Forum for the Application of Conservation Techniques) conference (Rodwell, 2001) in which he outlined the issues that had to be faced in thinking about a new vision for the uplands of Britain following the foot-and-mouth epidemic. He talked about a partnership between wildlife managers and academic ecologists.

> *We need to cultivate our imagination together, to conceive things that are at present out of mind and try and bring them to be. This is what will make these futures for the uplands present, give them life and make them last.*
>
> (p. 24).

He acknowledged that 'Scientific hypotheses do not a vision make. But neither do action plans, mission statements and conferences… We need to cultivate our imagination together' (p. 24). This emphasis on vision and imagination in scientific research is something we need to bring to the fore in the current climate of distrust in scientists and in scientific endeavour. As the Royal Society recognised in the 1980s the public perception of scientists as 'logical and unemotional individuals…may preclude recognition of the imaginative and humanistic aspects of the scientific endeavour' (1985, p. 15). Most people simply do not appreciate the part played by vision and imagination in scientific endeavour. Science may be objective in the sense that it is 'something real and external to the speaker' (Polanyi, 1962, p. 403), but the process of enquiry is guided by a vision of reality which suggests the questions which it will be worthwhile to explore. 'Without a scale of interest and plausibility based on a vision of reality, nothing can be discovered that is of value to science' (Polanyi, 1962, p. 135). Science is important in giving generality to ideas that start off as anecdotal happenings and, through the rigour of collecting data, tests hypotheses. However, science cannot be useful to site managers if it insists on a degree of rigur that excludes any relationship to the real world. In the Bedelands experiment, provided we check at the beginning of the experiment that the field is not obviously zoned in relation to the areas that we are treating in different ways, we can be reasonably sure that large differences observed after the treatments have been applied are due to the treatments. By proceeding on this basis we can build in the complexities of the actual situation and draw conclusions about the management options that are being tested. This type of research will be seen as being relevant to wildlife managers and should encourage them to adopt similar procedures. The *Journal of Applied Ecology* is now billed as the journal 'through which ecologists speak to each other and to related disciplines in environmental management' (*Journal of Applied Ecology*, 2001, vol 38, p. 2), so, hopefully, there is a medium through which such voices will be heard.

Implications

This chapter has demonstrated the teaching goal of genuine participative research using the voices of the adults involved, and has begun the process of setting the Meadow Management Experiment in its scientific ecological setting. The issues raised go beyond the local setting and have implications for policy makers in nature conservation bodies and local government as well as for science education in Britain and overseas.

The professional worlds of education and nature conservation are sinking under the weight of paper. We have endless paper exercises from teaching and learning strategies to Biological Action Plans, and the feeling in both worlds is that if you have a strategy it will do. Unfortunately, the bulk of our time and energy is going towards adding to this mountain of paper, leaving little left over for implementation. Our research at Bedelands demonstrates the sort of action that is needed to fulfil a limited local target. It will enable us to implement appropriate management for the meadows on this reserve, but it will be difficult to extrapolate from this specific example to general principles. If, on the other hand, there was a body of data derived from this type of experiment going on up and down the country we would be in a much stronger position to make this leap. For instance, on our clay site there have been problems implementing aftermath grazing when wet weather has delayed the September haycut. Similar data from other MG5 grassland sites on clay soil might enable us to say that for such sites it is better to cut in July and ensure the aftermath grazing takes place than to wait for a later cut with greater seed-set, but an increased risk of missing out on the grazing. There is a great need for this type of 'performance monitoring' which is specifically designed to assist decision-making and management (Possingham *et al*, 2001).

County Wildlife Trusts have large numbers of volunteers who would like to do more than raise funds, but apart from the occasional two-hour course on very basic surveying skills my county trust does little to harness this resource. Meanwhile, reserves are managed and management plans are introduced with little or no biological monitoring to see if the conservation objectives are being met. As the student voices relate in Chapter 5, biological monitoring and surveying skills take time to acquire and rather than short courses, the trust resources would be better employed in setting up and coordinating monitoring schemes that would allow the training of new volunteers under the leadership of volunteers who already have the necessary skills.

So far we have been discussing vegetation monitoring, but the principle could be extended to other types of biological monitoring. Two recent studies which used volunteers concluded that the data collected by the volunteers compared well with that collected by professional researchers. In the first of these volunteers collected data to map the distribution and abundance of common marine organisms occurring between high and low tide on the shores of the Isle of Cumbrae in Scotland (Foster-Smith *et al*, 2003). In the second, volunteers took part in mammal monitoring that included small mammal trapping, badger surveying, counting deer droppings to estimate population size, and transect surveys for mammal field signs (Newman *et al*, 2003). Both studies also found that, as in the Meadow Management Experiment, there had been educational spin-offs. Through taking part, volunteers had increased their understanding of woodland ecology or marine issues, and had become more aware of environmental issues and the way in which scientific studies are undertaken.

The type of ecological experiment that we have been discussing fits within the growing realisation within ecological circles that in order to tackle urgently needed studies that deal with complex situations of the real world, such as the management of habitats, we will have to be satisfied with less statistical certainty than is associated with highly reductionist experiments (Grime, 2000). It also demonstrates the type of research that can bridge the gap between university academics and wildlife managers.

In this chapter we have been concentrating on experimental research, but this is not the only way we find out about the natural world. Observation is equally important. Amateur astronomers look for objects in space and make measurements, and in this way contribute to the body of knowledge along with professionals. Archaeologists when they are carrying out an excavation make very precise measurements and record accurately, but the research is not experimental. To an engineer such as John (Chapter 6, p. 127) this is probably more like science than the Meadow Management Experiment.

Similarly, some biological recording is simply observing and recording what is there: adding to our knowledge about the distribution of plants and animals. Arguably this is as important as finding out how things change following manipulations, but as Kohler recounts (2002). the history of field biology has been bedevilled with a perceived need to be experimental. In the next chapter we look at research based on observation rather than experimental manipulation.

CHAPTER 8

Research in the countryside: wildflower meadows

Unimproved meadows have been studied because they provide an important habitat for wildlife, are a feature in the landscape and because the sights, scents and sounds associated with them in summer are amongst the most evocative of a bygone era (Hazel, undated, p. 3).

This chapter is about teaching and researching science as a university CE lecturer, and demonstrates the essential synthesis between the two. Recently, there has been considerable debate over a possible move to create a two-tier system of British universities, with some engaged in research as well as teaching, while others become essentially teaching only. Quite rightly, this move is being resisted. University teaching is about equipping people not only to be independent learners, but also to be original thinkers. Although it is no longer true that a university education is aimed at creating research workers, it is still expected that the best students will go on to do research, and that all graduates will need to be able to think creatively in new situations. This is essentially the difference between a university engineering course and learning how to be an aeroplane mechanic at a college of further education. In order to be able to teach people to be original thinkers it is essential that the teachers are engaged in original thinking themselves and this means original research. I also think that this is most effective when there is a connection between the research topic and the subject of the teaching.

So what sort of research should a CE field biology or natural history teacher be engaged in? Earlier chapters in this book have set out a philosophy of teaching that relates to fostering independent learning while preparing people to take part in biological conservation either as volunteers or as a career. So, most importantly, the research should contribute to our knowledge of declining species and habitats. Soule and Orians (2001a) set out the research priorities for biological conservation research for the next decade, stressing throughout that we lack basic information about declining species and habitats, and that until we have this information our attempts to deal with the threats to biodiversity posed by climate change and land-use are unlikely to be effective. This chapter shows how such information can be gathered readily by botanically-minded CE lecturers and also by conservation professionals. If the research is going to relate to teaching natural history students, it should be field-based and not rely on complicated equipment. It should be a natural extension to class exercises, which will take them into the world of original research, and one where there will be aspects in which they will be able to participate fully.

The research described here depends on collecting floristic data sets from selected sites in the countryside, which are then analysed by comparison with standard data sets in the National Vegetation Classification (NVC) system in a similar way to that described in relation to class exercises in Chapter 2. In this way, species-rich examples can be used to inform conservation practice. As well as relating to students, such observational techniques will be familiar to site managers and those assessing wildlife habitats. This is important because the research should also connect with the aspirations of the students, whether they be career aspirations or the desire to be involved on a voluntary basis with nature conservation. The habitat will need to be accessible: it will not be much good studying mountain-top vegetation from a location in southern Britain, however threatened such a habitat might be; but it will also need to be a topic in which not much research is currently being undertaken. And ideally the habitat will be geographically widespread, allowing extension of the topic beyond the local scene. Here, we take lowland neutral grassland as the habitat. It is geographically widespread, but has received much less scientific attention than more geographically restricted grasslands such as calcareous or flood-plain grasslands (Vickery *et al*, 2001). Recently it has suffered biological degradation on an unprecedented scale because of an economically-driven, but ultimately unsustainable, culture of intensive land management. Local species-rich examples are examined first, and then the study is extended to the Republic of Ireland where, on the coastal fringes of the north and west, magnificent flower-rich grassland still flourishes under extensive grazing systems. A site in Norfolk is used to illustrate the difficulty of maintaining such grassland by conservation means.

This chapter is also addressed across the academic divide to conservation professionals who find that university research does not provide answers to the practical questions with which they are concerned. The sort of biological conservation research illustrated here can be done without expensive equipment or sophisticated computer software, and there is an urgent need for it to be undertaken. I hope that my account will inspire more people to undertake such research. The future of much of our wildlife may depend on this.

Wildflower meadows

Traditionally, the lowland neutral grassland with which we are concerned has been full of wildflowers. However, English Nature and the Wildlife Trusts estimated in 1994 that only 4000 ha of this flower-rich grassland remained in Britain, and that much of this was in small scattered patches (Sussex Wildlife Trust, 1995). A similar picture now exists across much of the Republic of Ireland, where, although more than two-thirds of the land is covered in some type of grassland, most of it is now agriculturally improved with more than 200,000 acres being ploughed and reseeded annually (Dwyer, 1997). The coastal fringe of north-west Ireland is exceptional because here there are areas where the centuries-old practice of open grazing of cattle and sheep at low levels of intensity has continued on common land, resulting in a very special type of flower-rich grassland known as machair, some of which occurs on neutral soils. In the second section of this chapter we look at three examples of Irish machair on neutral soils, and use the British National Vegetation Classification (NVC) and a site in Norfolk to explore their extraordinary biodiversity within the context of the British Isles. We start, though, by looking at meadows local to the Meadow Management Experiment and look at how species-rich examples can be used to define conservation goals for the Bedelands meadows.

Surveying local meadows

Setting the Meadow Management Experiment in its local context

The wildflower meadows at Bedelands are reasonably species-rich, and the Meadow Management Experiment shows that with appropriate management they can become more colourful, with a higher proportion of wildflowers to grass in the sward. But we need a a picture of what we were aiming for. The Meadows Research Group (Chapter 5, p. 3) had a good understanding in a general way of what such a meadow might contain from the NVC description, but that description is an average picture taken from 194 samples up and down the country of which only four came from our area, although we have 17 per cent (Sussex Wildlife Trust, 1995) of the area of this type of grassland remaining in Britain. The local picture might differ from the NVC description considerably, so we were interested to know how the Bedelands meadows compared with the best examples of local wildflower meadows. This would give us a clear picture of what we could hope to achieve on our site. Ten of the best remaining meadows in Sussex were selected from records at the County Biological Records Centre and a vegetation survey was carried out by the Meadows Research Group at each site. The results were analysed using the National Vegetation Classification system and the floristic characteristics applicable to the local context determined.

Choosing the meadows

Wildflower meadows represent the species-rich end of the spectrum of so-called neutral grasslands: that is grasslands occurring on soils that are neither very acid nor alkaline. They contain a wider range of herb and grass species than agriculturally improved grassland (Haines-Young *et al*, 2000, p. 132), and so are important for biodiversity. They are also, as the quotation at the head of this chapter suggests, one of the most evocative landscapes of our countryside heritage, captured in literature, paintings and early photographs and representing to many people a golden era of harmony between man and nature (Hazel, undated). However, since they occur on naturally fertile lowland soil, such meadows have been prime targets for agricultural improvement or conversion to arable, and this process is continuing. A recent assessment of habitats in the UK countryside, *The Countryside Survey 2000* (Haines-Young *et al*, 2000) found that there has been a steady loss of the surviving parcels of such grassland (p. 49) accompanied by declining frequencies of typical meadow flowers and grasses, and increasing levels of fertility in England and Wales. Sussex is a relative stronghold for unimproved neutral grassland, but many of the meadows in Sussex surveyed in the late 1980s and early 1990s (Barton and Fisher, 1987; Allwright, 1988; Stevens, 1990) were no longer in existence in 1999 when we did our survey. Of those that remained we chose ten of the best examples to give a good spread of location over the county and to include a mixture of amenity and farmland. We included both 'hay meadows', where, as we discussed in Chapter 5, the grass is grown for hay and then the aftermath grazed in autumn, and 'grazing meadows', which traditionally were on land too poor to grow a satisfactory hay crop and so were made available for grazing throughout the year (Hazel, undated, p. 3). Site details with notes on current management are given in Table 8.1.

The National Vegetation Classification for this type of grassland in Sussex is MG5, defined as grassland having crested dogstail grass and common knapweed as constants, accompanied typically by red fescue, common bent grass and sweet vernal grass plus birdsfoot trefoil, red clover, common sorrel and green-winged orchid ('Habitat definition for unimproved neutral grassland in Sussex', from *Habitat Action Plan for Sussex*, Sussex Biodiversity Partnership in conjunction with Weald Meadows Group). This is the wildflower meadow of popular imagination. The sample meadows were used to build up a picture of this type of grassland in our part of the country.

Table 8.1   Site location and designation of wildflower meadows in 1999 Sussex survey with notes on current management.

These ten meadows, chosen as the best remaining examples of unimproved neutral grassland in Sussex, give a good spread of location over the county and include both land used for amenity and farmland. Traditionally there were two categories of meadow: 'hay meadows' where the grass was grown for hay and then the aftermath grazed in the autumn, and 'grazing meadows' where grazing took place throughout the year because the land was too poor to grow a satisfactory hay crop.

Site location	Site designation	Site management
Big Meadow, Pulborough, West Sussex	Farmland	Annual hay cut, aftermath grazed by sheep
Bosham Hoe, Chichester Harbour, West Sussex	Amenity Site of Special Scientific Interest Managed by Residents Association	Annual hay cut, no grazing
Hogs Common, Chilgrove, in dip slope of chalk, West Sussex	Amenity Managed by local council	Unmanaged 3 years. Previously cut annually with forage harvester
Jamieson's, Ashburnham, High Weald, East Sussex	Farmland	Not cut, grazed by cattle over winter
Montague, Hankham, Pevensey Levels, East Sussex	Farmland Site of Special Scientific Interest	Annual hay cut, aftermath grazed by cattle, then sheep
Paige's Meadow, Haywards Heath, Mid Sussex	Amenity Local Nature Reserve Managed by local council	Annual hay cut, no grazing
Sapperton A, Heathfield, High Weald, East Sussex	Farmland Site of Special Scientific Interest	Annual hay cut, aftermath grazed by cattle
Sapperton B, Heathfield, High Weald, East Sussex	Farmland Site of Special Scientific Interest	Not cut, grazed by cattle throughout year
Tommy's Meadow, Pulborough, West Sussex	Farmland	Annual hay cut, aftermath grazed by sheep
Willingford, Burwash, on Purbeck limestone, High Weald, East Sussex	Farmland Site of Special Scientific Interest	Annual hay cut, aftermath grazed by cattle

Survey method

As discussed in Chapter 2, the NVC uses a very pragmatic and sensible approach to sampling and data analysis, with which non-professionals can readily identify. Uniform areas of vegetation are chosen, and within these the plants present in a representative sample are listed and a quantitative score given as a measure of abundance. The emphasis is on careful identification and 'the old-fashioned virtue of accurate recording' (Rodwell, 1991a, p. 267). Analysis depends on a direct comparison of the data collected with standard data in a floristic table. Here, common sense and judgement in interpretation are paramount rather than elaborate statistical treatments, which claim to be more objective but require considerable mathematical expertise. For grassland, 2 m by 2 m quadrats are used, set out in the uniform part of each meadow, avoiding discontinuities such as paths and the atypical border around the edge. We recorded from five quadrats in each meadow, which gave us a sufficiently large sample and also made it easy to calculate the frequency with which a species occurred in the quadrats (because frequency values go from I to V). There is no requirement to put out the quadrats in any particular pattern, but we wanted to sample the whole meadow and also to avoid selecting patches such as those containing ox-eye daisy which catch the eye as you look across the sward (Figure 8.1). So we used a similar technique to that used by soil surveyors (Rowell, 1994, p. 14) and set out our quadrats along a zig-zag path with five sections which just fitted into the homogeneous area of the meadow. We generated a random number for each section and the quadrat was placed the appropriate number of paces along the section. In this way we sampled in all parts of the meadow and within each part placed our quadrat at random, a technique known as 'stratified random'. With only five quadrats a completely random placement might have led to all the quadrats occurring in only one part of the meadow. We made our visits to the chosen sites between late May and early July 1999. Figure 8.2 shows the research group recording plant species in quadrats in Sapperton Meadow.

Although all the meadows were expected to occur on neutral soil, this was likely to cover a range of pH values, and indeed the three sub-communities found *within* MG5 relate to the acidity of the soil. Soil pH also varies within meadows, so we needed an average value for each meadow. Using a bulb-planter to go down to a depth of 10cm, two soil samples were taken for each quadrat and the pH was estimated using a Whatman pHScan meter and the standard technique described in chapter 2 (p. 5). In Figure 8.3, a soil sample has just been collected with the bulb planter and is being added to the 50 ml of distilled water in the calibrated bottle to bring the level up to the 70 ml mark. The bottle will then be shaken for 5 minutes, allowed to settle and the reading taken as soon as the display has stabilised.

Figure 8.1 Ox-eye daisy growing in patches in Valebridge Common Field. During the Sussex meadow survey, quadrats were set out using a 'stratified random' technique to avoid over-selection of patches such as these.

Figure 8.2 Students from the Research Group recording plant species in quadrats in Sapperton Meadows in the High Weald of Sussex. (Photograph by author, June 1999)

Soil acidity involves more than just the pH of the soil solution which we are measuring, but by using a standard method of measurement comparisons between soils can be made (Rowell, 1994). We had discovered the difficulty of getting consistent results measuring soil pH in previous years and the method used here was developed during detailed testing in which we compared field estimations using different recipes with laboratory determinations on the same bulk samples. The standard method used here was found to give consistent results.

Figure 8.3 Students from the Research Group estimating the pH of the soil, Sapperton Meadows in the High Weald of Sussex. A soil sample has just been collected with the bulb planter and is being added to a measured amount of distilled water in a calibrated bottle. (Photograph by author, June 1999)

Building up a picture of a typical local meadow

Within each quadrat the students listed all the plants present and assigned a quantitative score as a measure of abundance. Here we just consider the frequency values: that is how often a species occurred in the five quadrats.

In the NVC method, it is the consideration of the frequency of community constants that leads to decisions about community type. Preferential species are then used to distinguish between sub-communities. Associate species fill in the fine detail of the community. For the sake of clarity these three steps are dealt with in separate sections below and the quadrat data have been organised into separate floristic tables as follows: (a) species constant for MG5 crested dogstail – common knapweed grassland – Table 8.2a; (b) species preferential to each of the three subcommunities of crested dogstail – common knapweed grassland (MG5a, MG5b, MG5c) – Table 8.2b; and (c) other species, which although not constants for crested dogstail – common knapweed grassland attained a frequency of V in at least one Sussex meadow – Table 8.2c. Frequency values for the three sub-communities (taken from the standard floristic table, Rodwell 1992, pp. 64–5) are given on the right of the table, with the sub-communities ordered to reflect their characteristic pH – the most acid-soil-loving community coming first. The average soil pH for each meadow is also given and these meadows have been ordered in a similar way – the most acidic, Sapperton Meadow A, coming first. These rather complicated tables will be explained over the next few pages, and as the discussion progresses all will become clear.

MG5 community: crested dogstail – common knapweed grassland

Constant species
We start our analysis, then, by looking at the constant species, that is those species that are expected to occur in almost all the quadrats, and compare the values given for the three sub-communities of MG5 in the standard floristic table with our data from the local meadows (Table 8.2a). It is immediately obvious that some of the local meadows lack a number of constant species and other constant species are only present in a small number of the quadrats. For example, Montague Meadow, which was a particularly fine example of a traditionally managed hay meadow (with an annual hay cut in August followed by aftermath grazing by cattle and then sheep, and which had not been ploughed within living memory), lacks four of the expected eleven constant species. The missing species are red fescue grass, ribwort plantain, cocksfoot grass and common knapweed. Two other meadows lacked one constant species: red fescue grass (in Sapperton B, one of the two meadows that were grazed rather than cut for hay) and cocksfoot grass in Sapperton A, the most acid meadow (which was cut for hay and aftermath grazed). The remaining meadows contained all the constant species, but with particularly high frequencies of Yorkshire fog grass and sweet vernal grass. In contrast, crested dogstail and birdsfoot trefoil, while present in all, occurred at a low frequency in several meadows. Birdsfoot trefoil occurred at a low frequency in two meadows, Tommy's and Big Meadow, with the same management history. Both had not been ploughed since at least 1894 (Allwright, 1988), but were still in successful hay production with herbage more than a metre high in mid June and a mass of grass roots right down to 10 cm depth in the soil. It may be that the vigorous growth of grass, albeit by traditional management rather than by

Table 8.2a Floristic table of frequency values for constant species comparing data from ten Sussex meadows with standard data for MG5 crested dogstail – common knapweed grassland (MG5c, MG5a and MG5b). Average soil pH values are included.

Meadow	Sapp A	Tom	Big	Paige's	Jamies	Sapp B	Mont	WillingF	Bosham	Hogs C	MG5c	MG5a	MG5b
Average soil pH	5.0	5.3	5.5	5.5	5.5	5.8	5.8	6.0	7.3	7.2	low	medium	high
red fescue grass	V	IV	V	IV	V			V	IV	V	V	V	V
crested dogstail grass	III	IV	V	V	II	V	V	IV	V	I	V	V	V
birdsfoot trefoil	V	III	II	V	IV	IV	V	V	V	I	V	V	V
ribwort plantain	V	IV	IV	V	V	IV		V	V	V	IV	IV	IV
Yorkshire fog	V	V	V	V	V	V	V	V	V	V	V	V	IV
cocksfoot		I	I	I	I	II		IV	I	III	V	V	IV
white clover	V	IV	V	IV	V	V	V	V	I	V	V	V	IV
common knapweed	V	III	II	V	V	V		V	V		V	V	IV
common bent grass	V	V	V	V	V	IV	V	V	II	III	V	V	IV
sweet vernal grass	V	V	V	V	V	V	V	V	V	IV	V	IV	IV
red clover	V	V	V	II	V	V	IV	IV	V	V	IV	IV	IV

Table 8.2b Floristic table of frequency values for preferential species comparing data from ten Sussex meadows with standard data (Rodwell, 1992) for the three subcommunities, MG5c, MG5b & MG5a, of crested dogstail – common knapweed grassland. Average soil pH is given for each meadow.

Meadow	Sapp A	Tom	Big	Paige's	Jamies	Sapp B	Mont	WillingF	Bosham	Hogs C	MG5c	MG5a	MG5b
Average soil pH	5.0	5.3	5.5	5.5	5.5	5.8	5.8	6.0	7.3	7.2	low	medium	high
Preferentials c													
selfheal	V		I	II	II	V	IV	V	IV		IV	III	III
autumn hawkbit					I			I			IV	II	II
field woodrush	IV	I	I	IV	V	II	II	V	V		IV	II	I
heath grass	I				II			I	III		V	I	I
tormentil					IV	I		II			V	I	I
devilsbit scabious					V			II			V	I	I
burnet saxifrage					I	I					III	I	I
betony					II					II	III	I	I
spring sedge								IV			II	I	I
pignut					V	II		III			II	I	I
Preferentials a													
perennial rye-grass		II	V	IV	I	IV	V	III	V	I	I	IV	III
daisy			I								I	III	II
meadow vetchling		V	II	III	III	IV	III	V	III		I	III	I
ox-eye daisy		II	I		III			V	I		II	III	I
meadow fescue		III	I		II			II			I	I	
field scabious	I										I	I	
hard rush						II	II						
Preferentials b													
lady's bedstraw							I	I	V	V	I	II	V
yellow oat-grass								V	IV	IV	II	II	IV
yarrow		II		III	V	I		II	V	V	III	III	V
glaucous sedge				III	III								
salad burnet	I			I	I	I	II		V	I	I	I	II
crested hair-grass									II	II		I	II
creeping bent grass	II	V	III	IV	II	III	IV	III	IV	IV	I	I	II
sheep's fescue grass													II
Designation	MG5c	MG5a	MG5a	MG5a	MG5c	MG5a	MG5a	MG5a	MG5a	MG5b	MG5c	MG5a	MG5b

reseeding and the application of artificial fertiliser, had left little room for the trefoil. The two amenity meadows, Paiges and Bosham, had a low frequency of either one or the other of the clover species, perhaps because they were outside the influence of the farming sector where the presence of clover is encouraged. Hogs Common, which had suffered from lack of management in recent years, had low frequencies of four of the community constants.

Preferential species – MG5 sub-communities
We now turn our attention to the preferential species, that is those species that are diagnostic for determining the sub-community, and again compare the values given for the three sub-communities in the standard floristic table with our data from the local meadows (Table 8.2b). Crested dogstail – common knapweed grassland has three sub-communities. The Meadow vetchling MG5a sub-community is the central type occurring on soils in the middle of the pH range for neutral grassland which Rodwell (1992) suggests is from pH 4.5 to 6.5. The heath grass MG5c sub-community occurs on the more acid of these soils, and the lady's bedstraw MG5b sub-community on the more alkaline. This is reflected in the frequency of the diagnostic preferential species which distinguish the sub-communities. Thus in Table 8.2b lady's bedstraw, yellow oatgrass, and yarrow all have frequencies of IV or V in the standard data for the lady's bedstraw MG5b sub-community and the first six species in the table (selfheal, autumn hawkbit, field woodrush, heath grass, tormentil and devilsbit scabious) have frequencies of IV or V in the standard data for the heath grass MG5c sub-community. The meadow vetchling MG5a sub-community is characterised by perennial ryegrass with a frequency of IV and three typical species (common daisy, meadow vetchling and ox-eye daisy) with a frequency of III.

In general, data for the Sussex meadows fit this picture (the sub-community to which each meadow belongs is indicated at the bottom of the table) with two MG5c meadows, Sapperton A and Jamieson's, and one MG5b meadow, Hogs Common. All the rest come within the MG5a sub-community, with high frequency values for perennial ryegrass and/or meadow vetchling. However, within the MG5a meadows there is no consistent movement of the frequency of species across the table reflecting the increasing pH value of the soil. For example, Bosham with the highest recorded pH of 7.3, contains high frequencies of selfheal, field woodrush and heath grass from the MG5c sub-community and only yarrow from the MG5b sub-community. Clearly much more than pH is determining the presence or absence of preferential species.

Seven of the local meadows surveyed belong to the central sub-community, MG5a (meadow vetchling) in which we are particularly interested because it is the sub-community to which the Bedelands meadows belong. This sub-community occurs on soils of medium pH, but in our case this spans a very wide pH range from the most alkaline soil we encountered (7.3 at Bosham) to one of the most acidic (5.3 in Tommy's Meadow). So this should give us a very good picture of the range of species likely to occur in the Bedelands meadows. Perennial rye-grass is low in two of the MG5a meadows surveyed, and common daisy is either absent or present at a very low frequency. Among the colourful flowers that sell the conservation of wildflower meadows to the general public, oxeye daisy tends to be absent or only present at a low frequency but meadow vetchling is likely to occur in abundance, and it is very unlikely that any Sussex meadows of this type will contain field scabious because none of the meadows we surveyed contained this species.

MG5 associate species
In the standard NVC data given in Rodwell (1992) the associates are species that occurred in at least 20 per cent of the 164 sites sampled, but not usually in more than 60 per cent. Within individual meadows, however, the frequency of these species may be higher than this, sometimes attaining the status of a constant species for a particular meadow. From Table 8.2c, which compares species that have attained a frequency of V in at least one Sussex meadow, special features of particular meadows can be seen and these can be linked to management. For example Big Meadow has a high frequency of meadow foxtail grass (V as opposed to I), which can be related to the long-term management of the meadow to give high yields of hay without agricultural improvement. Conversely, there has been no pressure on those managing the meadow at Bosham to produce a large crop of hay because this is an exclusive amenity area managed by the Residents Association. Here, several species attained high frequencies, including two species, green-winged orchid and adder's tongue fern, which are not even included as associates in the NVC standard data. Two species, meadow buttercup and common sorrel, attained constant status for all the Sussex meadows studied suggesting that these species are particularly frequent in meadows in this region.

How does this compare with Bedelands meadows?

Comparison with Bedelands meadows

Table 8.3 gives data for five Bedelands meadows compared with the best Sussex meadows in the 1999 survey that had similar soil pH. This shows that the Bedelands meadows are similar to the best Sussex examples, with meadow buttercup and common sorrel constant in all except Mill Pond Field and Valebridge Common Field, the two meadows that were part of the common grazing land of Valebridge Common until enclosure in 1828 (see map of Bedelands Farm, Figure 7.1 in Chapter 7). These two meadows also differed

Table 8.2c Floristic table of frequency values for other species which although not constants for crested dogstail – common knapweed grassland, attained a frequency of V in at least one Sussex meadow. Values from the ten Sussex meadows are compared with standard data (Rodwell, 1992) for MG5c, MG5a and MG5b sub-communities.

Meadow	Sapp A	Tom	Big	Paige's	Jamies	Sapp B	Mont	WillingF	Bosham	Hogs C	MG5c	MG5a	MG5b
Average soil pH	50	53	55	55	55	58	58	60	73	72	low	medium	high
hemp agrimony				V	I					III		I	I
meadow foxtail		IV	V			I	IV		V		I	I	I
false oat-grass		I	III	II						V	I	II	II
quaking grass				II	II			IV	V				
soft brome			II			I	V				I	I	I
lady's smock		IV	III		I	II	V				I	I	I
hairy sedge							V	V	V			III	
common mouse-ear	I		V	II	III	IV		V			II	III	II
common spotted orchid				V	V								
hogweed				II	I	I			V		III	II	II
cats-ear	V			V		III		V	V	IV	III	III	II
greater birdsfoot trefoil		I			IV			III	V				
green-winged orchid			I		I	I	I		V			I	I
adders' tongue fern			II			I	I				I	II	I
rough meadow grass				V	IV	II	V	I	V	IV		I	I
creeping cinquefoil				II	II	V	III	V	V	I	I		
meadow buttercup	V	I	V	V	V		V	V	IV	V	IV	IV	II
bulbous buttercup		V	I	V	III	V	I	I	I	III	III	III	II
creeping buttercup		IV	IV	V	V	IV	III	V	IV	II	III	II	I
common sorrel	IV	V	V		II		V		V	V	III	III	III
pepper saxifrage	V	V			III		II	III		IV		I	I
lesser stitchwort									V		I		
tufted vetch		I	I			II	II					I	I

from the other meadows at Bedelands in the high frequency of crested dogstail, and low frequency of meadow vetchling and tufted vetch. Crested dogstail performs better in pasture than in hay meadows (Grime *et al*,1990, p. 130) because it likes short turf, whereas meadow vetchling and tufted vetch have a tall, scrambling habit (Grime *et al*,1990, p. 216 and p. 352) and so are able to survive in tall herbage, but not under prolonged grazing. Such differences in the present-day vegetation of the Bedelands meadows may reflect their past history because these species have limited colonising ability and the species present in a meadow will depend on the availability of seed nearby. Centuries of grazing in the past on Valebridge Common may have determined the species occurring in this part of Bedelands Farm when the fields reverted to unimproved meadow in the 1900s. Sale particulars from 1918 tell us that the meadows on Valebridge Common were arable in 1918, and aerial photographs show that they have been grassland since 1946.

None of the Bedelands meadows match the species-richness of the best meadows if we measure this by the average number of species per quadrat. The best Sussex meadows are close to or more than the 22 species per quadrat of the standard data for MG5a, whereas all the Bedelands meadows are lower than this. There is a continuum between species-rich MG5 grassland and a more species-poor grassland dominated by perennial ryegrass (MG6) with species-richness related to low soil fertility (Rodwell 1992, p. 22). The ryegrass-dominated grassland has only 13 species per quadrat, so the Bedelands meadows are well on the way towards the species-rich end of the spectrum and with appropriate management it is hoped that this will improve. Ryegrass is adapted to fertile growing conditions and, like other competitive grasses, declines in relative abundance as the fertility declines leading to greater species-richness (Hindmarch and Pienkowski, 2000). Only very small amounts of perennial ryegrass were present in the quadrats, usually less than 10 per cent (for the sake of clarity, abundance score are not given in the tables). The frequency of perennial ryegrass in the Bedelands meadows is the same as the standard for MG5a in Mill Pond Field, but lower in all the other meadows.

Implications

As well as enabling us to see what we were working towards, this research contributes to an understanding of a nationally important and declining habitat. There is plainly a need for research into this type of grassland. From 1940 to 1980, 95 per cent of wildflower meadows were lost (Nature Conservancy Council, 1984, p. 50) and this trend is continuing. The latest survey of our countryside shows that overall between 1990 and 1998, 13 per cent of neutral grassland was converted to arable fields, woodland or urban development (Haines-Young *et al,* 2000, p. 49). As well as loss due to

Table 8.3 Comparison of frequency data from Bedelands meadows (shaded columns) with data from other Sussex meadows of similar pH

Meadow	Big	Watford	Common	Mill Pond	Old Arable	Tommy's	Big	Paige's	Sapp B	Montague	MG5a medium	MG5b high	MG5c low
Average soil pH	5.2	5.3	5.6	5.7	5.9	5.3	5.5	5.5	5.8	5.8			
Constants													
red fescue grass	V	I	I	III		IV	V	IV			V	V	V
crested dogstail grass	I	I	IV	IV	III	IV	I	V	V	V	V	V	V
birdsfoot trefoil	IV	II	V	III	I	III	II	V	IV	V	V	V	V
ribwort plantain	IV	V	V	IV	V	IV	IV	V	IV		IV	IV	IV
Yorkshire fog	V	V	V	V	V	V	V	V	II	V	IV	IV	V
cocksfoot	III	I	I	I	III	I	I	IV	V		IV	IV	V
white clover	III	III	V	V	IV	IV	II	V	V	V	IV	IV	V
common knapweed	V	II	V	V	II	III	II	V	IV		IV	IV	V
common bent grass	I	V	IV		II	V	V	V	V	V	IV	IV	V
sweet vernal grass	V	V	V	V	V	V	V	V	V	V	IV	IV	V
red clover	III	V	IV	IV	II	V	V	II	V	IV	IV	IV	IV
Preferentials for MG5a													
perennial ryegrass	III	III	II	IV	III	II	V	IV	IV	V	IV	III	I
daisy							I	III			III	II	I
meadow vetchling	IV	IV	II	II	V	V	II	III	IV	III	III	I	I
ox-eye daisy	I	I	III	II		II	I				III	I	II
Preferentials for MG5b													
yarrow	III		I	II	I	II	III	IV	III		III	V	III
creeping bent grass				I	V	V				IV	I	II	I
Preferentials for MG5c													
selfheal			IV	II			I	II	V	IV	III	III	IV
field woodrush	III	I	I	III		I	I	IV	II	II	II	II	IV
Site constants													
meadow buttercup	V	V	IV	V	V	V	V	V	V	V	IV	II	IV
sorrel	V	V	III	III	V	V	V	V	IV	V	III	III	III
tufted vetch	V	III	II		IV	I			II	II	IV	II	III
creeping buttercup	III	V	III	IV	IV	IV	IV	V	V	III	I	I	I
greater birdsfoot trefoil	I	III	III	III	V	I		V	III		II	I	II
Number of samples	45	21	35	12	24	5	6	5	5	5	137	42	15
Average number of species per sample	17 (13–27)	16 (7–19)	18 (10–28)	17 (8–25)	19 (15–26)	24 (20–28)	20 (17–31)	29 (26–30)	22 (19–30)	23 (22–26)	22 (13–32)	26 (12–38)	22 (18–27)

conversion to other categories, there was also loss in species-richness in the neutral grassland that remained. This loss was concentrated among the smaller and less competitive species such as meadow vetchling (p. 49), a species that was much more frequent in the Sussex meadows than in the average picture for this type of grassland given by the NVC standard data. This suggests that conservation of these Sussex meadows may be of national importance. Plant species such as cocksfoot and red clover, which are food sources for butterflies have also become less frequent, and birdsfoot trefoil has remained scarce (p. 47). These species occurred in many of the Sussex meadows in our sample, but were by no means frequent. Again, it is important to draw attention to this and the need to conserve what remains.

As well as being useful for conservation, this research was closely tied in with teaching. Being actively engaged in research using the NVC enables me to think creatively about what the students are doing in class exercises and I can draw on this experience when answering questions and discussing results because I am grappling with similar decisions in my own research. This, I am sure, has made me a more effective teacher. There is also a direct link because some of the students participated in the survey of the local meadows both in the field and in the subsequent data analysis. As with the Meadow Management Experiment, students from my Open Courses, the Field Biology Certificate and the Landscape Studies degree were invited to participate, but could only do so if they were available to attend for a day once a week during the Summer Term. In both cases this led to a preponderance of older learners with leisure for daytime activities, and to a large extent it was the same students who contributed to both pieces of research. From my point of view, I could not have covered the data collection in the time available on my own and the students benefited from participation in research. This was full participation, with the students involved in the data analysis as well as the data collection. In this respect, the participation was better than in the Meadow Management Experiment because the data analysis did not involve complicated statistics or access to computer software. All students were able to draw up their own tables for comparing the data from particular meadows with the standard NVC data and to draw their own conclusions. These were then discussed within the Research Group. Some of these students will be going on to be site managers at the end of their studies. Appropriate site management is informed by ecological research, but the research goals pursued by academic ecologists do not always provide answers to the questions posed by those responsible for practical conservation (Anderson, 1999), so it is important that these students can see the potential for a different sort of research such as that described here, based on observational techniques familiar to conservation professionals.

Irish wildflower meadows

This chapter is about doing science rather than about teaching science, and it would seen logical to extend our study of wildflower grassland to Ireland, that 'Emerald Isle' with its picturesque farm-scapes of orchid-filled meadows and hay-stooks which epitomise man in harmony with nature (Figure 8.4). This is now an out-of-date picture, because enthusiastic support for the Common Agricultural Policy has led very recently to the wholesale loss of species-rich grassland, but it still makes sense to look at what remains of this rich heritage before it all disappears. And there is an added advantage in that it shares a similar grassland flora to Great Britain. Another reason for choosing the Republic of Ireland is the reluctance of Irish botanists to use the British National Vegetation Classification system. On the face of it this reluctance is understandable because Irish sites were not sampled when the system was being developed, leading to the perception that the Irish vegetation will not fit into the same framework. However, as we have seen in the first part of this chapter, sampling was not uniform across Britain and the system does not require, or indeed expect, a perfect fit between particular sites and standard data. Much can be learnt from treating the British Isles as a biogeographical entity and here we use the NVC to set Irish wildflower meadows in this wider context and to develop a contextual appreciation of their special attributes.

Figure 8.4 Farmscape with hay-stooks surviving at Portacloy in an Irish-speaking part of county Mayo, Ireland. Traditional landscapes such as this, which epitomise man in harmony with nature, are becoming increasingly rare following Ireland's entry into the European Union. (Author's photograph, July 1998)

We start with three examples from Ireland of the now familiar MG5 grassland community to show that the fit for the Irish examples is as good as the fit for the local meadows we looked at in the first part of this chapter. We then move on to the special flower-rich grassland of Irish machair on neutral soils, comparing floristic data from three sites with standard NVC data. The continued presence of flower-rich grassland at these sites is linked to their history as common land with open grazing by stock. Data from a similar habitat in Norfolk provide an English example, and also demonstrate the loss of species-richness following cessation of grazing.

Survey method

The grassland community typical of neutral soils in Sussex, MG5 crested dogstail – common knapweed grassland (Rodwell, 1992) also occurs in Ireland, but is now very rare because the European Union support system has led to widespread reseeding and conversion of these meadows to silage production. Byrne (1997) looked at the occurrence of MG5 grassland in the province of Leinster in the east of the Republic and found only a few isolated examples of MG5b, the lady's bedstraw sub-community. The largest remaining area was in Phoenix Park, Dublin, and the area within the park east of Chapelizod Gate is also listed in *The Flora of County Dublin*. A homogeneous area of grassland on this slope was selected as the first MG5 example. The other two examples came from the north-west of Ireland, from Mullaghmore Hill above Bunduff in county Sligo and Sheskinmore in county Donegal (Figure 8.5).

Figure 8.5 Map of Ireland showing position of study sites.

Although most wildflower meadows of the MG5 grassland type have been converted into agriculturally improved, species-poor grassland in Ireland, we can still find flower-rich grassland on neutral soil on machair sites in Mayo, Sligo and Donegal counties. Machair is a mature grassland associated with coastal sand-dunes, which occurs where the sand-plain has been stabilised by the water table (Fay and Jeffery, 1995) leading to a low frequency of sand-binding species such as marram grass. It is breathtakingly beautiful with a profusion of wildflowers (see figure 8.6, p. 184) and much of it is still traditionally managed by extensive grazing. The distribution of machair is very limited because it requires a cool oceanic climate. In Ireland it occurs only on the north-west coast from Galway Bay to Malin Head (Bassett and Curtis, 1985). Much of the machair is very calcareous, but in Mayo, Sligo and Donegal counties there are areas of acidic bedrock where the machair grassland occurs on neutral soils. Three machair sites on neutral soil were selected from the Biomar survey (Crawford *et al*, 1996), one from each of these counties: Sheskinmore in county Donegal; Bunduff in county Sligo; and Garter Hill in county Mayo (Figure 8.5). Site visits were made in July 1998 and September 2001, and an area of fixed-dune grassland surveyed at each site. A similar type of grassland in Britain, at Beeston Regis on the north Norfolk coast (map reference TG 1642), was visited in July 1999 so that the Irish machair grassland could be set in a British context. Floristic data from these sites were analysed by comparing frequency values obtained from five sample quadrats with standard data for the appropriate fixed dune grassland community (SD8, red fescue – lady's bedstraw fixed dune grassland; Rodwell, 2000).

Soil pH at a depth of 10 cm was estimated in the field using a Whatman pHScan meter and the standard technique described in Chapter 2 (p. 26). Two samples were taken for each quadrat.

MG5 unimproved neutral grassland in Ireland

The three Irish examples of crested dogstail – common knapweed grassland contained lady's bedstraw, a diagnostic species for the MG5b sub-community, so they are compared with Hogs Common, the only Sussex example to contain lady's bedstraw, in Table 8.4. This table of frequency values is set out following the species order used in the standard floristic table for MG5 (Rodwell, 1992, pp. 64–65) giving site data in the first four columns followed by standard data for MG5a and MG5b in the two right-hand columns. Constant and preferential species are given in full, but associate species are only included if a frequency of V was attained in at least one site. As discussed below, this set of data suggests that the Phoenix Park grassland, from Dublin, with an average pH of 7.8, and the Donegal grassland, with a pH of 6.9 are MG5b like the Sussex example, and the Sligo grassland with an average pH of 5.3, is MG5a.

The designation of MG5 crested dogstail – common knapweed grassland is based on 194 British samples (Rodwell, 1992). None of these are from the Irish Republic, although key works by Irish botanists such as O'Sullivan (1965, 1982) were included in the interpretation of the data. Even within Britain the distribution of the samples is patchy and, as we discussed in the first part of this chapter, only four come from Sussex. This means that Sussex meadows may not fit the standard picture for MG5 because this is based on the frequency with which species occurred in 2 m by 2 m quadrats across these 194 sites. Quite apart from this, Rodwell (1992, p. 9) expected the widespread occurrence of stands that lacked one or more of the key species because of the different response of individual species to particular aspects of the management of the grassland. Different types of grassland are related to various combinations of treatments and these can cut across floristic differences based on soil characteristics and climatic factors. Individual species frequently respond differently to particular treatments, so this leads to meadows, which can be referred to a particular grassland type, that lack some of the diagnostic species. This was clear from our analysis of the ten Sussex meadows in the first part of this chapter, where we saw that fine examples of traditionally managed meadows, such as Montague Meadow, lacked community constants (Table 8.2a). When the context is extended to Ireland (Table 8.4) we find that the fit for constant species in the grassland surveyed in the three Irish sites is as good as that accepted for Sussex meadows, and that differences between the collected data and the NVC standard data can be linked to management. Samples from Phoenix Park (Dublin), a former deer park which is still grazed by deer, lacked two species. The first of these, common knapweed, is a species which does much better in terms of frequency, vigour and flowering in the absence of year round grazing (Grime *et al*, 1990, p. 110). Crawford *et al* (1996) note that it is poorly represented in grazed examples of this community from machair sites. The Donegal grassland in the present study was part of a lightly-grazed machair complex at Sheskinmore and here it reached the same frequency value as the standard for the community. The second, white clover, occurred at a very low frequency in the meadow at Bosham in Sussex. (Table 8.2a) where, in common with Phoenix Park, there was an absence of any agricultural interest in the land. The Sligo grassland, which is cut annually but not grazed, lacked only one constant species, common bent grass, but two species, birdsfoot trefoil and cocksfoot, occurred at very low frequencies. These species also occurred at low frequencies or were absent from some of the Sussex meadows (Table 8.2a). There are no consistent differences between the three Irish examples and the Sussex meadows. Sweet vernal grass is frequent in the Sligo meadow and the

Table 8.4 Floristic table giving frequency values (I–V) for grassland sites in counties Sligo, Donegal, and Dublin in Ireland and Sussex in England.

The table is set out following the species order used in the standard floristic table for MG5 crested dogstail – common knapweed grassland (Rodwell, 1992, pp. 64–5) with standard data for the sub-communities MG5a and MG5b in the last two columns. Average soil pH is given. P indicates that the species occurred at the site, but not in the quadrats.

Site	Sligo	Donegal	Dublin	Sussex	MG5a std	MG5b std
Average soil pH	5.3	6.9	7.8	7.2	medium	high
Constants						
red fescue	V	V	V	V	V	V
crested dogstail	III	V	IV	I	V	V
birdsfoot trefoilI	I	V	III	I	V	V
ribwort plantain	V	V	IV	V	V	V
Yorkshire fog	V	V	II	V	IV	IV
cocksfoot	I		V	V	IV	IV
white clover	IV	V		III	IV	IV
common knapweed	II	IV		V	IV	IV
common bent		III	II	III	IV	IV
sweet vernal grass	V	I	I	IV	IV	IV
red clover	III	V	III	V	IV	IV
Preferentials MG5a						
perennial ryegrass	**II**			I	**IV**	III
common daisy					**III**	II
meadow vetchling	**III**			I	**III**	I
ox-eye daisy	**II**			I	**III**	I
meadow fescue					**II**	I
field scabious					I	
hard rush					I	
Preferentials MG5b						
lady's bedstraw	I	**III**	**IV**	**V**	I	**V**
yellow oatgrass			**V**	**IV**	II	**IV**
yarrow		**I**	**V**		III	**V**
glaucous sedge		**I**	**V**	I	I	**II**
salad burnet			**III**	**II**	I	**II**
crested hairgrass					I	**II**
creeping bent	II	**V**	**III**	**IV**	I	**II**
Preferentials MG5c						
selfheal		I	I		III	III
autumn hawkbit					II	II
field woodrush			II		II	II
heath grass		IV	III		I	I
tormentil		I			I	1
devilsbit scabious		P			I	1
burnet saxifrage			I	II	I	I
betony					I	I
spring sedge					I	I
pignut					I	I
Site constants						
false oatgrass	V			V	II	II
quaking grass		P	V		II	III
common mouse-ear	V	IV			III	II
cats-ear	V	IV			III	II
meadow buttercup		V		V	IV	II
common sorrel		II		V	III	III
yellow rattle	V			II		II
wood false brome			V			

Sussex meadows, but has a very low frequency in the Dublin and Donegal grasslands, where it may be selectively grazed. Conversely, birdsfoot trefoil has a very low frequency in the Sligo meadow and at Hogs Common and Big Meadow in Sussex, but approaches the standard value in the Dublin and Donegal examples, where the competing herbage is grazed. This illustrates that ecological sense can be made of Irish wildflower meadows by dealing with them within the NVC system.

If we now move on to the preferential species, which are used to determine the sub-community, we again find that the system works as well for Irish meadows as for Sussex meadows. The Irish examples are from two different sub-communities: Sligo, with an average pH of 5.3, is MG5a; and Dublin and Donegal, with an average pH of 7.8 and 6.9 respectively, are MG5b. Preferentials for the Dublin example fit the standard data for MG5b better than Hogs Common in Sussex, because yarrow is present in every quadrat as in the standard data, whereas it was absent from Hogs Common. Sligo, in common with most of the Sussex meadows which we assigned to the meadow vetchling sub-community, lacks common daisy, meadow fescue, field scabious and hard rush, and is characterised by meadow vetchling (Tables 8.2b and 8.4). Perennial ryegrass and ox-eye daisy are present, but again, as in Sussex, at reduced frequencies. The Donegal grassland, which showed a very good fit for the community constants, fits less comfortably within the MG5b sub-community. Although it contains four of the seven preferential species, three of these are present at a very low frequency and it has high frequencies of some associate species. The NVC is still useful even here, as we can describe this community by saying that it is the lady's bedstraw sub-community of crested dogstail – common knapweed grassland, but it lacks yellow oatgrass, salad burnet and crested hairgrass and has high frequencies of heath grass, common mouse-ear, meadow buttercup, cats-ear and common sorrel. This would enable a site manager in, for example, Scotland to picture the grassland that we are describing.

In Table 8.4 we have only included associate species that have attained constant status in at least one of the Irish examples. As with the Sussex meadows we expect these site constants to relate to regional differences or the management of the site. Perhaps not surprisingly, given the regional differences between the three Irish examples and the contrasting management regimes, no associates attained constant status in all the Irish examples, but again this suggests that Irish data should not be considered to lie outside the NVC system.

From this regional study of crested dogstail – common knapweed grassland, then, it can be seen that frequency values for diagnostic community constants and preferential species from different sites within a British county may deviate more from the standard NVC values than those from Irish sites.

Such differences should be viewed as a strength not a weakness in the NVC system, because attention is drawn to key features of the floristic composition of particular meadows, which can then be linked to management issues.

Irish machair on neutral soils

This theme can be developed further by a consideration of the more specialised flower-rich grassland of fixed-dune grassland on machair sites. Fixed-dune grassland, as its name suggests, is the stable grassland that develops behind sand-dunes. Marram grass, so much a feature of the sand-dunes themselves, is very rare and in the sub-communities with which we are concerned here, the common flowers of species-rich neutral grassland (lady's bedstraw, ribwort plantain, white clover, and birdsfoot trefoil) which we have already met in previous sections of this book, occur in profusion, giving the impression of wildflower meadow vegetation (Rodwell, 2000, p. 174). Such vegetation has developed around the northern coasts of the British Isles under the influence of sheep and cattle grazing combined with the moist climate (Rodwell, 2000, p. 179). The soils contain a substantial proportion of shell fragments in the sand and in Ireland are generally lime-rich, with a pH as high as 8.3 in some areas (Bassett and Curtis, 1985). For our study we are interested in the more neutral end of the range, and the three selected sites, arrayed around Donegal Bay, all occur on acidic deposits. The soil pH at the central site at Bunduff (Irish National Grid, G 7256) was comparable to the soil pH of our meadows, ranging from 5.8 to 6.4, because here the carboniferous limestone which underlies most of Ireland is replaced by an acid sandstone (Macdermot *et al*, 1996), giving rise to more acidic soils. The other two sites lie further west near the northern and southern extremities of the large bite in the land mass that is Donegal Bay; Sheskinmore (Irish National Grid, G 6895) to the north in county Donegal and Garter Hill (Irish National Grid, F 8040) to the south in county Mayo (Figure 8.5). Although these sites lie on similar acidic deposits, the soil pH was higher here, ranging from 6.9 to 7.8.

Quadrat data were collected from the richest example, Bunduff, in July 1998 and this site is considered first. The other sites were visited in July 1998 and full quadrat data collected on a re-visit in September 2001.

The fixed-dune grassland community at Bunduff

As you come over the sand-dunes from Mullaghmore beach, the area of fixed-dune grassland lies spread out below you, extending down into tall swamp vegetation at the edge of a lough to your left and bounded by hummocks covered in MG5 grassland to your right (Figure 8.6). A previous study of Irish Machair sites (Crawford *et al*, 1996) used the NVC to map very complicated mosaics within the fixed dune grassland community and created four new sub-communities to deal with the quadrat data collected. I found the mosaics difficult to interpret *on site* and the new communities meant that comparisons could not be made with the existing classification. Here we will take a different approach, treating the area of fixed-dune grassland as a whole and using the existing standard floristic table as a benchmark against which to highlight differences. This will lead us to a contextual understanding and appreciation of the species richness of this particular example of fixed-dune grassland.

In Table 8.5, quadrat data from Bunduff and the other sites are compared with red fescue – lady's bedstraw fixed-dune grassland (SD8, Rodwell, 2000, pp. 174–87). In this type of mature dune grassland, marram grass is no longer constant, and red fescue and a variety of other grasses, wildflowers and mosses form a generally closed sward (Rodwell, 2000, p. 174). In the Bunduff example, red fescue and three of the other five constants occurred in every quadrat. Affinity is shown to two sub-communities: SD8d, the common daisy – meadow buttercup sub-community, and SD8e, the selfheal sub-community.

Figure 8.6 View of Bunduff Machair from Mullaghmore Hill, county Sligo, Ireland. The extensive sand-dunes behind Mullaghmore beach (left of photograph) are dwarfed by the height from which the photograph has been taken. The machair lies behind the dunes extending from the lough in the middle distance to hummocks of MG5 grassland on the right. (Author's photograph, July 1998)

In Britain these two sub-communities occur mainly in the north-west of Scotland and the Isles, where they cover extensive stretches of machair landscape (Rodwell 2000, p. 179). They are characterised by grasses such as Yorkshire fog and wildflowers such as common daisy, meadow buttercup, self heal, eyebright and red clover (Rodwell 2000, p. 178), all of which are present at Bunduff at a high frequency. In both sub-communities red fescue is likely to be the most abundant plant (Rodwell 2000) and this was particularly true at Bunduff, where the cover of red fescue was more than 50 per cent in all the quadrats (in order to make Table 8.5 easy to understand, abundance data have not been included). In SD8e, selfheal is most strongly preferential, and common daisy and meadow buttercup, which are preferential for SD8d, are only occasional (Rodwell 2000, p. 176). At Bunduff, the high frequency of meadow buttercup might suggest SD8d, but selfheal is constant and this, together with the balance of other preferentials, points to SD8e as being the sub-community here.

We now turn to the important differences between the standard picture for SD8e and the quadrat data from Bunduff. Two features stand out: first, the consistency of the species composition of the Bunduff quadrats is remarkable, with 15 species (shown in bold in Table 8.5) occurring in every quadrat. This consistency supports our decision to deal with this area of vegetation as a single plant community. Second, the quadrats were also particularly species-rich, with 40–44 species recorded in each, compared with 16–32 in the standard table. This is due to special characteristics of the habitat. The groundwater table across this area of Bunduff machair is close to the surface, keeping the soil waterlogged through much of the year. This means that as well as having transitions to dune-slack vegetation in the depressions of an undulating plain, as described by Rodwell (2000, p. 181), the actual SD8 community contains elements from the slack vegetation as constants. Thus species such as carnation sedge, marsh pennywort, grass of Parnassus and bog pimpernel were present in all the quadrats. The waterlogged nature of the soil and the low height of the grazed sward also allowed mire species such as common butterwort, flea sedge, lesser clubmoss, toad rush and tormentil to come in from areas of sphagnum bog within the mosaic, thereby increasing the species-richness still further. Finally the uneven nature of the terrain and free draining properties of the soil allowed an intimate mix of plants from drier grassland habitats amongst these wet-loving plants. Thus heath grass and quaking grass from the crested dogstail – common knapweed grassland community, had frequency values of V and IV respectively within the fixed-dune grassland community.

Table 8.5. Comparison of quadrat data from the three Irish machair sites and a similar English site, with standard data from two fixed-dune grassland communities (SD8d and SD8e, Rodwell 2000, p. 183–86).

All community constant species have been included and preferential species for SD8d and SD8e. Otherwise, only key species attaining a frequency of IV or V in at least one site are included. P indicates that the species occurred at the site, but not in the quadrats.

	Sheskinmore	Garter	Bunduff	B. Regis	SD8d std	SD8e std
pH	7.2 – 7.5	6.9 – 7.8	5.8 – 6.4	6.3 – 7.1	7.5 – 8.9	7.7 – 8.6
Constants SD8						
red fescue	V	V	**V**	IV	V	V
lady's bedstraw	III	P	I	I	IV	V
ribwort plantain	V	V	**V**	III	V	V
white clover	IV	V	**V**	III	V	I
birdsfoot trefoil	V	IV	**V**	III	IV	I
smooth meadow grass		I			IV	IV
Preferentials SD8d						
common daisy		III	III		IV	II
meadow buttercup	IV	V	IV	III	IV	II
creeping bent	V	V	II		II	I
tufted vetch		III		I	I	
Preferentials SD8e						
ragwort	I		II		III	IV
eyebright	IV	III	**V**		IV	V
Yorkshire fog	IV		IV		III	V
fairy flax	IV		II		II	IV
bellflower	P				I	IV
selfheal	V	V	**V**	II	II	IV
shaggy moss					I	III
spear moss	I		II	II	II	III
red clover	IV		**V**	V	II	III
glaucous sedge			III	II	II	III
felwort					I	III
common knapweed	P			IV	I	II
creeping buttercup	III				I	II
pincerwort					I	II
wild carrot		I			I	II
wavy flat moss	II				I	II
creeping willow	P					I
ox-eye daisy			I			I
Associate species						
common horsetail	I	II	**V**	V	I	I
Associates SD8a and b						
spring sedge			**V**			
Species not in SD8						
carnation sedge	IV	V	**V**			
heath grass	III	II	**V**	I		
tormentil	I		**V**	V		
grass of Parnassus	V	V	**V**	II		
bog pimpernel		V	**V**	III		
marsh pennywort	IV	V	**V**	III		
lesser clubmoss		V	IV			
flea sedge			IV	I		
toad rush			IV			
quaking grass	P		IV	III		
lesser hawkbit	**V**	V	III			
Average no. of species per sample	26	25	41	28	20	24
	(23–29)	(23–29)	(40–44)	(24–34)	(14–30)	(16–32)

Importance of grazing for maintenance of species-richness

An essential feature of this species-richness is low-level grazing by cattle. This area of fixed dune grassland is unenclosed commonage which is lightly grazed by free-roaming cattle (Crawford *et al*, 1996). The cattle shown in Figure 8.7 roamed freely over the beach, dunes and machair areas and into Bunduff Lough. Much of the machair site at Sheskinmore in county Donegal (Figure 8.8) is also lightly grazed by cattle (Crawford *et al*, 1996), but some areas have been fenced. As Crawford *et al* (1996) point out, this allows the exercise of individual initiative in a way not possible on commonage, with the possibility of agricultural improvement or over-stocking. This was evident in one area where a closely grazed turf had been further degraded by rabbits to give a much less species-rich turf dominated by silverweed. In the area surveyed in 2001, the sward was longer than at Bunduff and was not being grazed by stock at the time. Garter Hill in county Mayo (Figure 8.9) provides a contrast because, although still unenclosed, Crawford *et al* (1996) record this site as sheep- rather than cattle-grazed. When visits were made in 1998 and 2001 as part of this study, the site was being very heavily grazed by sheep and there was evidence that cattle had also grazed there in the past. The turf was very short with bare patches. A study of the quadrat data from these sites should allow us

Figure 8.7 Cattle grazing extensively at Bunduff machair. An essential feature of the species-richness of these sites is the low level of grazing on what is still unenclosed commonage. (Author's photograph, July 1998)

Figure 8.8   View of Sheskinmore machair looking west from Sheskinmore Hill. The open sea can just be glimpsed behind the extensive sand-dunes in the middle distance. The machair grassland covers the relatively flat area between Sheskinmore Hill and the dunes. (Author's photograph, July 1998)

Figure 8.9   View of Garter Hill machair site with fixed-dune grassland in the foreground, dunes in the middle distance and open sea beyond. The area is unenclosed, but is heavily grazed by sheep resulting in a very short turf with bare patches. (Author's photograph, July 1998)

to relate differences in the species composition of the machair grassland to these different grazing patterns.

Data from both Sheskinmore and Garter Hill (Table 8.5) present a similar picture to Bunduff for the community constant species and in the high frequency of selfheal, the characteristic species of the SD8e sub-community. Lady's bedstraw did not occur in any of the quadrats at Garter Hill, although it was present in the area, and it was more frequent at Sheskinmore than Bunduff perhaps reflecting its sensitivity to grazing pressure (Grime *et al*, 1990, p. 180). Common daisy was absent from the longer sward at Sheskinmore. Species-richness was much less at these two sites than at Bunduff, with only 23–29 species per quadrat, compared with 40–44, but at an average of 25 and 26 species per quadrat respectively, this is still above the average of 24 for this the richest sub-community of fixed-dune grassland. In spite of the impoverished state of the turf at Garter Hill, most of the additional constants from Bunduff, such as carnation sedge, grass of Parnassus, bog pimpernel, and marsh pennywort, were constant here too. From the mire vegetation, lesser clubmoss is constant and common butterwort is present at the same frequency as at Bunduff, but tormentil, flea sedge, and toad rush are absent. Crawford *et al* (1996) stress the importance of cattle- rather than sheep-grazing on these machair sites. In the wet Atlantic climate nutrients are quickly leached out of the sandy soil and there is no build up of nutrients. Grazing is essential for the maintenance of species-richness, but sheep severely cut back the vegetation, leading to degradation and erosion, especially where over-stocking occurs. European Union subsidies for sheep encourage over-stocking. Such grazing pressure is a particular problem on Irish machair sites where year-round grazing is unrelieved compared with Scottish sites, where arable cropping provides respite from grazing (Crawford *et al*, 1996). The quadrat data indicate that the site would recover quickly should grazing rates be reduced.

Similarly, the grassland at Sheskinmore contains thirteen of the Bunduff site constant species, with only bog pimpernel and lesser clubmoss being absent, perhaps excluded by the longer sward, but several of the Bunduff constant species are much less frequent. Apart from the difference in grazing, this site resembled Bunduff, with the fixed-dune grassland leading into dune-slack vegetation and the beautiful marsh helleborine present in quadrats in each. Heath grass from the crested dogstail – common knapweed grassland community had a lower frequency at both Sheskinmore and Garter Hill than at Bunduff, and quaking grass was absent. Instead, lesser hawkbit, another common plant of neutral grassland, is present in every quadrat from Sheskinmore and Garter Hill.

In the context of wildflower meadows the machair habitat, with its history of open grazing on common land, is becoming increasingly important in a country where agricultural improvement has led to a dearth of semi-natural grassland. Much of the machair is still unenclosed and grazed at a low level of intensity by cattle, leading to flower-rich grassland of great beauty and diversity. Across Europe, flower-rich grassland sustained by similar low-input, low-output grazing systems is being pushed to the fringes largely as a result of European Community Common Agricultural Policy subsidies (Bignal and Branson 1996, Mitchel 1996, Tubbs 1997).

The importance of the grazing element in the maintenance of species-rich fixed dune grassland can be seen in the British example looked at in this study. The site, at Beeston Regis on the North Norfolk coast, is also on common land. In the 1920s and 1930s the common was grazed by free-running ponies and horses and there were no trees (Ken Durrant, personal communication). In the 1950s, most of the common became covered in bracken following heather burning and, in the absence of grazing scrub and trees invaded. This has led to a gradual drying out of the site. In the last 16 years the Beeston Regis Management Group has cleared over 30 acres of bracken, but it is an uphill task carried out by a small band of dedicated volunteers. The site has the largest number of orchids and flowering plants in Norfolk and is now a Site of Special Scientific Interest. In many ways parts of the site are still reminiscent of Bunduff, but areas of scrub, tall rank grass and patches of bramble – Yorkshire fog underscrub illustrate how relaxation of grazing leads into the successive development of scrub and then woodland, the natural climax vegetation. Flower-rich red fescue – lady's bedstraw grassland is maintained as a plagioclimax, that is a stage in plant succession which precedes the natural climax (Lawrence, 1995, p. 443), by the grazing of stock or rabbits (Rodwell 2000, p. 118), and without the reintroduction of appropriate grazing the situation at Beeston Regis is unlikely to be sustainable.

In the open areas free from scrub and bracken, where the water table is close to the surface, a combination of uneven terrain and a free-draining soil has led to the development of a species-rich SD8e community (24 to 34 species per quadrat) similar to that at Bunduff, containing additional species from the slack community (grass of Parnassus, bog pimpernel, marsh pennywort and marsh helleborine), the mire community (common butterwort and tormentil), and the MG5 community (heath grass and quaking grass). Thus the species-rich grassland of one of the best machair sites in Ireland can be linked to the situation on this British site where the floristic diversity of the grassland is diminishing. By working within the NVC, Irish vegetation can be placed within a wider geographical context, leading to a proper appreciation of its particular attributes.

The Irish dimension

By widening our study of flower-rich grasslands to the Irish Republic, where widespread degradation has happened more recently than in England, we can see the importance of traditional farming practices for biological diversity. Within Europe as a whole, there are many examples of traditional farming practices that have created biological diversity at a range of ecological scales (Hindmarch and Pienkowski, 2000, p. v). Such systems also exploit natural resources within locally sustainable limits, and by studying them we can see that apparently successful, intensive land management has hidden costs in the form of environmental, economic and social damage. It is now widely recognised within the European Union that there needs to be policy shift from intensive production to more sustainable forms of land management: traditional farming practices with their proven record of sustainable production and high biological diversity provide compelling examples of what this could mean (Hindmarch and Pienkowski, 2000, p. v).

Implications

In this study of wildflower meadows we have shown how straightforward observational techniques can be used to increase our understanding of species-richness in habitats that are becoming degraded by human activities. This type of research is time-consuming, but uses exactly the skills of fieldwork and plant identification that students attending natural history classes acquire. These are also the skills possessed by site managers and conservation professionals, so there is great potential for us to fill in the gaps in our knowledge of existing habitats before it is too late. And yet, ecological journals are full of small-scale, tightly controlled, laboratory-type experiments which bear little relationship to actual habitats. This type of ecological research gets published because it is part of the ethos of university departments and publications are peer-reviewed. And what gets published ultimately controls the research that goes on, because research money follows departmental standing in the Research Assessment Exercise. This ethos extends right down to the new blood coming in as PhD students. Such students may be keen to do applied fieldwork, but will almost certainly have to include some laboratory experiments in order to make the project acceptable. Such difficulties seem to be widely recognised within the British Ecological Society which is trying to encourage more fieldwork within mainstream university programmes and more participation by conservation professionals at its conferences.

In this context, the current move to locate continuing education lecturers increasingly within mainstream departments (Chapter 1) is worrying. The very real possibility of engaging in the type of research required for effective biodiversity conservation, which has been open to continuing education lecturers with an interest in this field, becomes much more problematic from a location within a mainstream biology department. It would be very difficult for one lecturer to resist the dominant culture of the department. As well as the loss to the biodiversity conservation agenda of a change of research interest, there would also be a loss of connection between teaching and research because it will be more difficult to link the research to concerns of the older learner and to conservation professionals.

The problem of research funding may also need to be tackled at a higher level. Rothman *et al* (1996, p. 191) in their study of strategic research (that is 'research that someone pays for', p. 194) found that as the financial environment became more stringent in the 1990s, government funding focused on key areas of scientific research. Conservation biology was not one of these. More money was spent on human diseases and armaments than on trying to solve environmental problems because such concerns are higher up the agenda of people who lobby politicians, and it is the politicians who decide what research gets funded (Soule and Orians, 2001b, p. 280). It has been suggested that conservation biologists should be organising themselves to lobby the government for funding rather than just deciding on research priorities within the money allocated (Soule and Orians, 2001b, p. 279).

CHAPTER 9

Conclusions

The debate is really about our own world, our own futures. Skylarks are one of the government's 'indicators of environmental health', but it is our (spiritual) health that is meant, not that of the skylarks

(Marren, 2002, p. 316).

Summary

Skylarks were once so common in Britain that Jefferies (undated) writing a century ago could describe numbers so great that the ground was black with them. Now the presence of just one skylark is noted with pleasure and they continue to decline along with many of the other species that are associated with the general countryside rather than protected habitats: victims of modern agricultural practice, road building and housing development. Ecological citizenship is about reclaiming this general countryside for nature by building on the foundations laid by nature conservation groups. As scientists or amateur naturalists, we are concerned with managing habitats and with the associated biological monitoring and surveying which tell us that the management is achieving the objectives set. We are less concerned with campaigning and would couch our rhetoric in terms of our responsibilities towards understanding and maintaining the whole web of life of which we are one part, rather than assigning rights to physical features such as rivers and meadows, or to particular plants and animals. This does not mean that we are indifferent to the beauty and spiritual dimensions of the natural world. Indeed, it is clear to us that unless we start from an aesthetic appreciation that values nature, no amount of scientific rationalisation will achieve our objectives.

Today in Britain, we start from a point where many people are disconnected from a direct experience of nature, although passive interest in the subject, as measured by ratings for TV natural history programmes and membership of nature conservation organisations, is at an all time high. This has two consequences: on the one hand we have a lack of people with biological identification and fieldwork skills; while at the same time we have an appropriate starting point for developing such skills within local communities. This book has set out a philosophy of science teaching aimed at developing this type of ecological citizenship. As well as biological fieldwork skills, we also need citizens able to participate fully in current debates about the environment, and in today's technologically-driven world this requires an understanding of scientific method. We have seen how it is possible to begin with an interest in natural history or love of the countryside and, within this context, to develop science literacy and biological identification skills. We have looked at examples of open-ended investigations of heath and woodland vegetation using the National Vegetation Classification system; and at how long-term monitoring of bluebells in a local wood can be used to teach scientific method from formulating a hypothesis, through making measurements to test the hypothesis, to learning about uncertainty in biological data. The importance of learning about science through doing science has been stressed. The effectiveness of this approach has been verified using the voices of participating students. Such a problem-posing approach is the reverse of the traditional method of teaching science based on a lecture approach where a body of knowledge is built up in steps, and where science teaching at HE level requires the learners to have extensive foundation knowledge on which to build. For some science colleagues, biological fieldwork will seem like soft science, but there is no reason why the careful observation that is required to identify a species of moss or grass in the field should be seen as less rigorous than observations in a physics laboratory. Indeed, all natural science, as opposed to technology, is predicated on careful observation of the natural world: but what about that cornerstone of scientific discovery, experimentation? What sort of experiment will help to arrest the decline of biodiversity and can useful experiments be conducted outside the controlled environment of the laboratory or greenhouse?

In the Meadow Management Experiment students moved out from their course work to take part in an ecological experiment in a community setting. Here they were not just data collectors, but co-researchers who were able to influence the direction in which the research proceeded. They learnt about scientific research through doing research, while at the same time acquiring biological identification skills, and they were then able to go on and set up their own biological monitoring programmes. The project also linked site managers with academic research, and stepped outside the rigour of tightly controlled laboratory-type experiments to incorporate features of site management into the experimental design. This type of experiment, it is argued, is urgently needed alongside standard monitoring of site management if we are to reverse the continual decline in biodiversity in our open spaces. By working within a community setting, such projects also help to connect local people to their local wildlife.

As well as monitoring our efforts to manage habitats in such a way as to conserve biodiversity, we also urgently need basic information about species-rich examples of declining habitats. Again this requires an approach based on careful observation in the field, and so is open to conservation professionals and biological recorders as well as academic ecologists. To illustrate this approach, we looked at flower-rich meadow grassland, a habitat redolent of some midsummer rural idyll, that is now declining at an alarming rate. We chose particularly biodiverse examples from Sussex, Ireland and a site in Norfolk and used the National Vegetation Classification system to develop an appreciation of the particular attributes of meadow grassland. This demonstrated the importance of traditional farming practices in maintaining biodiversity. It is hoped that this book will contribute to a more knowledgeable appreciation of wildflower meadows and that this will follow through in action before, like Jefferies' skylarks black on the ground, they become a distant folk memory.

Implications for policy and practice

The student voices in this book demonstrate the potential for a new approach to lifelong learning directed towards education for ecological citizenship rather than paid employment. There are two aspects to such learning. The first concerns the development of scientific literacy, where it is important that they learn about the process of scientific investigation and about its self-imposed limitations, so that they are able to contribute to the process of making ethical decisions at the interface between science and society. The second concerns the development of the skills needed to participate in biological conservation work, which is not an optional leisure-time activity, but a crucial part of achieving the nature conservation aims to which the UK Government is committed. There is already insufficient professional manpower to cover site monitoring for nature conservation, and the need for biological monitoring expertise such as that acquired within the Meadow Management Experiment, will increase rapidly as local communities seek to meet their biodiversity targets within the international agenda agreed for the 21st century. Both these aspects of learning for ecological citizenship require proper government funding and the development of a new system of accountability which is not related to achieving academic credit.

The problem-posing approach to learning about science espoused in this book is relevant to all levels of science education from school to mainstream university. Fieldwork in the local countryside or urban green space provides open-ended investigation, builds on our innate curiosity about the natural world, and has a relevance to daily life which is lacking in laboratory work. Here, we have been concerned with one particular branch of science, field biology, but the same principles, which have emphasised the hands-on acquisition of data through careful observation, could be applied to the physical sciences using astronomy or geology.

As well as a change of emphasis in funding for adult education, the international conservation agenda requires governments generally to encourage more research in the area of conservation biology. In the UK, those of us concerned about the natural environment should be pressing the government to add conservation biology to the list of key areas of scientific research which are currently being funded. Already such research is showing the way forward for a sustainable agricultural policy based on traditional farming practices rather than the environmentally damaging, and in global terms economically unsustainable, system of intensive production.

This book has celebrated what can be achieved by local citizens, skilled in biological identification, working in and enjoying their local wildlife areas. This suggests that a change of emphasis is required within the nature conservation industry away from the current preoccupation with the writing of management plans and strategies towards the much more time-consuming but ultimately more important monitoring work which is being neglected at the moment. Partnerships between adult education institutions and local communities or wildlife trusts could facilitate such an approach.

The way forward

I believe that we need to embrace a lifelong learning approach to science teaching which is based on student-centred learning rather than knowledge acquisition. We need to recognise the potential contribution of the older citizen, not directly to wealth creation, but to equally essential work within the local environment which cannot readily be undertaken by those in paid employment because of the time-consuming nature of activities such as habitat monitoring. This will require flexible provision for education with a number of different progression routes. The current vertical progression model, in which credit is acquired and students pass rapidly through a series of courses to gain an award, can be adapted for lifelong learning for career development by providing appropriate entry and exit points. However, it should also be possible for students to return to the same class for a number of years while skills, such as fieldwork and biological identification are gradually developed. This horizontal mode of progression should be properly funded and recognised as being particularly appropriate for education for citizenship. In the ecological context this includes science literacy as well as biodiversity conservation work.

Peter Marren (2002), in a recent book in the New Naturalist series, takes a critical look at the state of our countryside and official efforts at nature conservation. His vision for the future lies in a rebirth of old-style natural history with all sorts of people taking a knowledgeable interest. The potential for science learning could be realised in a similar way. This book has presented a vision of field-based teaching and research which would put science on the adult education map – not as the current poor relation to arts-based studies, but with complementary numbers of staff and students. And in addition, ordinary adults up and down the country would be drawn into active participation in their local community as ecological citizens.

List of common and botanical names

Vascular plants (from Clapham AR, Tutin TG and Warburg EF, 1995, 3rd edition. *Excursion flora of the British Isles*. Cambridge University Press)

adder's tongue fern *Ophioglossum vulgatum*
alder *Alnus glutinosa*
ash *Fraxinus excelsior*
aspen *Populus tremula*
autumn hawkbit *Leontodon autumnalis*

beech *Fagus sylvatica*
bellflower *Campanula rotundifolia*
bell heather *Erica cinerea*
bent grass
    bristle bent *Agrostis curtisii*
    common bent *Agrostis capillaris*
    creeping bent *Agrostis stolonifera*
bilberry *Vaccinium myrtillus*
birch
    downy birch *Betula pubescens*
    silver birch *Betula pendula*
birdsfoot trefoil
    common *Lotus corniculatus*
    greater *Lotus uliginosus*
blackthorn *Prunus spinosa*
betony *Stachys betonica*
bluebell *Hyacinthoides non-scripta*
bog pimpernel *Anagallis tenella*
bracken *Pteridium aquilinum*
bramble *Rubus fruticosus*
bugle *Glechoma hedeacea*
bulbous buttercup *Ranunculus bulbosus*
burnet saxifrage *Pimpinella saxifraga*
buttercup
    bulbous *Ranunculus bulbosus*
    creeping *Ranunculus repens*
    meadow *Ranunculus acris*
butterwort *Pinguicula vulgaris*
carnation sedge *Carex panicea*
cats-ear *Hypochoeris radicata*

cherry plum *Prunus cerasifera*
cocksfoot *Dactylis glomerata*
common butterwort *Pinguicula vulgaris*
common daisy *Bellis perennis*
common horsetail *Equisetum arvense*
common gorse *Ulex europaeus*
common knapweed *Centaurea nigra*
common mouse-ear *Cerastium fontanum*
common sorrel *Rumex acetosa*
common spotted orchid *Dactylorhiza
    maculata*
cow parsley *Anthricus sylvestris*
crab apple *Malus sylvestris*
creeping cinquefoil *Potentilla reptans*
creeping soft grass *Holcus mollis*
creeping willow *Salix repens*
crested dogstail *Cynosurus cristatus*
crested hair-grass *Koeleria macrantha*
cross-leaved heath *Erica tetralix*

daisy *Bellis perennis*
devilsbit scabious *Succisa pratensis*
dogs mercury *Mercurialis perennis*
dogwood *Cornus sanguinea*
dog violet *Viola riviniana-reichenbachia*
dwarf furze *Ulex minor*
elder *Sambucus nigra*
enchanter's nightshade *Circaea lutetiana*

English elm *Ulmus procera*
eyebright *Euphrasia officinalis*
fairy flax *Linum catharticum*
false oatgrass *Arrhenatherum elatius*
felwort *Gentianella amarella*
field maple *Acer campestre*
field scabious *Knautia arvensis*

field woodrush *Luzula campestre*
flea sedge *Carex pulicaris*
foxglove *Digitalis purpurea*

glaucous sedge *Carex flacca*
goosegrass *Galium aparine*
gorse
    common gorse *Ulex europaeus*
    western gorse *Ulex gallii*
grass vetchling *Lathyrus nissolia*
grass of Parnassus *Parnassia palustris*
green-winged orchid *Orchis morio*
ground ivy *Glechoma hederacea*
guelder rose *Viburnum opulus*

hairy sedge *Carex hirta*
hard rush *Juncus inflexus*
hard shield fern *Polystichum aculeatum*
hawthorn
    common hawthorn *Crataegus monogyna*
    woodland hawthorn *Crataegus laevigata*
hazel *Corylus avellana*
heath grass *Danthonia decumbens*
hemp agrimony *Agrimonia eupatoria*
herb Robert *Geranium robertianum*
hogweed *Heracleum sphondylium*
holly *Ilex aquifolium*
honeysuckle *Lonicera periclymenum*
hornbeam *Carpinus betulus*
horse chestnut *Aesculus hippocastanum*
horsetail *Equisetum arvense*

ivy *Hedera helix*

juniper *Juniperus communis*

knapweed *Centaurea nigra*

lady's bedstraw *Galium verum*
lady's smock *Cardamine pratensis*
lesser celandine *Ranunculus ficaria*
lesser clubmoss *Selaginella selaginoides*
lesser hawkbit *Leontodon taraxacoides*
lesser stitchwort *Stellaria media*
ling heather *Calluna vulgaris*

marram grass *Ammophila arenaria*
marsh helleborine *Epipactis palustris*
marsh pennywort *Hydrocotyle vulgaris*
meadow buttercup *Ranunculus acris*
meadow fescue *Festuca pratensis*
meadow foxtail *Alopecurus pratensis*
meadow vetchling *Lathyrus pratensis*
mouse-ear *Cerastium fontanum*

nettle *Urtica dioica*

oak
    pedunculate oak *Quercus robur*
    sessile oak *Quercus petraea*
ox-eye daisy *Leucanthemum vulgare*

pepper saxifrage *Silaum silaus*
perennial ryegrass *Lolium perenne*
petty whin *Genista anglica*
pignut *Conopodium major*
primrose *Primula vulgaris*
purple moorgrass *Molinia caerulea*
pussy willow *Salix caprea*

quaking grass *Briza media*

ragwort *Senecio jacobea*
red fescue *Festuca rubra*
red clover *Trifolium pratense*
ribwort plantain *Plantago lanceolata*
rough meadow grass *Poa trivialis*
rowan *Sorbus aucuparia*

salad burnet *Sanguisorba minor*
Scots pine *Pinus sylvestris*
sedge
    carnation sedge *Carex panicea*
    flea sedge *Carex pulicaris*
    glaucous sedge *Carex flacca*
    hairy sedge *Carex hirta*
    spring sedge *Carex caryophyllea*
selfheal *Prunella vulgaris*
sheep's fescue *Festuca ovina*
silverweed *Potentilla anserine*
smooth meadow grass *Poa pratensis*
soft brome *Bromus hordeaceus*
sorrel *Rumex acetosa*

spindleberry *Euonymus europaeus*
spotted orchid *Dactylorhiza maculata*
spring sedge *Carex caryophyllea*
sweet chestnut *Castanea sativa*
sweet vernal grass *Anthoxanthum odoratum*
sycamore *Acer pseudoplatanus*

toad rush *Juncus bufonius*
tormentil *Potentilla erecta*
tufted vetch *Vicia cracca*

wavy hairgrass *Deschampsia flexuosa*
western gorse *Ulex gallii*
white clover *Trifolium repens*
wild carrot *Daucus carota*

wild cherry *Prunus avium*
wild service *Sorbus torminalis*
wood anemone *Anemone nemorosa*
wood avens *Geum urbanum*
wood dock *Rumex sanguineus*
wood false brome *Brachypodium sylvaticum*
wood sorrel *Oxalis acetosella*

yarrow *Achillea millefolium*
yellow archangel *Lamiastrum galeobdolon*
yellow oatgrass *Trisetum flavescens*
yellow-rattle *Rhinanthus minor*
yew *Taxus baccata*
Yorkshire fog *Holcus lanatus*

Mosses and liverworts (from Crawford CL, 2002. *Bryophytes of Native Woods: A field guide to common mosses and liverworts of Britain and Ireland's woodlands.* Ayr: The Natural Resource Consultancy)

Catherine's moss *Atrichum undulatum*
cupressus moss *Hypnum jutlandicum*
feather moss *Eurhynchium praelongum*
forest star *Mnium hornum*
fork moss *Dicranum scoparium,*
great fork moss *Dicranum majus*
hair moss *Polytrichum juniperum*
neat moss *Scleropodium purum*

ordinary moss *Brachythecium rutabulum*
pincerwort *Lophocolea bidentata*
shaggy moss *Rhytidiadelphus triquestrus*
spear moss *Calliergon cupidatum*
stripe moss *Eurhynchium striatum*
tamarisk moss *Thuidium tamariscinum*
wavy flat moss *Plagiothecium undulatum*

References

Akeroyd J, 1991. 'Illustrated Field Guides to the British Flora: a review'. *British Wildlife,* 2 (4), 214–218.

Ali Khan S, 1996. *Environmental Responsibility: A review of the 1993 Toyne Report.* London: Her Majesty's Stationery Office.

Allen RE (ed.) 1990 (8th edition). *The Concise Oxford Dictionary.* Oxford University Press.

Allwright R, 1988. *Survey of unimproved neutral grassland in West Sussex, Volume 2.* Peterborough: Nature Conservancy Council.

Ambrose P and Holloway G, 1994. 'Conclusions'. In: G Holloway (ed.) *All change! Accreditation as a challenge to Liberal Adult Education.* Brighton: Centre for Continuing Education at the University of Sussex, 83–91.

Anderson P 1999. 'A view from the edge'. In: *British Ecological Society Bulletin,* 30, (3), 6–8.

Apel H and Franz-Balsen A, 1998. 'Filling the gap – adult education and the implementation of Local Agenda 21 programmes in German local communities'. In: A Bron, J Field and E Kuantowicz (eds) *Adult Education and Democratic Citizenship II.* Krakow: Impuls, 169–76.

Barker S, Slingsby D and Tilling S, 2002. *Teaching Biology outside the classroom. A report on biology fieldwork in the 14–19 curriculum.* Field Studies Council Occasional Publication 72. Field Studies Council and British Ecological Society.

Barkham J, 1994. 'Climate change and British wildlife'. *British Wildlife,* 5 (3), 169–80.

Barr J, 1999. *Liberating knowledge.* NIACE.

Barton J and Fisher K, 1987. *Survey of unimproved grassland in West Sussex Volume 1.* Peterborough: Nature Conservancy Council.

Bassett JA and Curtis TGF, 1985. 'The nature and occurrence of sand-dune machair in Ireland'. *Proceedings of Royal Irish Academy,* 85B (1), 1–20.

Bignal E and Branson A (eds) 1996. *La Canada,* No 5.

Bourgeois E, Duke C, Luc-Guyot J and Merrill B, 1999. *The Adult University.* Buckingham: SRHE and Open University Press.

Braun-Blanquet J, 1932. (English translation by Fuller GD and Conard HS) *Plant Sociology. The study of plant communities.* New York: McGraw-Hill Book Company.

Byrne C, 1997. *Semi-natural grassland communities in Eastern Ireland: classification, conservation and management.* Trinity College, Dublin: PhD thesis.

Carlton S and Soulsby J, 1999. *Learning to grow older and bolder: A policy discussion paper on learning in later life.* Leicester: NIACE.

Carlton S, 2001. *Life, the Universe and Almost Everything.* Leicester: NIACE.

Clapham AR, Tutin TG and Warburg EF, 1962. *The Flora of the British Isles.* Cambridge University Press.

Clapham AR, Tutin TG and Warburg EF, 1995, 3rd edition. *Excursion Flora of the British Isles.* Cambridge University Press

Clare J, (1827), 1973 edition. *The Shepherd's Calendar,* edited by E Robinson and G Summerfield. Oxford University Press.

Clark JE, 1936. 'The history of British phenology'. *Quarterly Journal of the Royal Meteorological Society,* 62, 19–23.

Coare P and Johnston R (eds) 2003. *Adult Learning, Citizenship and Community Voices.* Leicester: NIACE.

Coare P and Thomson A, 1996. *Through the Joy of Learning.* Leicester: NIACE .

Collinson N and Sparks T, 2003. 'The science that redefines the seasons. Recent results from the UK Phenology Network'. *British Wildlife,* 14 (4), 229–32.

Crawford CL, 2002. *Bryophytes of Native Woods. A field guide to common mosses and liverworts of Britain and Ireland's woodlands.* Ayr: The Nature Resource Consultancy.

Crawford I, Bleasdale A and Conaghan J, 1996. *Biomar Survey of Irish Machair Sites, 1996.*

Darwin F (ed.) 1889. *The life and letters of Charles Darwin, Volume 1.* D. New York: Appleton.

Davis C 2001. 'When experts cost, enthusiasts count'. In: *The Times Higher Education Supplement,* November 30, p 22.

DETR, 1997. *Convention on Biological Diversity. The United Kingdom's first National report.* London: Department of Trade, Environment, Transport and Regions.

Doberski J, 2002. 'Teaching ecology in universities'. In: *The Bulletin,* August 2002. British Ecological Society, 20.

Dwyer RB (ed.), 1997. *Our Grasslands Heritage.* Irish Wildlife Trust.

Engel JR, 1993. 'The role of ethics, culture and religion in conserving biodiversity: a blueprint for research and action'. In: LS Hamilton (ed.) *Ethics, Religion and Biodiversity,* Cambridge: The White Horse Press, 183–214.

English Nature, 1994a. *The Great Nut Hunt.* Peterborough: English Nature.

English Nature, 1994b. *Managing Local Nature Reserves.* Peterborough: English Nature.

English Nature, 1997a. *High Weald Natural Area Profile.* Lewes: English Nature.

English Nature, 1997b. *Wealden Greensand Natural Area Profile.* Lewes: English Nature.

English Nature, 2000. *A provisional minimum intervention woodland reserve series for England with proposals for baseline recording and long-term monitoring therein.* English Nature Research Reports No. 385, Lewes: English Nature.

EntecUK, 2001. *The Millennium Biodiversity Report.* Newcastle on Tyne: EntecUK Ltd.

Eraut, M, Alderton, J, Cole, G and Senker, P, 1998. 'Development of knowledge and skills in employment'. Research Report No 5. Falmer: University of Sussex Institute of Education.

European Commission, 2001. 'Testing time for science'. In: *Science and Young People,* special edition of RTD info (magazine for European Research), November 2001. Brussels: European Commission.

Fay PJ and Jeffrey DW, 1995. 'The nitrogen cycle in sand-dunes'. In: DW Jeffrey, MB Jones and JH McAdam (eds) *Irish grasslands, their biology and management.* Dublin: Royal Irish Academy, 151–66.

Ferris T, 2002. *Seeing in the Dark. How backyard stargazers are probing deep space and guarding earth from interplanetary peril.* New York: Simon and Schuster.

Field J, 1995. *The Environmental Agenda.* London: Pluto Press.

Field J, 2000. *Lifelong Learning and the New Educational Order.* Stoke-on-Trent: Trentham Books.

Field Studies Council, 1988. *Key to grasses.* Slough: Richmond Publishing.

Fitter AH, Fitter RSR, Harris ITB and Williamson MH, 1995. 'Relationships between first flowering date and temperature in the flora of a locality in central England'. *Functional Ecology,* 9, 55–60.

Foster-Smith J and Evans SM, 2003. 'The value of marine ecological data collected by volunteers'. *Biological Conservation,* 113, 199–213.

Freire P, 1970, 1996. *Pedagogy of the Oppressed.* Harmondsworth: Penguin Books.

Freire, P, 1974. *Education: the Practice of Freedom.* Writers and Readers Publishing Co-operative.

Fuller JR and Warren MS, 1995. 'Management for biodiversity in British woodlands'. *British Wildlife* 7 (1), 26–37.

Gould CD, 1983. 'The impact of Nuffield O-level Biology – an agent of change in biology teaching?' *Journal of Biological Education,* 17 (3), 201–4.

Grace J, 2002. In: S Barker, D Slingsby and S Tilling. *Teaching Biology outside the classroom: Is it heading for extinction? A report on biology fieldwork in the 14–19 curriculum.* Field Studies Council Occasional Publication 72. Field Studies Council and British Ecological Society, 2.

Grayson FW, 2000. 'The financial and ecological implications of restoring grazing regimes to grassland of high conservation value suffering from long-term agricultural abandonment: a case study'. In: AJ Rook and PD Penning (eds) *Grazing Management, British Grassland Society Occasional Symposium,* 34, Reading: British Grassland Society, 215–20.

Green B, 1981. *Countryside Conservation. The protection and management of amenity ecosystems.* London: George Allen and Unwin.

Green T, 2000. 'Coppicing like a beaver'. *British Wildlife* 11 (4), 239–41.

Grime JP, 1993. 'Vegetation functional classification systems as approaches to predicting and quantifying global vegetation change'. In: AM Solomon and HH Shugart (eds), *Vegetation Dynamics and Global Change,* Chapman and Hall, 293–305.

Grime JP, Hodgson JG and Hunt R, 1990. *The Abridged Comparative Plant Ecology.* Chapman and Hall.

Grime P, 2000. 'Report on joint meeting of the BES and ESA, Orlando, Florida, USA 10–13 April 2000'. *British Ecological Society Bulletin,* 31 (3), 14–17.

Haines-Young RH *et al,* 2000. *Accounting for Nature: assessing habitats in the UK Countryside 2000.* London: Department of the Environment, Transport and the Regions.

Hambler C, 2004. *Conservation.* Cambridge University Press.

Hamilton LS (ed.), 1993. *Ethics, Religion and Biodiversity.* Cambridge: The White Horse Press.

Hazel V (undated) *Hampshire's Countryside Heritage. 9: Meadows.* Hampshire County Council.

Hepper NF, 2003. 'Phenology records of English garden plants in Leeds (Yorkshire) and Richmond (Surrey) from 1946 to 2002. An analysis relating to global warming'. *Biodiversity and Conservation,* 12 (12), 2503–20.

Heywood VH, 1995. *Global Biodiversity Assessment.* Cambridge University Press.

Hill D, Yates T, Treweek J and Pienkowski M (eds), 1996. *Actions for Biodiversity in the UK: approaches to implementing the Convention on Biological Diversity.* British Ecological Society, Ecological Issue no.6, Shrewsbury: Field Studies Council.

Hindmarch C and Pienkowski M, 2000. *Land Management: The Hidden Costs.* Cambridge: Blackwell Science Ltd.

Holden E, 1979 (11th edition). *A Country Diary of an Edwardian Lady.* Webb and Bower Ltd.

Holloway G, 1994. 'The interviews with CE departments'. In: G Holloway (ed.) *All Change! Accreditation as a challenge to Liberal Adult Education.* Brighton: Centre for Continuing Education at the University of Sussex, 31–55.

Hoskins WG, 1955, 1988. *The Making of the English Landscape.* Hodder and Stoughton.

Hubbard CE, 1954, 1984. *Grasses.* Penguin.

Hurlbert SH, 1984. 'Pseudoreplication and the design of ecological field experiments'. *Ecological Monographs,* 54, 187–211.

Irwin A and Wynne B, 1996. *Misunderstanding Science? The public reconstruction of science and technology.* Cambridge University Press.

Jefferies R, 1979. *The Pageant of Summer. Essays by Richard Jefferies selected and introduced by A Rossabi.* London: Quartet Books.

Jefferies R, undated. *Wild Life in a Southern County.* London: Thomas Nelson.

Kirby K, Saunders G and Whitbread A, 1991. 'The National Vegetation Classification in nature conservation surveys – a guide to the use of the woodland section'. *British Wildlife* 3 (2), 70–80.

Kirchin IM, 2000. 'Concept mapping in biology'. *Journal of Biological Education,* 34, (2), 61–8.

Knapper CK and Cropley AJ, 2000 (3rd Edition). *Lifelong Learning in Higher Education.* Kogan Page.

Knight D, 1995. 'Participative environmental research and the role of continuing education'. In: I Bryant (ed), *Vision, Invention, Intervention – Celebrating Adult Education: Papers from the 25th Annual Standing Conference on University Teaching and Research in the Education of Adults, Winchester 1995.* University of Southampton/SCUTREA, 108–12.

Kohler RE, 2002. *Landscapes and Labscapes.* London: University of Chicago Press.

Kolb DA, 1984. *Experiential Learning Experience as the Source of Learning and Development.* Englewood Cliffs.

Lawrence E (ed.), 1995. *Henderson's Dictionary of Biological Terms,* 11th edition. Harlow: Addison Wesley Longman Ltd.

Lister R, 1997. *Citizenship: Feminist Perspectives.* Macmillan.

Lock R, 1994. 'Nuffield Advanced Biology naff? No, not even after 26 years!' *Journal of Biological Education,* 28 (3), 191–4.

Mabey R, 1996. *Flora Britannica.* London: Sinclair-Stevenson.

Macdermot CV, Long CB and Harney SJ, 1996. *Geology of Sligo–Leitrim.* Dublin: Geological Survey of Ireland.

Marren P, 1992. *The Wild Woods.* Newton Abbott: David and Charles.

Marren P, 2002. *Nature Conservation*. London: Collins New Naturalist.

Marrs RH, 1990. 'Plant Communities', Chapter 10 in: MGR Cannell and MD Hooper (eds) *The Greenhouse Effect and Terrestrial Ecosystems of the UK*, ITE Publication No 4, Her Majesty's Stationery Office.

Mayhew G, 1994. 'Tutors' and Students' response to the accreditation of LAE: a case study'. In: G Holloway (ed.) *All change! Accreditation as a challenge to Liberal Adult Education*. Brighton: Centre for Continuing Education at the University of Sussex, 57–82.

Mayne M, 2001. *Learning to Dance*. London: Darton, Longman and Todd.

McClintock D and Fitter RSR, 1961. *Collins Pocket Guide to Wild Flowers*. Collins.

McDonald S, 1996. 'Authorising science: public understanding of science in museums'. In: A Irwin and B Wynne (eds), *Misunderstanding Science? The public reconstruction of science and technology*. Cambridge University Press, 152–71.

Mead C, 2003. 'The migration atlas – 90 years of bird-ringing and recording migration'. *British Wildlife*, 14 (5), 313–19.

Millar R, 1991. 'Why is science hard to learn?' *Journal of Computer Assisted Learning*, 7 (2), 66–74.

Ministry of Education, 1919. *The final and interim reports of the Adult Education Committee of the Ministry of Reconstruction 1918–1919*.

Mitchel K, 1996. *The Common Agricultural Policy and Environmental Practices: Proceedings of the seminar organised by the European Forum on Nature Conservation and Pastoralism at COPA, Brussels on 29 January 1996*. EFNCP Occasional Publication No 1.

Moore N, 2003. 'Ecological Citizens or Ecoterroists? Learning through environmental activism in Clayoquot Sound'. In: P Coare and R Johnston (eds) *Adult Learning, Citizenship and Community Voices*, 92–107. NIACE.

Nature Conservancy Council, 1984. *Nature Conservation in Great Britain*. Peterborough: Nature Conservancy Council.

Newman C, Buesching CD, and Macdonald DW, 2003. 'Validating mammal monitoring methods and assessing the performance of volunteers in wildlife conservation – "Sed quis custodiet ipsos custodes?"' *Biological Conservation*, 113, 189–97.

Nicholson J, 1998. 'The Science Starter Project: University of East Anglia'. In: *Good Practice in Non Award-Bearing Continuing Education* HEFCE September 98/49.

Nicholson JR, 2002. 'Stimulating science in rural areas'. In: F Gray (ed.) *Landscapes of Learning*. Leicester: NIACE, 86–103.

Nilsson C, 1992. 'Increasing the reliability of vegetation analyses by using a team of two investigators'. *Journal of Vegetation Science*, 3, 565.

O'Kane D, 2002. 'Lifelong learning and Higher Education – obstacles to success'. *Ad lib: Journal for Continuing Liberal Adult Education*, Issue 22 (October 2002), 5–9. University of Cambridge Institute for Continuing Education Public Programme.

O'Sullivan AM, 1965. *A phytosociological survey of Irish lowland pastures*. University College, Dublin: PhD thesis.

O'Sullivan AM, 1982. 'Lowland grasslands of Ireland'. *Journal Life Sciences, Royal Dublin Society* 3, 131–42.

Oosthuizen S, 2002. 'The Fenland Oral History Project'. In: F Gray (ed.), *Landscapes of Learning*, Leicester: NIACE, 143–57.

Osmerod SJ and Watkinson AR, 2000. 'The age of applied science'. *Journal of Applied Ecology,* 37, 1–2.

Parry J, 2002. 'Pressing the local account'. *Local Environment,* 7 (2), 177–87.

Peterken GF, 2000. 'The human element in long-term woodland studies'. In: KJ Kirby and MD Morecroft (eds) *Long-term studies of British woodland,* English Nature Science No. 34, 11–18.

Philander SG, 1998. *Is the temperature rising? The uncertain science of global warming.* Princeton University Press: Princeton, New Jersey.

Phillips M and Wilson S, 1995. *A guide to conducting a Local Habitat Survey.* Henfield: Sussex Wildlife Trust.

Pigott CD, 1982. 'The experimental study of vegetation'. *New Phytologist,* 90, 389–404.

Pilkington MC and Stuart M, 2001. 'Science for active citizenship: the challenge for lifelong learning'. *Journal of Access and Credit Studies,* 3 (1), 4–16.

Pilkington MC, 2003a. 'Woodland NVC and conservation management in Sussex'. In: E Goldberg (ed.) JNCC Report No 335, *National Vegetation Classification – ten years' experience using the woodland section.* Peterborough: Joint Nature Conservancy Council, 25–35.

Pilkington MC, 2003b. 'Citizens, the environment and scientific literacy'. In: P Coare and R Johnston (eds), *Adult Learning, Citizenship and Community Voices,* Leicester: NIACE, 152–64.

Plantlife, 1991. *Death Knell for Bluebells.* Salisbury: Plantlife.

Polanyi M, (1958) 1962. *Personal Knowledge. Towards a post-critical philosophy.* London: Routledge and Kegan Paul.

Polkinghorne J, 2002. *The God of Hope and the End of the World.* London: Society for the Promotion of Christian Knowledge (SPCK).

Possingham HP, Andelman SJ, Noon BR, Trombulak S and Pulliam HR, 2001. 'Making smart decisions'. In: ME Soule and GH Orians (eds) *Conservation Biology,* London: Island Press, 225–44.

Preston CD, Pearman DA and Dines TD, 2002. *New Atlas of the British and Irish Flora.* Oxford University Press.

Putman RJ and Moore NP, 1998. 'Impact of deer in lowland Britain on agriculture, forestry and conservation habitats'. *Mammal Review* 28 (4), 141–63.

Reynolds PJ, 1979. *Iron-Age Farm. The Butser Experiment.* London: British Museum Publications.

Reynolds PJ, 1999. 'The nature of experiment in Archaeology'. In: AF Harding (ed.) *Experiment and Design. Archaeological Studies in honour of John Coles,* Oxford: Oxbow Books.

Rodwell JS, 1991a. 'The National Vegetation Classification'. *British Wildlife,* 2 (5), 266–268.

Rodwell JS, 1991b. *British Plant Communities, Volume 2. Mires and heaths.* Cambridge University Press.

Rodwell JS, 1991c. *British Plant Communities, Volume 1. Woodlands and Scrub.* Cambridge University Press.

Rodwell JS, 1992, 1998. *British Plant Communities, Volume 3. Grasslands and montane communities.* Cambridge University Press.

Rodwel JS, 2000. *British Plant Communities Volume 5. Maritime Communities and vegetation of open habitats.* Cambridge University Press.

Rodwell JS, 2001. 'A vision for the uplands'. *GAP News,* No. 16, 20–24.

Rose F, 1981, 1991. *The Wild Flower Key.* Harmondsworth: Penguin.

Rose F, 1995. *The Habitats and Vegetation of Sussex.* Brighton: Booth Museum of Natural History.

Rothman H, Glasner P and Adams C, 1996. 'Proteins, Plants and Currents: rediscovering science in Britain'. In: A Irwin and B Wynne (eds) *Misunderstanding Science? The public reconstruction of science and technology.* Cambridge University Press, 191–212.

Rowell DL, 1994. *Soil Science Methods and Applications.* Longman Scientific.

Royal Society, 1985. *The Public Understanding of Science.* London: Royal Society.

Rubenson K, 2002. 'Adult education policy in Sweden 1967–2001: from recurrent education to lifelong learning'. In: D Istance, HG Schuetze and T Schuller (eds) *International Perspectives on Lifelong Learning,* Buckingham: Society for Research in Higher Education and Open University Press, 203–16.

Rudling D, 2003. 'A tale of two villas: Beddingham and Barcombe'. *ARA Bulletin of the Association for Roman Archaeology,* 15, 10–15.

Schemann M, 2001. 'Environmental rights as a component of citizenship rights. Reflections from an adult education point of view'. In: M Schemann and A Bron (eds) *Adult Education and Democratic Citizenship 4.* ESREA: Impuls.

Shaw PJA, Lankey K and Hollingham SA, 1995. 'Impacts of trampling and dog fouling on vegetation and soil conditions on Headley Heath'. *London Naturalist,* 74, 77–82.

Smith RS and Jones L, 1991. 'The phenology of mesotrophic grassland in the Pennine Dales, Northern England: historic hay cutting dates, vegetation variation and plant species phenologies'. *Journal of Applied Ecology,* 28, 42–59.

Smith RS, Sheil RS, Millward D and Corkhill P, 2000. 'The interactive effects of management on the productivity and plant community structure of an upland meadow: an 8-year field trial'. *Journal of Applied Ecology,* 37, 1029–43.

Soule ME and Orians GH (eds), 2001a. *Conservation Biology. Research priorities for the next decade.* London: Island Press.

Soule ME and Orians GH, 2001b. 'Conservation Biology Research. Its challenges and contexts'. In: ME Soule and GH Orians (eds) *Conservation Biology. Research Priorities for the next decade.* London: Island Press.

Sparks TH and Carey PD, 1995. 'The responses of species to climate over two centuries: an analysis of the Marsham phenological record, 1736–1947'. *Journal of Ecology,* 83, 321–9.

Sparks TH, Crick H, Bellamy D and Mason C, 1998. 'Spring 1998: a summary of the first pilot year of a revived UK phenology network'. *British Wildlife,* 10, (2), pp.77–81.

Stevens G, 1990. *A botanical survey of unimproved neutral grassland in East Sussex.* Lewes: English Nature.

Sussex Wildlife Trust, 1995. *Vision for the Wildlife of Sussex.* Henfield: Sussex Wildlife Trust.

Sutherland WJ and Hill DA, 1995. *Managing Habitats for Conservation.* Cambridge University Press.

Tilling S, 2001. 'Fieldwork: is it in terminal decline?' In: *The Bulletin*, May 2001, British Ecological Society, 32–3.

Tow PG and Lazenby A (eds) 2001. *Competition and Succession in Pastures*. Wallingford, Oxon: CABI Publishing.

Tubbs, CR 1997. 'A vision for rural Europe'. *British Wildlife*, 9 (2), 79–85.

Tuckett A and Aldridge F, 2003. 'Sharp fall in adult participation in learning'. *Adults learning*, 14 (9), 25–26.

UK Government, 1994. *Biodiversity: UK Action Plan*, Cm 2428, Her Majesty's Stationery Office.

van Marion P, 1995. 'Contacts between schools and institutions outside the school in environmental education: problems and promising experiences'. In: Proceedings of the conference on exchange of experiences in environmental education in Great Britain, 26–33.

Vickery JA, Tallowin JR, Feber RE, Asteraki EJ, Atkinson PW, Fuller RJ and Brown VK, 2001. 'The management of lowland neutral grasslands in Britain: effects of agricultural practices on birds and their food resources'. *Journal of Applied Ecology*, 38, 647–64.

Watkinson AR and Ormerod SJ, 2001. 'Grasslands, grazing and biodiversity'. *Journal of Applied Ecology*, 38, 233–7.

Watson EV, 1955, 1981, reprinted 1995. *British Mosses and Liverworts*. Cambridge University Press.

Wernham C, Toms M, Marchant J, Clark J, Stirwardena G and Baillie S, 2002. *The Migration Atlas. The movements of birds of Britain and Ireland*. Published for the British Trust for Ornithology by T and AD Poyser.

White G, 1789, first published by OUP in 1902, 1982 reprint. *The Natural History of Selbourne*. Oxford University Press.

Yearly S, 1996. 'Nature's advocates: putting science to work in environmental organisations'. In: A Irwin and B Wynne (eds) *Misunderstanding Science? The public reconstruction of science and technology*. Cambridge University Press, 172–90.

Subject index

Index of vascular plants and mosses